T0360398

Golfonomics

G⬤lfonomics

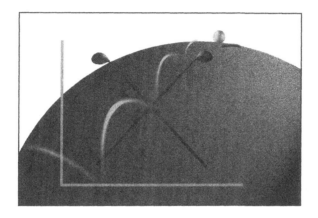

Stephen Shmanske
California State University, Hayward, USA

 **World Scientific**

NEW JERSEY · LONDON · SINGAPORE · SHANGHAI · HONG KONG · TAIPEI · BANGALORE

Published by

World Scientific Publishing Co. Pte. Ltd.

5 Toh Tuck Link, Singapore 596224

USA office: Suite 202, 1060 Main Street, River Edge, NJ 07661

UK office: 57 Shelton Street, Covent Garden, London WC2H 9HE

British Library Cataloguing-in-Publication Data
A catalogue record for this book is available from the British Library.

GOLFONOMICS

ISBN 981-238-677-7

Printed in Singapore by World Scientific Printers (S) Pte Ltd

This book is dedicated to:

Peggy Stevens

Economists who love Golf

and Golfers who love Economics

Preface

This book could not have been written without freely-supplied assistance from many sources, including professional golfers and their agents, amateur golfers, golf courses, golf course managers, friends, and family. To all those who helped, whether it was supplying data, offering opinions or advice, or answering what may have seemed to be bizarre questions, I am truly grateful.

My first thanks are for the professional golfers who helped by completing my survey about practice regimens. Without this information, my very first research paper on golf and economics, included here as Chapter 10, could not have been completed. Whenever I decide to root for one golfer or another in a professional tournament, the following golfers who took part in my survey have a special place in my heart: Paul Azinger, John Cook, Rick Fehr, Raymond Floyd, Scott Hoch, Bernhard Langer, Bruce Lietzke, Greg Norman, Nick Price, J. C. Snead, and D. A. Weibring. Although they will remain unnamed, I also thank the agents who delivered my survey into the hands of these and other golfers.

I am deeply indebted to the golf course managers and the golf course superintendents who helped me put together the data on public-access golf courses in the San Francisco Bay area. Without their agreement to submit to my prying questions, the rich data set that led to three published articles, and that forms the backbone of Part II of the book, could not have been assembled. To the people and golf courses in the following list I am especially grateful:

Mr. Peter Dempsey, Golf Course Superintendent
Adobe Creek Golf Course, Petaluma

Mr. John Flachman, Golf Course Superintendent
Bennett Valley Golf Course, Santa Rosa

Mr. Bob Wagner, Golf Course Superintendent
Blue Rock Springs Golf Course, Vallejo

Mr. Bob Boldt, PGA Class A Pro
Boundary Oak Golf Course, Walnut Creek

Mr. Roger Billings, Golf Course Manager
Chardonnay Club, Napa

Mr. Danny Plato, Golf Course Superintendent
Mr. Fred Framsted, Manager
Chuck Corica Golf Club, Alameda

Mr. Charlie Leider, Director of Golf
Crystal Springs Golf Course, Burlingame

Mr. Dan Brown, Manager of Golf Operations
Diablo Creek Golf Course, Concord

Mr. Bob Tyler, Golf Course Superintendent
Fountaingrove Resort & Country Club, Santa Rosa

Mr. Gill Flynn, Golf Course Manager
Franklin Canyon Golf Course, Rodeo

Mr. Bill Blest, Controller
Half Moon Bay Golf Links, Half Moon Bay

Mr. Bill Costanzo, Danville

Mr. Bruce Carpenter, Golf Course Superintendent
Indian Valley Golf Course, Novato

Mr. Tony Acosta, Park Services Manager
Lake Chabot Golf Course, Oakland

Mr. Mulkh Raj, Golf Course Superintendent
Las Positas Golf Course, Livermore

Mr. Hugh McKay, Director of Golf
Lew F. Galbraith Golf Course, Oakland

Mr. Jim Manion, Golf Course Superintendent
Lincoln Park Golf Course, San Francisco

Mr. Wayne Lindelof, Golf Course Superintendent
Mr. Pat Cain, Manager
Lone Tree Golf Course, Antioch

Mr. Sam Singh, Golf Course Superintendent
Mountain Shadows Golf Resort, Rohnert Park

Mr. Robert Swan, Golf Course Manager
Napa Municipal Golf Course, Napa

Mr. Dick Huff, Director of Golf
Oakhurst Country Club, Clayton

Mr. Lon Rickey, Manager
Mr. Dean F. James, Director of Golf
Oakmont Golf Course, Santa Rosa

Mr. Paul Dias, Golf Course Superintendent
Palo Alto Golf Course, Palo Alto

Mr. Jeremy Duda, Regional Manager
Mr. Tim McCoy, Golf Course Superintendent
Paradise Valley Golf Course and
Rancho Solano Golf Course, Fairfield

Mr. Richard Lavine, Golf Course Superintendent
Peacock Gap Golf and Country Club, San Rafael

Mr. Carl King, Golf Course Superintendent
Mr. Joe Fernandez, Manager
Pittsburg's Delta View Golf Course, Pittsburg

Mr. David Michael, Golf Course Superintendent
San Geronimo Golf Course, San Geronimo

Mr. Bob McGrath, PGA Class A Pro
San Jose Municipal Golf Course, San Jose

Mr. Dulbag Dubria, Golf Course Superintendent
San Mateo Golf Course, San Mateo

Mr. Richard Muzzy, Golf Course Manager
San Ramon Royal Vista Golf Course, San Ramon

Mr. Rich Taylor, Golf Course Manager
Santa Clara Golf & Tennis Club, Santa Clara

Mr. Jim McGrath, Golf Course Manager
Santa Teresa Golf Course, San Jose

Mr. Bob Killian, San Francisco Recreation & Parks
Harding Park Golf Course, San Francisco and
Sharp Park Golf Course, Pacifica

Mr. Scott Hall, PGA Class A Pro
Shoreline Golf Links, Mountain View

Mr. Rick Silva, Golf Course Manager
Ms. Cheryl Pastore, LPGA Class A Pro
Skywest Golf Course, Hayward

Mr. Steve Shimano, General Manager
Sonoma Golf Course, Sonoma

Mr. Rick Jetter, Director of Golf
Mr. Greg Jetter, Golf Course Superintendent
Spring Valley Golf Course, Milpitas

Mr. Bob Clark, General Manager
Summitpointe Golf Course, Milpitas

Mr. Curtis Black, Golf Course Superintendent
Sunnyvale Golf Course, Sunnyvale

Mr. Dan Russel, General Manager
Sunol Valley Golf Club, Sunol

Mr. Paul Henderson, Manager
Mr. Dave Smith, Golf Course Superintendent
Tilden Park Golf Course, Berkeley

Mr. Ken Schwark, Golf Course Superintendent
Mr. Steve Elbe, PGA Class A Pro
Tony Lema Golf Course, San Leandro

Mr. Rene Viviani, Golf Course Manager
Willow Park Golf Course, Castro Valley

Mr. Rick Hansen, Golf Course Superintendent
Mr. Charlie Gibson, Manager
Windsor Golf Course, Windsor

Mr. Kevin Roberts, President
American Golf Corporation

I also wish to thank the more than 900 volunteers who took a few minutes to answer my survey questions about the nature of the golf course they had just finished playing. Without their subjective opinions, the data series on quality variables like golf course beauty and golf course condition would not exist. Many of these volunteers were curious to know when the book would be completed. At the time, 1994, I remember telling them that it would be a long process. I apologize for the extent to which procrastination on my part lengthened the process, except, of course, for the part of my procrastination that was spent golfing.

The material in several of the chapters was presented at conferences. The material on price discrimination in Chapter 5 was presented at the 1996 Western Economic Association, International (WEAI) meetings in San Francisco in a session chaired by Francois Melese. I especially thank Torben Anderson who was the discussant for the paper. The material on gender discrimination in Chapter 12 was presented at the 2000 WEAI meetings in Vancouver, B.C. in a session organized by Larry Hadley and Elizabeth Gustafson, and chaired by Thomas Bruggink. Useful comments were made by Larry Hadley and Michael Ransom. The material on the golf course bottleneck in Chapter 8 was presented at the 2001 WEAI meetings in San Francisco in a session organized by Larry Hadley and Elizabeth Gustafson, and chaired by John Fizel. Helpful insight was offered by the discussant, Stacey Brook.

I have also presented much of my research in the Economics Workshop at California State University, Hayward. Chapters 3, 5, 6, 10, and 12 have been improved from the comments of students and faculty present at those workshops. I thank my colleagues at California State University, Hayward who also helped with comments, conversations, and suggestions offered outside of the workshop itself: James Ahiakpor, Charles Baird, Greg Christainsen, Leo Kahane, Shyam Kamath, Tony Lima, Nan Maxwell, and Paul Staudohar. Over half of these people do not even play golf. They deserve extra thanks for helping me with the economics even though they could not match my enthusiasm for the subject matter itself.

I would also like to thank the editors and anonymous referees at several professional journals where parts of this material were originally published. The material in Chapter 10, "Practice Makes Perfect," appeared in Shmanske, Stephen, "Human Capital Formation in Professional Sports: Evidence From the PGA Tour," *Atlantic Economic Journal*, Vol. 20, No. 3, (Sept. 1992) pp. 66-80. Some material in Chapter 5, "Price Discrimination," appeared in, Shmanske, Stephen, "Price Discrimination at the Links," *Contemporary Economic Policy*, Vol. 16, No. 3, (July 1998), pp. 368-378. Chapter 4, "Bad Mood Bias," includes material that originally appeared in, Shmanske, Stephen, "Subjective Measurement and 'Bad-Mood' Bias," *Briefing Notes in Economics*, 35 (July 1998) pp. 1-4. The essence of Chapter 6, "Replace Your Divots, and Please Don't Eat the Daisies," was published as Shmanske, Stephen, "The Economics of Golf Course Condition and Beauty," *Atlantic Economic Journal*, Vol. 27, No. 3, (Sept. 1999) pp. 301-313. Finally, Chapter 12, "Gender Discrimination," was originally published in part, in, Shmanske, Stephen, "Gender, Skill, and Earnings in Professional Golf," *Journal of Sports Economics*, Vol. 1, No. 4, (Nov. 2000), pp. 400-415.

I would also like to thank Ronald Ehrenberg and Michael Bognanno who did the research that I report on in Chapter 11, "Tournament Compensation in the Boardroom." Their paper appeared as: Ehrenberg, R. G. and M. L. Bognanno, "Do Tournaments Have Incentive Effects?," *Journal of Political Economy*, 98 (December 1990a), pp. 1307-24, and they allowed me to paraphrase their theory and report on their statistical results.

Hans Kramer, Executive Director of The Transamerica, a Senior PGA Tour event held at the Silverado Country Club & Resort in California's Napa Valley, helped me during an extended telephone conversation by supplying the information about how a golf tournament is organized. Later, he also read and commented on a draft of what became part of Chapter 9, "The Business of Professional Golf." Without his patient assistance, this part of the book simply would not have been written.

Other types of support that I have received are less specific to particular chapters. For example, financial support, in the form of minigrants to purchase publications from the National Golf Foundation, and sabbatical and release time from teaching assignments, came from my university. I thank

Dr. Norma Rees, the President of our campus, for her ongoing interest in, and support of, my research agenda.

I am deeply indebted to Peggy Stevens, who read and edited the entire manuscript, even though it distracted her from her true loves, poetry and the piano. Cheerful and steadfast, even in the face of serious health concerns, it was a delight to exchange chapter after chapter with her as the book rounded into final form. Her attitude and fortitude, as well as her prowess with words and language, are truly inspirational.

Thanks are also appropriate for all of my golf partners. Over the years I have played golf with hundreds of different people who have politely listened (in some cases whether they wanted to or not), to recaps of my latest academic work on golf and economics. A handful of these partners stand out, for teaching me more about golf, for igniting and fueling my love of the game, for teaching me more about economics, and in some cases, for all of the above. Extra gratitude is due to these special golf partners: Bernard F. Shmanske, Sr., Joe Fuhrig, Ed Martin, Dave Lidstone, and Scott Specht.

When it comes to partners, however, none is more important than my spouse and life partner, Tina Stevens. She has practically made a career out of challenging my economics, vicariously enjoying my latest round of golf (if it was good, consoling me if it was bad), reading and editing my research papers, sharing all of our decisions, our joys, and our sadness, and generally bringing focus and direction to my life. This is all in addition to her own career as an historian, teacher, and author. It is hard to imagine how this book could have been written without her love and support. For this, I am deeply grateful.

Stephen Shmanske

Contents

Part I

Warming Up

Chapter 1

Introduction

I am sure that I am one of the happiest people alive. I have all the required elements: a lovely, intelligent, loving spouse, a caring and interesting extended family, devoted pets, and a comfortable home. Of course, I do have to work to support all this, but on that score I have one of the best jobs that I can imagine. I am an economics professor at a bustling commuter campus, California State University, Hayward. Okay, maybe I do not have the best imagination in the world, but I do love economics.

One of the best parts of being an economist is that I get to research and study just about whatever I want to, because almost everything has an economic side to it. Not only do I continue to learn--another required element for happiness--but I can choose to learn about things which interest me. After becoming stuck in traffic jams, I started thinking, researching, and writing about the economics of traffic congestion. When a mid-life crisis started to hit, I undertook research on consumption, saving, and happiness over one's life cycle. When I did this research several years ago, I was pleased when one of my simulated life-cycles showed that happiness peaks when you reach the age of 42. (I am no longer happy about this result.) When our school was changing its curriculum, and the bureaucratic mentality started to get to me, I theorized and wrote about the economics of college enrollment and its relationship to the difficulty of the curriculum. And, while waiting to tee off on a backed-up golf course, I started thinking about the economics of golf course management.

Doing research on the economics of golf is a double blessing. I love economics, and I also love golf. I cannot say which I love more.

Economically speaking, it must be that I love golf more, because I willingly pay to play golf, while they have to pay me to teach economics. Economics is my job and golf is my hobby. But I have often thought that it might be the other way around. If I had the talent, and was willing to work hard enough to be a professional golfer, then my hobby would be learning and teaching economics. They would pay me to golf, and I would pay to take economics courses, and to attend lectures on the economy. Either way, I would be able to combine the two. Dr. Norma S. Rees, president of our university, is very astute on these matters. She is neither a golfer nor an economist. Nevertheless, in approving my sabbatical leave to write this book and, in generally supporting my research agenda, she wrote to me that she supposed, "everything boils down to economics, . . . or is it that everything boils down to golf?" Either way, she is right, and I am happy.

Combining these two loves, golf and economics, led me down several different paths, ultimately to a nice little collection of articles on golf and economics and a growing list of future topics to research. I decided to collect them all in a book, *Golfonomics*. I thought briefly about adding an overused subtitle to this book, *Golfonomics: Everything You Wanted to Know About the Economics of Golf but Were Afraid to Ask*. I quickly realized, however, that it would not be appropriate. First of all, the book is far from encyclopedic. There is much more about golf and economics that remains uncovered. Furthermore, I probably never even get to many of the questions that most readers would immediately think of asking. A better subtitle would be, *Golfonomics: Some Ideas About the Economics of Golf that You Never Would Even Think of Wanting to Know or Think of Asking About, but that You Might Find Amusing or Interesting*. In the end, I mercifully decided to forego the subtitle altogether.

An issue that one would probably never think about is how to calculate the dollar value of practice time to PGA TOUR professionals. This issue is covered in the book. By contrast, an example of something that one might ordinarily think of asking about, if the topic was the economics of golf, is the golf course feasibility study. Feasibility studies for new courses, or profitability studies for existing courses, or for major capital improvements to existing courses, are of obvious interest to those seeking to develop or invest in a golf course. These studies consist of forecasting the land acquisition costs and the design and construction costs of a new golf course, and comparing these with the expectations of future net revenues from green fees, cart operations, the restaurant, pro shop, and so on. These studies are also very useful to public agencies that are considering the development of a municipal golf course. Although these are all economic issues, *Golfonomics* does not go into such things. First of all, the National Golf Foundation has devoted considerable energies along these lines. Secondly, the type of detail that would be necessary in order for the book to be useful to prospective investors would be tedious and boring to the rest of us.[1]

A book could be written about the pros and cons of municipal golf courses, but it is not this one. The economics in this book is typically much more "micro" than that. I do not directly discuss the costs and benefits of golf course development. I look at the effect of hilliness on the demand for golf cart rental, but not at the overall profitability of managing a fleet of golf carts. I look at the relationship between maintenance expenditures and the condition of the golf course, but not at the overall establishment of a maintenance budget. I look at the form of a golf course's pricing structure much more than at the level of prices. Instead of asking whether prices should be higher or lower, I ask whether there should be a greater or lesser number of different price categories. I have some things to say about golf course location, but very little in the way of forecasting population growth trends and their effect on growth in the golf industry as a whole. It has been said that the United States needs a new golf course to open every day to keep up with the growth in demand. This may or may not be true, and it is an economic question, but that is not what this book is about. It has also been noted how Tiger Woods has fostered an explosion in youth golf that will soon lead to unprecedented growth in the demand for golf courses and golf equipment. Whether, or how soon, golf will become a $100 billion industry, or a trillion dollar industry, are also economic questions. But they are not what the book is about either.

That is not to say that tracking trends in the golf industry is not interesting. Tables of growth rates are often necessary to size up the topography of the subject matter. Table 1.1, for example, offers several

---

[1]That is not to say that there are no interesting comments to make about feasibility studies or profitability studies. In fact, I would like to criticize two common errors that such studies often make, especially in relation to municipal golf course development. Please see the appendix to this chapter.

different measures of the growth or size of the golf industry. Although the growth trends of golf course facilities, tournament purses, and charitable giving are all somewhat different, a consistent story is told from the whole-- golf is huge, and golf is growing. Professional golfers are particularly proud of their record of charitable giving. Week in and week out on the professional tours volunteers donate money and time to make the tournament a success. Invariably, some of the proceeds of a successful tournament are earmarked for charities. Comparisons of charitable giving across professional sports is another fascinating economic topic to research. Again, however, it is not the subject of this book.

So what is *Golfonomics* about? Perhaps the most straightforward answer comes from simply introducing the chapters. Part I, entitled, Warming Up, includes this introductory chapter and a chapter that illustrates how economists use and interpret a statistical technique called regression analysis. The results in Chapter 2, entitled, "Get Your Weight Behind It," show the relationship between a golfer's weight and how far he can drive the golf ball. Admittedly, this is a topic without serious economic theory or consequences. The main purpose of this chapter is to help introduce econometrics to those who are unfamiliar with regression analysis. Seasoned economists could bypass most of the chapter, and skip to the results which they might find amusing.

The body of the book is divided into two main subject headings: "The Front Nine: Golf Course Economics," in Part II; and, "The Back Nine: The Economics of Professional Golf," in Part III.

For "The Front Nine," I was fortunate to be able to gather a unique data set on golf course operations during 1994. The data refer to 1993, a year in which there were 48 public access golf course facilities with at least 18 holes, par of at least 68, and located roughly within a one-hour drive from San Francisco. Forty-six of these facilities allowed me to interview the superintendent and/or the manager to obtain information about maintenance costs, pricing practices, patterns of play, and different categories of revenues. I also interviewed at least 20 golfers from each course as they finished their rounds of golf on the eighteenth hole. The resulting data actually formed two subsets: one composed of 46 observations at the level of the golf course; and one composed of over 900 observations at the level of the golfer.

The data is more fully explained as it is employed in the succeeding chapters, especially in Chapter 4. The different types of information collected can be deduced from the following brief introductions to the chapters in Part II.

Chapter 3, "To Ride or Not to Ride," could also be called "Golf Cart Economics." The chapter introduces the concept of the demand curve for the benefit of the non-economist. The demand curve itself is then estimated for the case of the demand to rent golf carts. As expected, the demand curve is downward sloping--as the price goes up, fewer people use carts. Also as expected, the demand at each course is systematically influenced by the hilliness of the course. Golfers are more willing to walk on flatter courses, and more willing to rent carts on hillier courses. The most curious thing about golf cart economics, however, is the policy adopted by some golf courses of making golf carts mandatory. Many golfers and golf course insiders simply dismiss this as a profit grab on the part of the owners, but simple economics shows that making carts mandatory for everyone will actually decrease demand and profits if some golfers prefer to walk. Mandatory golf cart rental is somewhat of an economic riddle or puzzle that begs for a coherent explanation. This chapter presents, criticizes, and dismisses the usual explanations as inadequate. A possible solution to the riddle involves price discrimination, the topic of Chapter 5.

Chapter 4[2] describes the development of the data set that was collected through my survey of golfers as they finished their rounds of golf. The main reason for the survey was to measure subjective qualities like golf course beauty and golf course condition. Economic studies of the demand for golf should include objective variables like price, golf course yardage, golf course difficulty, and so on, but they should also include things, like beauty and condition, which are primarily subjective. The chapter discusses several types of bias that might pollute survey results, ultimately concluding that the subjective measurements are probably okay. As they say, "The proof is in the pudding." The remaining chapters in Part II show that the subjective variables are used successfully. Local golfers and local golf course

---

[2]This chapter draws on and extends research previously published in, Shmanske, Stephen, "Subjective Measurement and 'Bad-Mood' Bias," *Briefing Notes in Economics*, No. 35, (July 1998), pp. 1-4.

Table 1.1 Measures of golf's growth.

	total PGA TOUR purses[a]		leading money winner[a]	
year	actual $	2003 $	actual $	2003 $
1950	$ 459,950	$ 3,505,926	$ 35,759	$ 272,569
1951	460,200	3,251,490	26,089	184,329
1952	498,016	3,452,284	37,033	256,716
1953	562,704	3,871,487	34,002	233,939
1954	600,819	4,102,990	65,820	449,485
1955	782,010	5,360,269	63,121	432,662
1956	847,070	5,720,836	72,836	491,910
1957	820,360	5,362,994	65,835	430,388
1958	1,005,800	6,393,268	42,608	270,834
1959	1,225,205	7,734,369	53,168	335,635
1960	1,335,242	8,286,620	75,262	467,083
1961	1,461,830	8,981,210	64,540	396,521
1962	1,790,320	10,890,124	81,448	495,430
1963	2,044,900	12,276,080	128,230	769,799
1964	2,301,063	13,635,652	113,285	671,294
1965	2,848,515	16,611,814	140,752	820,830
1966	3,704,445	21,003,286	121,945	691,398
1967	3,979,162	21,885,387	188,998	1,039,489
1968	5,077,600	26,803,304	205,169	1,083,033
1969	5,465,875	27,359,158	164,707	824,432
1970	6,751,523	31,965,326	157,038	743,501
1971	7,116,000	32,276,767	244,491	1,108,963
1972	7,596,749	33,385,709	320,542	1,408,697
1973	8,657,225	35,818,290	308,362	1,275,813
1974	8,165,941	30,427,650	353,022	1,315,418
1975	7,895,450	26,958,995	298,149	1,018,029
1976	9,157,522	29,564,791	266,439	860,190
1977	9,688,977	29,370,707	310,653	941,699
1978	10,337,332	29,125,270	362,429	1,021,138
1979	12,801,200	32,390,910	462,636	1,170,610
1980	13,371,786	29,810,640	530,808	1,183,367
1981	14,175,393	28,647,077	375,699	759,251
1982	15,089,576	28,724,920	446,462	849,898
1983	17,588,242	32,439,354	426,668	786,937
1984	21,251,382	37,573,422	476,260	842,049
1985	25,290,526	43,177,223	542,321	925,877
1986	25,442,242	42,643,608	653,296	1,094,986

Table 1.1 Measures of golf's growth.

	PGA TOUR charitable contributions[a]		Golf Course Facilities in
year	actual $	2003 $	Northern California[b]
1950			70
1951			71
1952			76
1953			83
1954			88
1955			90
1956			97
1957			103
1958			109
1959			114
1960			122
1961			133
1962			145
1963			149
1964			157
1965			170
1966			182
1967			190
1968			197
1969			208
1970			222
1971			224
1972			227
1973			230
1974			241
1975			246
1976			247
1977	$ 3,300,000	$ 10,003,465	252
1978	4,300,000	12,115,182	255
1979	4,400,000	11,133,332	256
1980	5,100,000	11,369,780	264
1981	6,800,000	13,742,133	268
1982	7,200,000	13,706,112	273
1983	7,800,000	14,386,143	275
1984	9,400,000	16,619,632	276
1985	11,300,000	19,291,911	278
1986	16,100,000	26,985,126	283

Table 1.1 Measures of golf's growth.

	total PGA TOUR purses[a]		leading money winner[a]	
year	actual $	2003 $	actual $	2003 $
1987	$ 32,106,093	$ 51,918,034	$ 925,941	$ 1,497,318
1988	36,959,307	57,391,581	1,147,644	1,782,098
1989	41,288,787	61,167,334	1,395,728	2,067,703
1990	46,251,831	65,007,349	1,165,477	1,638,088
1991	49,628,203	66,936,124	979,430	1,321,008
1992	49,386,906	64,664,103	1,344,188	1,759,995
1993	53,203,611	67,636,695	1,478,557	1,879,660
1994	56,416,080	69,930,047	1,499,927	1,859,221
1995	61,650,000	74,311,703	1,654,959	1,994,856
1996	70,700,000	82,776,219	1,780,159	2,084,226
1997	80,550,000	92,193,361	2,066,833	2,365,590
1998	96,150,000	108,360,460	2,591,031	2,920,076
1999	135,808,500	150,108,430	6,619,585	7,313,277
2000	164,025,325	174,776,390	9,188,321	9,790,572
2001	185,350,000	191,285,350	5,687,777	5,869,913
2002	198,650,000	202,846,040	6,912,625	7,058,639
2003	225,000,000	225,000,000		

annualized growth rates[c]

1950-1960	11.2%	9.0%	7.7%	5.5%
1960-1970	17.6%	14.5%	7.6%	4.8%
1970-1980	7.1%	-0.7%	13.0%	4.8%
1980-1990	13.2%	8.1%	8.2%	3.3%
1990-2000	13.5%	10.4%	22.9%	19.6%

Table 1.1 Measures of golf's growth.

	PGA TOUR charitable contributions[a]		Golf Course Facilities in
year	actual $	2003 $	Northern California[b]
1987	$ 17,600,000	$ 28,460,559	284
1988	18,390,000	28,556,574	286
1989	19,779,000	29,301,628	291
1990	20,191,000	28,378,625	296
1991	19,534,000	26,346,515	308
1992	22,223,055	29,097,467	316
1993	22,752,137	28,924,339	320
1994	24,701,631	30,618,685	330
1995	25,487,489	30,722,121	337
1996	30,122,841	35,268,103	348
1997	33,995,646	38,909,653	358
1998	39,700,000	44,741,653	362
1999	44,766,824	49,480,537	376
2000	49,607,157	52,858,670	387
2001	50,785,553	52,411,830	393
2002	59,000,000(est.)	60,246,246(est.)	397
2003			

annualized growth rates[c]

1950-1960			5.7%
1960-1970			6.2%
1970-1980			1.7%
1980-1990	14.8%	9.6%	1.2%
1990-2000	9.4%	6.4%	2.7%

Notes:

[a] From *1999 PGA TOUR Media Guide* and *2003 PGA TOUR Media Guide*.

[b] From *NCGA Golf 1999 Bluebook Edition*, 19, 1, (Winter 1999), *NCGA Golf 2003 Bluebook Edition*, 23, 1, (Winter 2003), and author's calculations.

[c] Author's calculations.

managers will enjoy the "top-ten" lists ranking the 46 golf courses on several different measurements. These lists also illustrate the types of results that are possible with survey data.

Chapter 5[3], "Price Discrimination," will be of interest to golfers who are looking for good deals on golf, golf course managers who are seeking ways to increase revenue and manage demand at their golf courses, and professional economists who are interested in the statistical analysis of pricing behavior. Surprisingly, price discrimination, the practice of selling different units of a good for different prices, can simultaneously help golfers who are willing to seek out bargain prices, and enhance the revenues and profits of the sellers. The basic logic and arithmetic of how this works is presented in the first part of the chapter. The payoff for economists, is the statistical analysis of the most detailed data set ever compiled to address the estimation of demand in the presence of price discrimination. For reasons of simplicity, many economic models assume uniform pricing, that is, each unit of a firm's output is sold for the same price. Furthermore, for reasons having to do with the expense of data collection, practically every existing statistical demand study has employed the same uniform-price assumption. It is simply too bad that this is so. Theory and logic clearly suggest, and a casual look at the real world confirms, that no firm ever should, or ever does, use uniform pricing. It is time for the statistical work to catch up with the theory. This chapter illustrates that it can be done, shows how, and presents the results of my research on 46 golf courses, each of which uses a multiple price strategy.

Chapter 6[4], analyzes the basic economics of quality decisions that business managers must face. The quality decisions in question concern the condition of the course, the beauty of the course, and how condition and beauty effect costs and revenues. Higher quality enhances demand, but it also costs more. The theory of comparing and equating the marginal costs

---

[3]This chapter draws on research previously published in, Shmanske, Stephen, "Price Discrimination at the Links," *Contemporary Economic Policy*, Vol. 16, No. 3, (July 1998), pp. 368-378.

[4]This chapter draws research previously published in Shmanske, Stephen, "The Economics of Golf Course Condition and Beauty," *Atlantic Economic Journal*, Vol. 27, No. 3, (Sept. 1999), pp. 301-313.

and benefits of increased quality is clearly illustrated in the beginning of this chapter. Then, the theory is applied to the consideration of quality by the managers of a golf course. Several basic economic principles are illustrated nicely by the statistical results.

Spatial economics is explored in Chapter 7, "Location, Location, Location." The 46 golf courses in the study compete with each other in the sense that someone, such as myself, living near the center of the San Francisco Bay area, could easily drive to any one of the courses for a round of golf. From a different vantage point, however, each course has somewhat of a local monopoly over nearby residents. This tension between competition across geographic areas and local monopoly is the essence of what economists call spatial competition. This chapter explains how best to consider which portion, and how much of the total population each course can look forward to counting among its loyal, captive consumers.

The final chapter of Part II, "The Economics of Slow Play," presents totally new research on the problem of slow play on golf courses. Using insights from economic production theory, from management science, and from operations research, in particular, from models of production smoothing and inventory management, I offer a better and more complete understanding of golf course backups. The USGA has tried to help golf course managers deal with slow play, but its efforts are hampered by an incomplete understanding of the problem. A manifestation of the outright failure on the part of the USGA to fully understand the problem is seen when the flow of professional golfers playing in the U.S. Open Championship is completely broken by a backup of groups waiting to play a tough par three hole. If long rounds of golf are a problem on your course, this chapter alone is worth the price of the book. Following the implications of my analysis, and employing the suggestions in this chapter, or getting the management of your golf course to follow the suggestions will help in two ways. First, it can save you time by speeding up play on the golf course. Second, it can simultaneously increase the capacity of the golf course by obtaining a sustainable flow of golfers around the course.

The look at golf course economics in Part II was helped by the economic models of demand and supply, optimal production of quality, price discrimination, spatial economics, and production smoothing. Part III turns to look at the economics of professional golf. Here, we are guided by the insights and techniques from cartel theory, labor economics, optimal input usage, wage determination models, and models of discrimination.

Professional golf is described from three perspectives--the individual golfer, the professional golf association (for example the PGA TOUR), and the tournament sponsor or promoter--in Chapter 9, "The Business of Professional Golf." Although each of these three interests has its own incentives and goals, each must interact, and cooperate in order to stage the actual tournament events. In a nutshell, the golfer wants to showcase his talents and compete with others at nice venues for large prize funds, but the golfer wants to avoid economic competition of the type that would lower prize funds. This tension between sporting competition and economic competition is a common theme in the economics of sports, and here we see it played out in the game of golf. Team owners in many league sports limit their economic competition, and act as a cartel by establishing drafting procedures for new talent, and by implementing salary caps and arbitration procedures. In golf, the PGA TOUR is the governing body of the cartel, and sets up its own rules and regulations to police the individual golfers, and to negotiate with the tournament sponsor.[5]

Two levels of economic analysis are combined in Chapter 10, "Practice Makes Perfect," to study the relationship between professional golfers' practice regimens and their earnings. At one level, the professional golfer uses his skills, as measured by a variety of the statistics that are kept on driving distance, putting, and so on, to perform well in tournaments, and win prize money. By using multiple regression analysis, the dollar return to each type of skill can be calculated. Thus, we have production theory at one level; the golfer uses his inputs, the skills, to "produce" tournament winnings. We also have production theory at another level, the professional golfer uses his practice time to develop and maintain his skills. By using regression analysis at this level we can determine the marginal product of practice on a skill-by-skill basis; that is, we can estimate how much improvement comes from practicing an additional hour per week on a certain skill. Combining the two levels leads to an estimate of the value of the marginal product of practice,

---

[5]This chapter draws on and extends Rex Cottle's excellent article: Cottle, Rex L., "Economics of the Professional Golfers' Association Tour," *Social Science Quarterly*, 62 (December 1981) 721-34.

which economic theory shows should be equalized across all skills. These theories are explained and applied in the chapter.[6]

Some fascinating research on salaries and incentives by Ronald Ehrenberg and Michael Bognanno is the centerpiece of Chapter 11, "Tournament Compensation in the Boardroom."[7] Ehrenberg and Bognanno follow an important insight from modern labor economics which suggests that the overwhelmingly large salaries of many corporate executives may best be explained as an efficient form of labor contract. These salaries can be understood as rewarding past superlative performance, so the theory goes, rather than predicting current or future superlative performance. Only a few employees will be promoted to the highest positions, but the potential large financial reward gives all workers the incentive to work hard, and such hard work translates into higher profit. This explanation for large executive salaries rests on the proposition that the greater the potential reward, the greater the effort expended. This chapter explains the tournaments/ compensation model and discusses Ehrenberg and Bognanno's ingenious testing of this proposition by examining fourth-round scores in golf tournaments in relation to how much a particular golfer reasonably has at stake.

My research comparing skills and earnings on the PGA TOUR to those for the LPGA is reported in Chapter 12, "Gender Discrimination?"[8] Statistical examinations of gender or racial discrimination in labor markets are difficult to carry out because of the many unmeasurable aspects of any job. If pay is lower or higher for seemingly identical jobs, is it discrimination or is it some unmeasurable aspect of job performance that causes the

---

[6]The statistical results in this chapter were originally published in, Shmanske, Stephen, "Human Capital Formation in Professional Sports: Evidence from the PGA Tour," *Atlantic Economic Journal*, 20 (September 1992) 66-80. I have a soft spot in my heart for this paper because it was my first publication in the field of golf and economics.

[7]See, Ehrenberg, R. G. and M. L. Bognanno, "Do Tournaments Have Incentive Effects?," *Journal of Political Economy*, 98 (December 1990a) 307-24, and Ehrenberg, R. G. and M. L. Bognanno, "The Incentive Effects of Tournaments Revisited: Evidence from the European PGA Tour," *Industrial and Labor Relations Review*, 43 (supp. February 1990b) 74S-88S.

[8]See, Shmanske, Stephen, "Gender, Skill, and Earnings in Professional Golf," *Journal of Sports Economics*, Vol. 1, No. 4, (November 2000), pp. 400-415.

difference? The economics of sports has made inroads into this area because of the, arguably, better job performance measures that exist because of the sports fans' love of statistics. This chapter explains how economists go about attempting to ferret out discrimination with statistical analysis. The theory is then applied to comment on gender inequality in professional golf, reaching the provocative conclusion that, relative to their skills, women professional golfers are not underpaid compared to men.

A single chapter constitutes Part IV, "The Nineteenth Hole." It summarizes the findings of the preceding chapters, and highlights the areas where potentially fruitful research could be undertaken.

Any book is more than the sum of the individual parts, and this book is no exception. Two themes provide unifying structures to the whole. Certainly, the material is about golf and economics, but instead of one integration of two subject areas, I see it more as a two-way street. Economics can illuminate things about golf, and golf can illustrate things about economics. In each case, one helps us to learn and understand the other.

The first of these themes, economics illuminating golf, may seem the more obvious. Supply and demand modeling can help us analyze the market for golf carts. Analysis of marginal costs and benefits, and subjective measurements of golf course condition can inform us about the proper level of golf course maintenance. Production theory and operations research improve our understanding of the causes of long rounds of golf. Cartel theory explains a lot about the operation of the PGA TOUR. These are not the only examples, but they illustrate the first theme.

Whether any of these examples will actually improve golf course operations or make professional golfers more efficient is hard to say. I am not in the business of running a golf tournament or a golf course. I will say, however, that it was not until I sat down, and worked out the model of slow play and waiting on a golf course, that I felt I had a true understanding of each different variety of the slow play problem. Careful economic analysis showed me that some of my preconceived ideas about slow play and golf course backups were mistaken. Economic analysis and application has the potential to teach many things to golf professionals and economists alike.

The economics of sport in general, and *Golfonomics* in particular, is not solely limited to frivolous illustration and application. There are a number of important and nettlesome issues in economics that are addressed fruitfully with the help of golf and golf statistics. And so, I hope that many of you will be equally intrigued by the second theme, golf illustrating economics. The data on golf course pricing, for example, gives economists the ability, for the first time, to examine multiple price strategies in a competitive, multiple firm setting. Similarly, the data on population and location shows economists the best way to measure certain things in a spatial economic setting. The data on fourth round scores allows a clean test of propositions about how the reward structure affects effort. Also, the tests comparing men and women illustrate nicely many important issues about gender equality or inequality.

The two themes can certainly become intertwined, as Chapter 5 on price discrimination clearly illustrates. On the one hand, golf course managers have much to gain from the analysis of how those pricing structures influence demand and revenues. This is the first theme, economics helps golf. On the other hand, economists doing statistical demand studies have much to gain from my analysis and measurement of the pricing structures used by golf courses. This is the second theme, golf helps economics.

Having met with a modicum of success in my early research projects on golf and economics, I knew that I wanted to continue having fun learning, researching, and writing about golf and economics; in essence, being a student of the combined subject area. My goal became to present, in a book to a wider audience, my collected and extended research and writings in these areas; a book that students of golf and economics would enjoy. But I do not think that one needs to be a student of both to enjoy the finished product. There is enough in the book to satisfy several audiences.

Casual golfers may be predominantly interested in golf either as fans of the sport at the professional level or as stakeholders in the management policies of their own local golf course. I am sure there is enough golf in the book to keep all of you interested. This book will most certainly be uniquely differentiated from the other books in your golf library. And, if you have just an inkling of interest in, or curiosity about economics, and perhaps a dab of patience to wade through the numbers and the related economic arguments, you will be rewarded with an increased appreciation for the breadth and variability of application of my chosen profession. Readers in this audience do not need to have prior knowledge of economics to enjoy this book or to find it useful. Regression analysis, demand, supply, elasticity, marginal product, value of marginal product, and all the jargon are illustrated and defined when they first come up in the book. Who knows, you may yet become an economist.

For those in the professional business of golf course management, Part II should be of immediate interest. From an insider's perspective, you may have much to disagree with in my conclusions. But you might also find something of value from my outsider's perspective as an avid amateur golfer informed by academic training in economics and management. Also, it is extremely likely that golf course managers and superintendents are also fans of professional golf, and will enjoy Part III of the book.

For those who are predominantly interested in economics, whether it be as a teacher or as a student, I am also confident that *Golfonomics* has much to offer. Teachers will certainly get nice classroom applications of economics in the areas of demand estimation, price discrimination, demographics, production theory, measurement of the value of marginal product, measurement of gender discrimination, and spatial economics. Students, as well, will learn about each of these topics. Those who need economic research topics will find several suggestions. I have certainly found that in my study of golf and economics, the more I find out, the more interesting things there are to find out. Each question answered poses two new questions. I suspect you will find the same.

Finally, even without noticing that all of the examples are about golf, golfers, or golf courses, the book works as applied economics. But *Golfonomics* is more than just general applications, it is a book about sports, golf in particular. As such, it will easily fit on the shelf next to other books in the rapidly growing field of sports economics.

Appendix to Chapter 1

There are two errors that commonly appear in profitability studies whether the object of study is a golf course, a park, or any type of municipal expenditure. First, it is fairly typical for a municipality that is thinking about building a municipal golf course to count the expenditure on golf course construction as something that is good for the local economy. Construction workers, irrigation and concrete subcontractors, architects, and consultants all will earn income from the project, and will, in turn, spend some of it, thus helping other local businesses who in turn spend part of their income, and so on. The original expenditure leads to subsequent rounds of secondary expenditures that add to the level of economic activity in the community. Thus, the original expenditures are said to be multiplied in these subsequent rounds leading to a multiplied effect on the economy. If the original expenditure was $10 million, and if the "multiplier" was three, then total income would be increased by $30 million according to this argument.

If the above argument sounds familiar, perhaps it is because you have recently heard it in conjunction with government-financed sports stadiums. The argument is just as fallacious there as it is here. Such arguments are pure rhetorical snake oil put forth by proponents of the project to persuade people who may not directly benefit from the new government facility. To see this, ask yourself a simple question. If a golf course could be constructed for free, or if the golf course in question were already built, would the community be worse off than having to build it from scratch? Surely, having a freely supplied golf course is better than having to spend $10 million to get one. The construction cost is a *cost*, pure and simple; it is not a benefit. Nevertheless, pro-golf-course-development interests will invariably offer the argument about increased economic activity as a benefit.

What is conveniently left out of the argument, and why it is a fallacy, is that the $10 million spent on construction is *exactly* offset by the $10 million decrease in consumer or municipal expenditure elsewhere. Simply put, the money and the resources have to come from somewhere. If the local government spends the $10 million on a golf course, then it does not have it to spend elsewhere. If there was nothing else for the local government to spend on, then they could rebate the money to the taxpayers who surely could find ways to spend the money on meals, entertainment, education, and other services in the community. The $30 million of multiplied expenditure due to the golf course construction is exactly offset by the $30 million of multiplied *lost* expenditure due to the tax collections. Borrowing the funds to construct the golf course complicates, but does not change, the logic of this deductive argument. The borrowed funds, along with accrued interest will eventually have to be repaid from future taxes, or from money that could be used in place of future tax levies, thus delaying, but not avoiding the negative multiplier consequences.

The snake oil argument is convincing enough to fool many because it is half true. Income will be earned by those doing the construction, and will be spent again and again in multiplied fashion. This much is visible to everyone. What is hidden from view, is the expenditure that does not take place because of the taxes collected to pay for the project.[9]

The second error often comes up in discussions of the operations of municipal golf courses. In many, but not all, cases, municipal golf courses earn enough revenues to cover all the costs of operations, and still have money left over to subsidize other city activities. Supporters see such courses as win-win situations. But positive cash flows from golf course operations are neither necessary nor sufficient for the golf course to be the best possible use of the land. Beside the fact that cash flows ignore other benefits that the community receives from a golf course, such as subsidized recreational opportunities for residents and pleasant views for neighbors, focusing on whether the cash flow is positive or negative is tantamount to comparing the golf course to a costless and valueless alternative use of the

---

[9]The original, and much more complete, presentation of this argument and its implications was written in 1946, and is reprinted in, Hazlitt, Henry, *Economics in One Lesson*, Laissez Faire Books, San Francisco, CA, 1996.

land. Perhaps the alternative use of the land was an ugly, barren, possibly dangerous, abandoned landfill that costs the local government money for police time spent keeping the site free from trespassers and hooligans. If so, a golf course with a negative cash flow might still be a good idea. Going the other way, if the alternative use of the land is a housing development that expands the tax base and tax collections by more than the cost of the additional governmental services provided to the new neighborhood, then a meager positive cash flow from golf course operations might pale in comparison. A proper accounting of the costs and benefits of the golf course in question compared to the costs and benefits of the alternative use of the land is required, not a simple comparison of the golf course facility's net revenue to zero.

Chapter 2

Get Your Weight Behind It

Armchair advice frequently given to Little League baseball players is: "get your weight behind it." This advice is usually given to batters with weak swings, or to fielders attempting to throw farther and faster. The advice might also be given to boxers, shot putters, snow shovelers, or to anyone evidencing a lack of power. The target of such counsel might even be the proverbial ninety-eight pound weakling suffering from both a lack of strength and a lack of technique. Notwithstanding the mental image of a more efficient weight transfer designed to foster improved technique, does weight, itself, have anything to do with it?

At 220 pounds, John Daly is among the heavier PGA TOUR professional golfers; he is also among the longest drivers. In fact, he won the long distance crown in 1998 by averaging 299.4 yards. However, the heaviest golfer by far, at six feet seven inches and 245 pounds, Phil Blackmar, had only average length off the tee at 275.9 yards in 1998. Moreover, the second longest in 1998, and one of the longest ever since, was Tiger Woods, who at the time was listed at 160 pounds. The lightest golfer at 140 pounds, Jeff Sluman is a relatively short driver at 266.5 yards. But among the five golfers who, at 150 pounds, were the next lightest on the PGA TOUR in 1998--Skip Kendall, Jodie Mudd, Corey Pavin, Tom Pernice, Jr., and Willie Wood--1995 U.S. Open champ Corey Pavin was the shortest driver on tour (249 yards), and Tom Pernice, Jr. (278 yards), was longer than average.

Endless recounting of weights and distances, that is to say, anecdotal evidence, is not sufficient to get a clear picture of the relationship between a golfer's weight and how far he can hit the golf ball. Economists use a statistical device called regression analysis to get a more complete picture. Readers familiar with statistical regression analysis can skip ahead to the results. The next few sections provide a simple introduction to regression analysis, showing how the regression coefficients are related to slopes on graphs.

2.1 A Simple Example

To illustrate the concept of regression analysis, consider the information in Table 2.1 about five of the longest drivers on the PGA Tour. For these five

Table 2.1 Five long drivers.

golfer	distance	weight	height	age	experience
John Daly	299.4	220	71	32	197
Harrison Frazar	289.8	190	72	27	27
Fred Couples	289.1	185	71	39	404
David Duval	286.8	180	72	27	118
Steve Flesch	281.6	155	71	31	33

Notes: Distance is measured in yards, weight in pounds, height in inches, age in years as of 1998, and experience is the number of PGA TOUR events the golfer has played through 1998.
Source: *1999 PGA TOUR Media Guide.*

golfers there is a consistent relationship between distance and weight; as weight decreases, so does driving distance. There is no such relationship between distance and any of the other variables: height, age, or experience. By measuring driving distance on the vertical axis, and weight on the horizontal axis, five data points can be plotted as in Fig. 2.1.

The points line up pretty well but not exactly. Regression analysis is designed to find the algebraic formula for the line which best approximates the points. In this case the formula is:

$$\text{Driving Distance} = 237.97 + 0.276(\text{Weight}) , \qquad (2.1)$$

and the line is plotted along with the points in Fig. 2.1. In Eq. (2.1), 237.97 is called the constant term, and 0.276 is called the coefficient estimate or the regression coefficient.

The constant term is simply the point at which the regression line crosses the vertical axis; in this case, about 238 yards. The literal interpretation is that a golfer with a weight of zero would average about 238 yards on the drive. Obviously, the literal interpretation is suspect because the relationship between weight and driving distance does not remain linear once one moves outside the range of usual weights. For example, no one would want to use the equation to predict how far a 700 pound person could drive a golf ball. In this case, the formula would give, $137.97 + 0.276 \times 700 = 431.17$ yards.

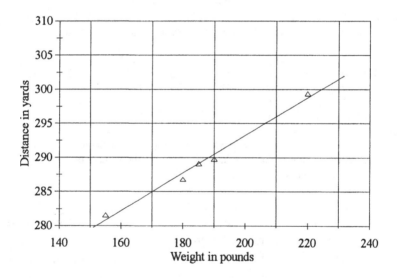

Fig. 2.1 Data points and Eq. (2.1).

More attention is usually given to the estimate of the coefficient of the independent variable, which in this case, is the golfer's weight. The coefficient is a positive number, 0.276, meaning that the slope of the line is positive; thus the line is upward sloping. The upward-sloping regression line indicates that golfers who weigh more, hit the ball farther on average. This positive correlation between weight and driving distance is what is known as a qualitative result. But the regression coefficient also gives us a quantitative result--it puts a number on the positive slope. In this case, each extra pound of weight corresponds to about .276 yards, or about 9.9 inches.

In Fig. 2.1, the coefficient estimate is diagrammatically represented as the slope of the regression line. The slope between two points, mathematically, is the vertical distance between the two points divided by the horizontal distance between the points. In less technical language, the division calculation that yields the slope is also known as "rise over run." So if we take the two points on the regression line corresponding to the weights 150 pounds and 151 pounds, the horizontal distance, or run, is one pound. The vertical distance, or rise, between the two points is 0.276 yards. And 0.276 divided by 1 is 0.276, the slope of the line. On the diagram, every time we move to the right by one pound, we go up by 0.276 yards. If the regression coefficient were larger, the slope of the regression line would be steeper.

Perhaps this is as good a time as any to point out the difference between correlation and causation. Regressions like the one presented here only illustrate the presence or absence of a correlation between the variables. In this case, we have a positive correlation between driving distance and weight. But there is no way that a regression can prove causation. That is, these results do not prove that gaining weight will make you hit the ball farther any more than they prove that hitting the ball farther will make you gain weight. There is simply no way to determine logically from the statistics which way, if any, the causation goes. For the determination of causation, one must fall back on a prior notion or theory of why two variables should be related.

Usually the underlying theory is obvious, but sometimes it is not; and sometimes the underlying theory is ambiguous, or suggests causation running simultaneously in both directions. For the most part this book deals with rather simple underlying theories as is the case with this first simple example. Weight and driving distance were not chosen randomly from among hundreds of data series that could be collected. They were chosen because of the possibility that being a "heavy hitter" is more than just a cliché. So here, the theory is that extra weight allows the golfer to transfer more power to the golf ball, resulting in lengthier shots. According to the data presented so far, an economist or statistician would say that the evidence supports, or is consistent with, the "heavy hitter" hypothesis.

Besides the coefficient estimates, there are a few other statistics that are important to understanding and interpreting the results. Because of these other statistics, and to present the results in a uniform manner, regression results are usually presented in a tabular form as opposed to the equation form given above in Eq. (2.1). Table 2.2 presents the results for the regression of driving distance, measured in yards, on the golfer's weight and a constant term. The column headed by "coefficient" gives the same information that is in Eq. (2.1). The other columns tell us something about the statistical properties of the estimates.

The standard error helps us determine how good the estimate is, that is, how much degree of error is included in the estimate. Like political polls that claim accuracy within a margin of plus or minus 2 percentage points, the standard error allows one to calculate the plus-or-minus margin around the estimate.

Table 2.2 Regression of driving distance on weight.

dependent variable: Driving Distance			
variable	coefficient	standard error	t-statistic
constant term	237.97	3.53	67.35
Weight	0.276	0.0189	14.63

r-squared .986   adjusted r-squared .982   n = 5

How much plus-or-minus margin one ultimately chooses depends on the degree of probability one desires in order to be sure that the true relationship falls within the margin. The narrower the range, the greater the probability that the truth falls outside the range. Conversely, the greater the probability one desires of having the range around the estimate hold the truth, the wider the plus-or-minus margin must be. As a rule of thumb, a range of plus or minus one standard error will contain the truth about two-thirds of the time; a range of plus or minus two times the standard error will contain the truth 95% of the time; and a range of plus or minus three times the standard error will contain the truth about 99% of the time.

Therefore, the larger the standard error, the larger the range of uncertainty around the estimate. For the constant term of 237.97, the standard error is 3.53. Is this large? For the estimate of the weight coefficient of 0.276, the standard error is a tiny 0.0189. Is this small? The answer depends on one's purposes. Three and one-half yards is a suitable margin of error for some things, perhaps driving distance among them, but certainly not for others, such as putting accuracy. For driving distance, adding and subtracting two times the standard error will create a 95% confidence interval that will run from 237.97 +/- 7.06, or from 230.91 to 245.03. This seems to be a relatively narrow range, but not as narrow in absolute terms as the 95% confidence interval around 0.276, from 0.2382 to 0.3138.

The rough rule of thumb that economists use to determine whether the standard error is too large to make the estimate useful, is to compare it to the estimate itself. If the coefficient estimate is more than twice as big as the standard error, then a 95% confidence interval will not contain the value zero. This is an important result to look for in interpreting statistical results. For example, if the estimate is 1.5, and the standard error is 1, then the 95% confidence interval goes from negative 0.5 to positive 2.5, and includes the value zero. Even though the estimate says that there is a positive relationship with a slope of 1.5, the margin of error of plus or minus two means that there may be no relationship, or even a negative relationship between the two variables.

The easiest way to capture the relative size of the standard error is to divide the coefficient estimate by the standard error in order to see how many times larger the estimate is. This is precisely what the t-statistic does. Therefore, a t-statistic of two or greater (in absolute value) is the signal that the 95% confidence interval does not include the value zero.[1] Both estimates in our practice example have t-statistics much greater than two and are, as such, estimated with great precision. They are said to be "statistically significant." Statistical significance is important, and is one of the first

---

[1] For a 90% confidence interval to avoid including zero, the t-statistic only has to be about 1.67. Actually, the 1.67 and the 2.0 figures are not absolutes, they both depend upon the size of the sample.

things to look for in evaluating a regression model. However, as we shall see
below, it is not the only important thing.

In most tables of regression, results of both the standard error and the t-
statistic are not reported. Since one is simply derived from the other in the
formula:

$$\text{(coefficient estimate)/(standard error)} = \text{t-statistic} \quad , \qquad (2.2)$$

usually only one or the other is given. Which one is a matter of the author's
taste. It is my practice to report t-statistics and after this chapter the rest of
the tables in the book are arranged as such.

There is another type of information in the Table 2.2, namely, the r-
squared. The r-squared is a measure of how well the regression equation as
a whole explains or captures the dependent variable, in this case, driving
distance. Driving distance varies from 281.6 yards to 299.4 yards in our
sample of five golfers, with the average being 289.34 yards. The regression
equation uses the explanatory variable, weight, to explain why some golfers
are long, like the 299.4 yards of John Daly, and why others are (relatively)
short, like the 281.6 yards of Steve Flesch. This model does so with great
accuracy. The r-squared of .986 indicates that 98.6% of the variation
around the average of 289.34 in driving distance is captured or explained by
considering the golfer's weight. Since 100% would be a perfect fit, the
theoretical maximum for the r-squared is 1, and an r-squared of .986 is very
good. But whether an r-squared of .986 is good enough depends on the
nature of the model, particularly the nature of the dependent variable. Some
variables tend to fluctuate very predictably, and r-squareds of .999 are
possible. Other types of data vary very randomly; capturing 20% or 30% of
the variation is the best that can be done. In the simple regression here, the
leftover 1.4% of the variation is unexplained by this model, and may be due
to other factors such as height, age, experience, or other unmeasurable
differences. For the purposes of the diagram, the high r-squared means that
the regression line, as drawn, goes very close to the five data points in the
sample.

The adjusted r-squared makes a technical adjustment to the r-squared.
One can always increase the r-squared simply by adding more explanatory
variables, or by eliminating variation by trying to explain fewer data points.

The adjusted r-squared takes into account how many data points the model is trying to explain, and how many factors the model is using to explain them. Roughly put, the more data and the fewer explanatory variables, the higher will be the adjusted r-squared in relationship to the r-squared. Its interpretation is similar to that given for the r-squared in the preceding paragraph, and most economic researchers report only the adjusted r-squared.

The last piece of information in the table is: n = 5. This is a simple reminder that the number of observations, n, equals 5. That is, the regression model is explaining or illustrating the relationship between weight and driving distance for the five golfers in Table 2.1. Five observations are woefully inadequate to achieve results that will not be changed by the consideration of more data points. Generally speaking, economists require at least 30 observations to overcome a severe small sample bias. I am using only five observations here for simplicity. The remainder of the chapter delves into what kinds of things change as we consider more golfers.

2.2 Small Sample Bias

The five golfers listed in Table 2.1 had driving distances that could be explained by a constant term and a weight variable. Now consider the following five golfers in Table 2.3 who were among the shortest in driving

Table 2.3 Five short drivers.

golfer	distance	weight	height	age	experience
Larry Rinker	256.5	155	69	41	459
Lee Porter	259.1	165	69	32	87
Olin Browne	263.3	175	69	39	154
Bob Friend	264.2	180	68	35	77
Paul Goydos	266.9	190	69	34	186

Notes: Distance is measured in yards, weight in pounds, height in inches, age in years as of 1998, and experience is the number of PGA TOUR events the golfer has played through 1998.
Source: *1999 PGA TOUR Media Guide*.

distance in 1998. Again there seems to be a relationship between distance and weight. As weight increases, so does driving distance. There is no such uniform relationship between distance and any of the other variables in the table. A statistical regression analysis, the results of which appear in Table 2.4, confirms the relationship.

Table 2.4 Regression of driving distance on weight.

dependent variable: Driving Distance			
variable	coefficient	standard error	t-statistic
constant term	209.03	3.26	64.19
Weight	0.306	0.0188	16.30

r-squared .989   adjusted r-squared .985   n = 5

The five data points and the regression line are plotted in Fig. 2.2 along with the original five points and the first regression line. As the diagram illustrates, and as Table 2.4 enumerates, the constant term is lower and the slope is slightly higher than in the first regression. Indeed, the constant term

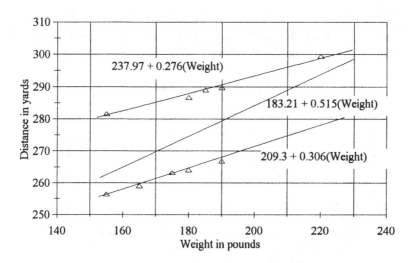

Fig. 2.2 Data points and regression lines.

is 209.03, down from 237.97, and the slope is 0.306, up from 0.276. There is a positive relationship between weight and driving distance for the short hitters in the second example, but it is different from the one before.

The statistical properties of the second regression are very similar to the first regression. The r-squared is very high, and so are the t-statistics. The closeness of the data points to the regression line in the diagram goes hand in hand with the high t-statistics and r-squared, but the sample is still small.

Notwithstanding the fine statistical properties of each of the two equations presented so far, a quick look at the diagram tells us that, if we were to combine the samples, one line will not capture all ten data points. Indeed, the results of the regression of driving distance on weight for all ten golfers appears Table 2.5, and is illustrated in Fig. 2.2. The regression line

Table 2.5 Regression of driving distance on weight.

dependent variable: Driving Distance			
variable	coefficient	standard error	t-statistic
constant term	183.21	38.72	4.73
Weight	0.515	0.2146	2.40

r-squared .419   adjusted r-squared .346   n = 10

is still upward sloping, in fact, it is even steeper than before, but it does not nearly capture the ten points as closely. Indeed, the line splits the difference between each of the two sets of five points, but does not capture any one of the points with great accuracy. While it is easy to see from the diagram what is going on, the information required to interpret the results is also contained in the table. Note that the standard errors are much higher than previously and, therefore, the t-statistics are lower. To get a rough estimate of a 95% confidence interval for the coefficient estimate, one must add and subtract two times the standard error to the estimate. Adding and subtracting (2 x .2146) to .515 yields an interval from .0858 to .9442. This confidence interval does not contain any negative numbers, so the result that weight and driving distance are positively related is still statistically significant. But note that the lower end of the range means that a gain in weight of one pound is associated with a .0858 yard increase in driving distance. This is a whopping 3.09 inches; not very much on which to stake a claim for the "heavy hitter" hypothesis. Also note that the r-squared and adjusted r-squared have fallen dramatically. The equation now only captures about 42% of the variation in driving distance.

The deterioration in the r-squared continues as we consider more and more data. It is too tedious to list all the data points by name but we can calculate the regression line, listing the results in Table 2.6, and plot all the

Table 2.6 Regression of driving distance on weight.

dependent variable: Driving Distance			
variable	coefficient	standard error	t-statistic
constant term	248.186	6.322	39.26
Weight	0.126	0.0345	3.668

r-squared .095   adjusted r-squared .088   n = 130

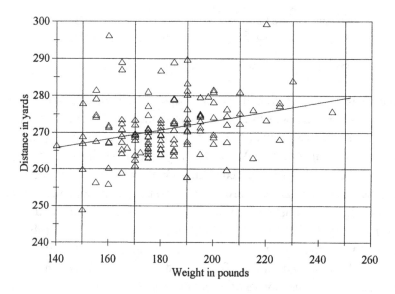

Fig. 2.3 Data points and regression line from Table 2.6.

data points and the regression line in Fig. 2.3. This time, the sample includes all 130 PGA TOUR professional golfers who played enough official rounds in 1998 to be included in the official statistics for 1998. The sample size is 130.

Table 2.6 shows that there is still a positive relationship between weight and driving distance, and it is statistically significant as evidenced by the low standard error and the t-statistic of 3.668. According to the regression, each extra pound is associated with 0.126 extra yards of driving distance, or about four and one-half inches. But there is a lot of unexplained variation in the data. According to the r-squared in the table, only about 9.5% of the variation in driving distance can be attributable to weight differences among professional golfers, leaving over 90% of the variation due to other factors. Diagrammatically speaking, the regression line plotted in Fig. 2.3, although upward sloping, only very roughly captures the spread of the data points.

2.3 Multiple Regression Analysis

It is clear from Fig. 2.3 that something else beside weight must be going on to cause the large variation in driving distances. The data in Table 2.1 and Table 2.3, and the diagram in Fig. 2.2, point to a possibility that will be explored here. Fig. 2.2 shows that two separate upward sloping functions can capture the two sets of five points very precisely. Tables 2.1 and 2.3 show that there is a systematic difference between the two data sets; namely, each of the five long drivers in Table 2.1 is taller than 70 inches, while each of the five short drivers in Table 2.3 is less than 70 inches tall. Perhaps it is not only weight, but height as well, that influences how far one can hit a golf ball. In fact, the theory for such a finding would be straightforward. Taller people can develop wider arcs in their swings, thus developing more clubhead speed and greater distance.

As before, anecdotal evidence on long and short hitters, tall and short golfers, the lithe and the rotund, will not be conclusive. Tiger Woods has a tall, lightweight body and prodigious length off the tee. Tiger's data point might indicate that it is height not weight that is important. But Phil Blackmar at six feet, seven inches and 245 pounds, has both height and weight, but he has below average driving distance. Examples such as these supply interesting barroom conversation, but not much understanding of any underlying relationship that might exist. Economists, however, have a tool to simultaneously factor in the effects of height and weight. It is called multiple regression analysis.

Fortunately, there is nothing new to learn about the interpretation of multiple regression analysis. The slope coefficients, the t-statistics, and the r-squared have the same meanings as above. Unfortunately, we will no longer be able, as before, to picture the results in a two-dimensional diagram because there are now three dimensions of interest: namely, driving distance, height, and weight. Therefore, to understand the results of multiple regression analysis, it is necessary to picture the results in your mind's eye, in two dimensions at a time. To do this, let us consider an example chosen specifically to work well: namely, the ten golfers from Tables 2.1 and 2.3.

Table 2.7 lists the results of a regression of driving distance on both height and weight for the hand-chosen sample of ten golfers. These results are best contrasted to the results in Table 2.5. Weight is still a statistically significant explanatory variable that is positively related to driving distance. Each pound is associated with extra distance of 0.337 yards; and the t-statistic has increased while the standard error has decreased. Therefore, the size of the plus-or-minus confidence interval around the estimate of 0.337 has decreased. Furthermore, the r-squared has increased from just under 42% to just under 92%. In the three-dimensional picture that will not be attempted in this book, the data points lie very close to the three-dimensional regression line. Actually, the regression analysis yields a two-dimensional plane situated in three-dimensional space, but common usage refers to it as the regression line.

Table 2.7 Regression of driving distance on weight and height.

variable	coefficient	standard error	t-statistic
dependent variable: Driving Distance			
constant term	-333.686	80.19	-4.161
Weight	0.337	0.0899	3.751
Height	7.829	1.192	6.569

r-squared .919   adjusted r-squared .896   n = 10

The new factor which causes the improvement in the results is the golfer's height. Each inch of height is associated with tee shots that are 7.829 yards longer on average. This estimate is fairly precise; the standard error of 1.192 when doubled is still less than two and one-half yards, so that the plus-minus range around the estimate for a 95% confidence interval is less than five yards wide.

If one could picture the results two dimensions at a time, the regression line would have a positive slope of 0.337 yards per pound in the weight-driving distance diagram, and a positive slope of 7.829 yards per inch of height in the height-driving distance diagram. The ten data points would fall closely to the line.

The t-statistics and the r-squared increased when height was added to the regression model. This is a sign that the new model is better than the first one. In reality, however, we still have a model based on a small sample, and what is worse, based on a hand-picked, as opposed to a randomly-picked, sample. I chose the sample to illustrate what happens when multiple regression analysis works to improve a two-dimensional model, specifically, that the t-statistics and the r-squared increase. What happens in the larger sample of 128 golfers (heights were not reported for two of the 130 golfers in the *1999 PGA TOUR Media Guide*) is not such a clear improvement.

The results of the regression of driving distance on height and weight for the full sample are listed in Table 2.8. Height and weight are still positively related to driving distance. The weight variable is statistically significant with a t-statistic of 2.181, but the low t-statistic on the height variable

Table 2.8 Regression of driving distance on weight and height.

dependent variable: Driving Distance			
variable	coefficient	standard error	t-statistic
constant term	227.326	21.20	10.771
Weight	0.0943	0.0432	2.181
Height	0.374	0.346	1.081

r-squared .097   adjusted r-squared .083   n = 128

indicates that the margin of error around the estimate of 0.374 is large enough to contain zero and negative numbers. One cannot be sure that taller golfers hit the ball farther.

By comparing Table 2.8 with Table 2.6, we see an example of a multiple regression equation that does not improve over the simple, two-dimensional linear model. The percentage of the variation in driving distance explained by the model, that is, the r-squared, increased by only two-tenths of a percentage point from 0.095 to 0.097. The new variable, height, is not a statistically significant factor, and the inference about whether weight and driving distance are linked is hardly changed. On the basis of the regressions reported in Tables 2.6 and 2.8, one would conclude that there is a statistically significant relationship between a golfer's weight and the distance he can hit the driver. Quantitatively speaking, the relationship is on the order of 0.09-0.12 yards of extra distance per pound or about 3.5 inches per pound. Big deal.

2.4 Economic Significance

I have been careful, so far, to consistently repeat the tongue-tying, "statistically significant," when discussing the regression results. Without statistical significance (t-statistics larger than two in absolute magnitude for 95% confidence, or t-statistics larger than 1.67 for 90% confidence), you cannot reject the hypothesis that the two variables are not related. While this mouthful of jargon sounds like a confusing double negative, all it really means is that you probably have only random variation. But too many people rely too much solely on statistical significance. For example, driving in the rain (a car, not a golf ball), may increase the risk of an accident in a manner that is statistically significant, say from one chance in 100,000 to one chance in 90,000, but for all practical purposes the change is inconsequential. Taking a drug with potentially negative side effects, or a health food extract with supposedly positive effects, may double or halve the risk of contracting a certain form of cancer. But if the risk is small to begin with (say, one case in a million), doubling or halving the risk is hardly consequential.

Statistical significance is determined by comparing the size of the regression coefficient to the standard error. But we must also determine the economic or practical significance of a result by comparing the magnitude of any regression coefficient to a common-sense notion of its importance. In this comparison, the three and one-half inches of extra driving distance per pound of body weight is laughably small. But here is where one needs to be guarded with respect to the rhetoric surrounding any issue. It is true that there is a significant *statistical* relationship between weight and driving distance; heavier golfers hit the ball farther on average. Quantifiably, however, if the effect is so small, as it is in this case, is it really worthwhile to place any importance on it?

Perhaps the simplest way of determining whether a result that passes statistical muster has any real consequence is to examine, as we have done, the magnitude of the coefficient. We found a result of roughly 3.5 inches per pound. Now, if the result was 3 yards per pound we might have something. I suppose that many golfers, professional and amateur, would commence a weight-gain program to gain ten pounds if it meant hitting a drive 30 yards farther, but I doubt that golfers would do it to gain 35 inches. To examine the results this way requires that the reader have some familiarity with the subject matter, at least enough to be able to determine that 30 yards is worthwhile, whereas 35 inches is not. For most of the golf statistics presented in this book, it is probably the case that the reader has enough prior knowledge to interpret the economic significance, but such is not always the case. There is, however, one more technique that is often useful. That technique is the calculation of an elasticity.

In general, an elasticity is a ratio of percentage changes. By focusing on percentage changes one can determine whether an increase in driving distance of 3.5 inches is large or small, and whether an increase in one pound of weight is large or small. Taking the result of Table 2.8., the slope coefficient for the weight variable is 0.0943 yards per one pound. To determine whether 0.0943 yards is a lot or a little, we place it in perspective by dividing it by the average driving distance in the sample, in this case, 271.36 yards. Therefore, the percentage change in driving distance is 0.0943/271.36 = 0.0003475. This change in driving distance of 0.0943 yards is associated with a change in weight of one pound. To determine whether one pound is a lot or a little, we place it in perspective by dividing it by the average weight of the 128 golfers in the sample, which in this case is 182.63 pounds. Therefore, the percentage change in weight is 1/182.63 = .005476. Finally, the elasticity of driving distance with respect to weight is formed by the ratio of these two percentage changes, .0003475/.005476 = .063.

Whenever elasticity is less than one in absolute value, and in this case, it is close to zero, the effect is called inelastic. Alternatively, if the elasticity is greater than one in absolute value, the effect is called elastic. For an inelastic relationship such as we have calculated, you can change the denominator by a great deal in percentage terms, that is, gain a lot of weight, and the effect on the numerator is still very small. Such an inelastic relationship will not lend itself to exploitation because the change one would have to make is too large and the return is too inconsequential.

Pointing out that the elasticity is close to zero is really just another way of saying that gaining weight will not have a very big effect on how far one hits a golf ball. Using the following formula for elasticity, some numerical examples can be quickly calculated:

$$0.063 = (\text{\% change in distance})/(\text{\% change in weight}) \quad . \quad (2.3)$$

Multiplying each side by the % change in weight yields:

$$0.063 \times (\text{\% change in weight}) = \text{\% change in distance} \quad . \quad (2.4)$$

According to Eq. (2.4), a 10% change in weight would lead to a six-tenths of 1% change in driving distance. Another way to think of it is that in order to get a 6.3% change in distance (about 17 yards), one would have to endure a 100% increase in weight!

We are left with the conclusion that although there is a statistically significant positive relationship between a golfer's weight and the distance he hits the driver, the elasticity is so small that there is no economically significant relationship between the two. The "heavy hitter" hypothesis does not hold water. Oh well, time to go back on my diet.

2.5 Epilogue

Knowledge about nutrition, exercise, and weight management, has been developed at light speed over the past quarter century. Athletes now know that for most purposes it is not sheer weight that is important. Sumo wrestling, tug-of-war, and certain positions in American Football may be exceptions. In most sports, however, measures of muscle mass or body fat percentages are the indicators of optimum physical fitness leading to optimum performance.

In a recent issue of *Golf Magazine*, Harry Blauvelt reports on the exercise routines of five PGA TOUR golfers--Jesper Parnevik, Stuart Appleby, Rocco Mediate, Grant Waite, and Scott McCarron.[2] These golfers are clearly interested in aerobic fitness, muscle tone, and turning fat into muscle. It is interesting to compare the weights reported for these golfers as of January 2001 with the weights reported in the *1999 PGA TOUR Media Guide*. Jesper Parnevik is listed at the same 175 pounds. Rocco Mediate, who at one point was 250 pounds, has actively been trying to lose weight because of back problems and has, indeed, dropped another 5 pounds from 190 to 185. The other three golfers have actually gained weight. It would be interesting use some measure of muscle mass or body fat percentage as an additional variable in the driving distance-weight regressions reported above.

It might also be interesting to look at the relationship between weight and driving distance over a period of years. Interestingly, four of the five golfers listed above have increased their driving distance from 1998 to 2001, and the fifth, Scott McCarron, has exactly the same 289.1 yards in 1998 and 2001. With some of the five golfers losing weight and some gaining, and with all driving farther or at least as far, perhaps the notion of fitness rather than weight holds the key to the relationship. Conclusions will be difficult to come by, however, because over the same period, there have been changes in the technology of balls, clubheads, and shafts that also lead to the increasingly prodigious distances that the professionals can drive the golf ball. Discovering the degree to which technology and fitness each influence driving distance will be left to future research.

---

[2]See, Blauvelt, Harry, "Survival of the Fittest," *Golf Magazine*, Vol. 43, No. 1, (Jan. 2001) pp. 120-5.

Part II

The Front Nine:

Golf Course Economics

Chapter 3

To Ride or Not to Ride

There is no doubt that golf is much more difficult than economics. It is evident that top golfers earn more than top economists do; justifiably so. The higher earnings of golfers are called for on both the supply and demand sides. Indeed, the demand for Tiger Woods' services is higher than for the services of a Nobel Prize winning economist like Milton Friedman, because Tiger Woods creates more value or more enjoyment for his "customers" than does Friedman. Likewise, the demand is higher for other top professional golfers than it is for top professional economists. On the supply side, it is simply harder to develop the skills of a professional golfer than the skills of a professional economist, so the supply of golfers is lower. The golfer has too many things to learn: keep your head down, light grip pressure, left arm straight, stop at the top, KISS (keep it slow, stupid), correct weight shift, and so on. Comedian Tom Smothers jokes about writing a book entitled, *The 57 Swing Keys to Remember in the Two Seconds Between Takeaway and Impact.* The corresponding joke about economists is that one could teach economics to a bird brain, to wit, a parrot with a two-word vocabulary, "supply" and "demand."

This chapter concentrates on the concept of demand and its measurement. The demand curve is described first and applied to the demand to ride in golf carts. A brief discussion of golf cart economics follows. This discussion includes treatment of a curious policy that some golf courses employ, namely, making carts mandatory. A recognition of the competition between carts and caddies concludes the chapter.

3.1 Demand

Fig. 3.1 presents a generic, downward-sloping demand curve labelled, D. Price per unit is measured on the vertical axis, and some measure of quantity is on the horizontal axis. The diagram is interpreted in the following manner. Take any price, say p_0, draw a horizontal line over to the demand curve, and then from the point on the demand curve extend the line down to the horizontal axis to get a quantity, say q_0. This quantity, goes with the original price, and is called the "quantity demanded" at that price. For a different price, p_1, out comes a different quantity, q_1. Note that for a downward sloping demand curve, since p_1 is a lower price than p_0, it must be the case that q_1 is a higher quantity than q_0. When price goes down, quantity demanded goes up, duh.

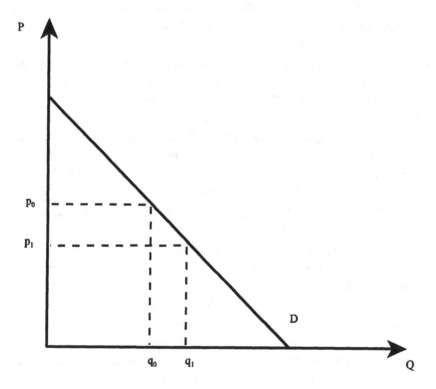

Fig. 3.1 The demand curve.

Quantitatively, the relationship between price and quantity depends on the position and shape of the demand curve. In turn, the position and shape of the demand curve depends on how the market is defined. For example, the demand curve in Fig. 3.1 might represent the yearly demand for one individual to ride a golf cart. Consider the demand for a person who golfs once per week. Suppose that a relatively high price for today's market might be $15 to rent a cart and at that high price the golfer might take a cart half the time or about 26 times per year. So p_0 would be $15 per cart and q_0 would be 26 cart rentals per year. The same golfer might take a cart three quarters of the time if the price were only $10 per rental. Thus, p_1 would be $10 and q_1 would be 39 cart rentals per year. For a different golfer the numbers would be different depending on the golfer's age, physical condition, and the golfer's enjoyment of walking versus riding. For golfers on different courses, the hilliness of the course and whether or not carts are restricted to cart paths would also make a difference.

For the interpretation of the demand curve at the level of the golf course, however, the numbers would be different. The vertical axis would still be the price per cart rental. But now, the horizontal axis would be the number of carts rented per day or year, or perhaps the percentage of golfers taking carts. So the high price of $15 might lead about 50% of the golfers to rent carts while a lower price of $10 might lead about 80% of golfers to rent carts. For a busy golf course that sells about 240 rounds of golf per day, q_0 would be 50% or 120 cart rentals per day, and q_1 would be 80% or 192 cart rentals per day.[1]

Given any demand curve such as the one depicted in Fig. 3.1, whenever the price changes, the relevant point on the demand curve changes and the associated quantity also changes. This is the change in quantity demanded and is brought about by the change in price. In fact, a change in price is the only thing that causes the movement up and down the demand curve because that is precisely what the demand curve is, a relationship between price and

---

[1]Perhaps we should be calling this "half cart" rentals since carts normally accommodate either one or two riders at the same time. Some golf courses will charge the full price to rent a cart whether one or two golfers are using it. Other golf courses will discount a "half cart" rental by as much as 50%.

quantity demanded. It is crucial, however, to understand the following distinction between a change in quantity demanded and a change in demand.

Consider again the golfer who plays 52 rounds a year and takes a cart one half of the time because the price is $15. If this golfer sprains his wrist and plays only once every other week (but keeps the proportion of times he rents a cart the same) then his cart rentals will fall to one half of what they used to be, even though the price has not changed. This is illustrated in Fig. 3.2 as the movement from point A on demand curve D_1 to point B on demand curve D_2. Alternatively, suppose that the golfer's employment status changes and he now plays golf twice per week. Now he rents twice as many carts per year even though the price has not changed. This is illustrated by a movement from point A on demand curve D_1 to point C on demand curve D_3, still at a price of $15 but now with 52 cart rentals per year. Either of these changes is called a change in demand (as opposed to a change in quantity demanded) and is illustrated by a change in the position of the whole demand curve (as opposed to a movement along a single demand curve).

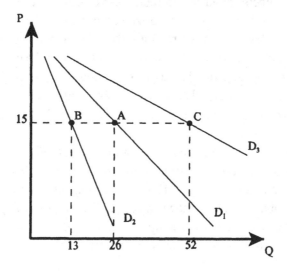

Fig. 3.2 Changes in demand.

Anything other than price can change the demand. For an individual it could be an injury, a change in income, a change in employment status, or simply growing older. It could also be a change in the golf course, for example, a redesign that makes the course hillier (or flatter), a change in policy regarding whether carts have to stay on cart paths, or even a change in the availability and price of caddies. Anything, except price, that changes the nature of the consumption of the good in question, changes the position of the demand curve and is called a change in demand. The only thing that can never change the demand is the price itself. When price changes, the demand curve stays put and one slides along it to choose a different point corresponding to the changed price. As previously named, this is called a change in quantity demanded.

3.2 The Demand For Carts

Let us try to quantify these relationships by looking at the demand to rent golf carts. Using a sample of 46 public access golf courses in the San Francisco Bay area in 1993, data was collected on cart usage, cart policy, cart pricing, golf course characteristics such as hilliness and yardage, and demographic characteristics such as income of the golfers at a particular course. Potentially, each of these variables has an influence on the demand and quantity demanded for golf cart rental. Using regression analysis we will estimate the demand for golf cart usage as a function of price, hilliness, yardage, cart policy, and demographic characteristics.

The dependent variable in the regressions is the percentage of golfers who take golf carts. This number was obtained from the golf course personnel. An alternative to the percentage of golfers taking carts is the absolute number of cart rentals that the golf course makes. But the absolute number of cart rentals will be harder to estimate because it also depends on the number of golfers in total which in turn depends on the popularity and price of the golf course itself. By taking the percentage of golfers who take carts, those factors that influence only the total number of golfers but not the percentage who take carts can be ignored. For example, one golf course that sells twice the number of rounds as another course because it is closer to a population center, will rent twice the number of carts if the two courses have the same percentage rental rate. Therefore, population will be a necessary control variable if the number of cart rentals is the dependent variable but not if the percentage taking carts is the dependent variable. Therefore, using the percentage taking carts will make for a simpler regression. Summary statistics for the dependent variable and all the explanatory variables are listed in Table 3.1. As is shown in the table, cart rental percentages range from a low of 11% to a high of 100% with an average of almost 50%. As might be expected, the 100% figures are reached on several courses that require carts to be taken and the 11% figure is reached for a very flat golf course.

Table 3.1 Summary statistics.

Variable	Mean	Std. Dev.	Minimum	Maximum	N
% Taking Carts	49.713	26.410	11	100	46
Price	9.48	2.14	0	12	46
Hilliness	2.50	0.97	1.04	4.54	46
% Carts Required	0.13	0.30	0	1	46
Cartpaths Only	0.14	0.34	0	1	46
Income	59.38	17.14	37.25	118.8	46
Elevation Change	78.72	81.43	3	330	46
Yardage	6573.6	362.67	5149	7131	46

Notes: Price is in 1993 dollars for a single cart rental. Hilliness is the average opinion of all surveyed golfers for the course on a scale of 1-5 with 1 being flat and 5 being most hilly. % Carts Required is the percentage of time that carts are required at a particular facility. Cartpaths Only is a dummy variable equal to one if carts are required to stay on paved paths. Income is measured in thousands of 1993 dollars. Elevation Change is measured in feet. Yardage is measured in yards.

The first factor to consider in a demand curve study is the price per cart rental. The price is measured in dollars and stands for the price for a single golfer to rent a shared cart. As Table 3.1 shows, these prices ranged from zero to $12. The only peculiar thing to note is that some courses require you to take a cart and some courses require you to pay for a cart whether or not you take it. When carts are mandatory, some courses just quote a combined price for green fees and cart rental; other courses quote two different prices, but make you pay them both. Some of these courses actually ring up the cart rental and the green fee on separate cash registers. To avoid confusion and to keep the same measurement protocol, I have measured the price of carts as equal to $10 (which is the median price) for courses that require carts and do not list separate prices.[2] However, in cases where carts are not mandatory but paying for them is (that is, you can walk the course if you want but you still have to pay for the cart), the true opportunity cost of the cart to the golfer is zero. In these cases the price has been entered as zero, carts truly carry a price of zero to the golfer and although most people take them in these cases, not all do.

In fact, this author is one of those who would rather walk if allowed to do so. Moreover, I actually paid more to walk on one occasion. My friend and I went to a golf course with a two-for-one coupon that required the rental of a golf cart. It was about 1990 at the time. Green fees were $24 and the cart rental fee for two was $22. Use of the coupon would have cost us $46 and we would have received a cart which we did not want. When we asked if we could use the coupon, pay for the cart but not use it, we were told that we could not do so. The result was that we did not use the coupon and paid $48 to walk rather than $46 to ride. I have not been back to that golf course since.

Another main factor in determining the demand for cart rental is the hilliness of the golf course. Obviously, it is easier to walk and carry one's golf clubs on a flat golf course than on a hilly one. The statistical problem we face is how to measure the hilliness of the golf course. I tried two methods to get a measure of hilliness.

The first measure of hilliness is the difference in elevation between the highest point on the golf course and the lowest point. Table 3.1 shows that this difference ranged from a low of 3 feet to a high of 330 feet with an average of about 79 feet. There are a couple of reasons why this measure is not ideal. First, there is a measurement problem. Some of the golf course

---

[2]This is an interesting issue in itself. In some cases it makes no difference whether money collected for golf is attributed to green fees or cart rentals, especially if all the money accrues to the same owners. In other cases, perhaps the green fee revenues go to one owner or set of owners and the cart revenues go to another owner or in different proportions to a set of owners. In some cases perhaps different tax rates apply to green fee revenue and cart revenues. In other cases coupons for free green fees or free cart rental might require a breakdown of the total price into parts attributable to either cart rental or green fees. The point is that the somewhat arbitrary treatment of these revenues by golf courses can occlude the underlying relationship between price and quantity unless the prices are treated uniformly across all the observations.

superintendents with whom I spoke quoted me an exact figure from memory. Others brought out topographic maps of the golf course property. Still others seemed simply to make an educated guess. It is not at all clear that these figures carry the same degree of accuracy. While this is not a fatal problem in statistical analysis, it does cloud the interpretation of the results somewhat. The second problem is that the difference from highest to lowest elevation does not really determine how hilly the golf course plays. Equally important, or perhaps even more important, is how many times the golfer has to go up and down the hills that are there. For these reasons, a second approach to hilliness was tried.

The second measure of hilliness is a subjective one. In interviews of golfers, I asked them to rank the hilliness of the golf course on a scale of one to five with one being flat and five being most hilly. Using at least 20 interviews for each of the 46 golf courses, I obtained over 900 separate rankings of course hilliness. I then took the average ranking for each golf course as the measure of that course's hilliness. This method is not as objective as the measurement of actual elevation change. Nevertheless, perhaps because of its subjectivity it is an even better measure in that it captures what the golfers think the hilliness is. And it is what golfers think about hilliness that is important when the decision to rent a cart is made.

Table 3.1 shows that the 1-5 rankings range from 1.04 to 4.54 with a average of 2.50. Table 3.2 compares the objective elevation change measure with the subjectively measured hilliness for the five flattest and five hilliest courses in the sample. There is a close but not exact correspondence between the two measures. The two hilliest and two flattest courses in the sample are ranked as such by either measure. But note, for example, that the fourth and fifth most hilly by the subjective Hilliness measure are only the eighth and seventh most hilly in actual elevation change. Overall, the correlation coefficient between the two measures is 0.83. In the statistical regressions, the subjective Hilliness measure leads to better results.

Another variable that might represent the difficulty of walking, thus being a factor associated with an increased demand to rent carts, is the overall length of the golf course. The variable, Yardage, from Table 3.1 lists the course yardage from the longest tees. Unfortunately, this is still only a rough measure of how far one would have to walk. The distance from one green to the next tee can vary greatly from course to course. Furthermore, the course layout may allow golf clubs to be left at convenient in-between places (for example, when walking back to a tee or after hitting a nice approach shot to the green with the next hole being played back along a parallel fairway) so that a portion of the walking is done without the necessity of carrying the whole golf bag. As it turns out in this data set, the overall yardage from the back tees is not a significant determinant of the demand to rent a cart.

Table 3.2 Comparison of hilliness and elevation change.

course	Hilliness	Rank	Elevation Change	Rank
Lake Chabot	4.542	1	330	1
Pittsburg Delta View	4.325	2	300	2
Indian Valley	4.26	3	200	T4
Tilden Park	4.188	4	170	8
Summitpointe	4.119	5	175	7
Sunnyvale	1.333	42	10	T37
San Jose Municipal	1.111	43	7	T43
Chuck Corica	1.093	44	10	T37
San Mateo Municipal	1.067	45	4	45
Skywest	1.04	46	3	46

Notes: Hilliness is a 1-5 scale with 1 being flattest. Elevation Change is in feet. Rank is among the 46 courses with 1 being the hilliest. "T" before a number indicates a tie.

There are two direct golf course policy issues that influence cart usage, namely, whether or how often carts are mandatory, and whether carts must remain on paved cart paths. The variable, % Carts Required, measures the percentage of the rounds at a golf facility for which cart rental was required. Some golf course facilities always require carts to be taken, others never do. And there are a variety of intermediate cases. For example, one facility in the sample has two 18-hole courses and carts are mandatory on one of them after 8:00 AM. A couple of the semi-private facilities[3] allow members to walk but require non-members to rent a cart. Other courses require carts on

---

[3]A semi-private facility allows open play for a daily fee but also has members who, in return for yearly or monthly fees, receive special privileges such as preferred tee times and the right to walk.

weekends but not weekdays, and so on. As Table 3.1 shows, by far the most common case is for walking to be allowed with carts optional. It is expected that courses that require carts more of the time will have a higher overall percentage of cart usage.

The second golf course policy issue is whether or not carts must remain on paved paths. Most golf course facilities allow carts to drive on the fairways, but some facilities restrict carts to paths. When carts are restricted they are not as useful as otherwise and thus we should expect the restriction to lower the overall cart usage rate. Cartpaths Only is a dummy variable equal to one for golf courses that restrict carts to paths.

Finally, I attempted to consider income as a determinant of golf cart usage. Income is an important determinant of demand for most goods, and is one of the things that economists naturally try to measure and control for in a demand study. In this case, I was ultimately unsuccessful in capturing any effect of income on cart rental frequency. One might think that since carts add an extra expense to a round of golf, that those with higher incomes will rent golf carts more often. That means that golf courses with a wealthier clientele might rent carts a higher percentage of the time. So I set out to measure income.

During my interviews of golfers on the 46 golf courses, I asked for some demographic information including income. A significant number of interviewees declined to state their incomes. Some, however, were not concerned with such issues of privacy. Thus, I was able to obtain an average income figure by course for the golfers who stated their incomes. Table 3.1 shows that these average figures ranged from $37,000 to almost $119,000, with an average of $59,000 in 1993 dollars.

These figures are suspect for at least two reasons. First of all, they seem high. While golfers are wealthier on average than the non-golfing public, the difference is not as great as these figures would make it seem. These figures are skewed by the nature of the self-reporting and the small sample. While I had at least 20 interviews at each golf course, perhaps only five or six agreed to report income at some of the courses, and thus the average would be taken from a small sample and would be a very unsure measure of the average income of all golfers on the course. Such an average would easily be skewed upwards by one high-income person proudly reporting that fact.

The second reason for skepticism about the income figures is that the interviews were not all performed on the same day of the week. On some golf courses a portion of the interviews came from ladies' foursomes who were golfing on ladies' day. On some golf courses a portion of the interviews were taken from senior citizens who had teed off early during a time reserved for them. Furthermore, none of the interviews were taken on weekend days when the demographic characteristics of the golfers might significantly differ from the usual weekday clientele.

To properly measure the income of a golf course's customers requires a much more thorough canvassing of the golfers. This was beyond the scope of my investigation. The sampling that I performed was designed foremost to obtain subjective measures of hilliness, condition, and beauty, and was adequate for that task. But it was not adequate to capture income levels.

Using the variables as explained above, the following equations were estimated with multiple regression analysis:

$$\% \text{ Taking Carts} = b_0 + b_1\text{Price} + b_2\text{Hilliness} + b_3\text{Yardage} + \\ b_4\% \text{ Carts Required} + b_5\text{Cartpaths Only} + \quad (3.1) \\ b_6\text{Income} \quad ;$$

$$\% \text{ Taking Carts} = b_0 + b_1\text{Price} + b_2\text{Elevation Change} + \\ b_3\text{Yardage} + b_4\% \text{ Carts Required} + \quad (3.2) \\ b_5\text{Cartpaths Only} + b_6\text{Income} \quad .$$

The results of these regressions appear in Table 3.3. Eq. (3.1) includes all the variables that have been introduced above with the subjective Hilliness variable used to capture the effect of hilliness. Eq. (3.2) was estimated with Hilliness replaced by Elevation Change. As the Table shows, the Hilliness variable works better than the Elevation Change variable. The t-statistic is higher for Hilliness than for Elevation Change, and the r-squared and adjusted r-squared are higher for the regression with Hilliness. None of the estimates of the other coefficients are dramatically changed by the substitution of one variable for the other. In the discussion and diagrams below I use the figures from Eq. (3.1).

The results confirm most of our expectations about the demand for cart rental. Overall, these sets of variables explain about 75% of the variation in cart rental rates. Judging by the t-statistics, the most important explanatory variables are price, hilliness and whether carts are required. The variables which do not seem to matter are income, the overall yardage, and whether carts are restricted to cartpaths only.

Table 3.3 Regression coefficients and (t-statistics).

Equation	3.1	3.2
Dep. variable	% Taking Carts	% Taking Carts
Independent variable		
Constant	18.186	28.554
	(0.417)	(0.598)
Price	-3.564	-3.180
	(-2.939)	(-2.359)
Hilliness	12.387	
	(5.114)	
Elevation Change		0.120
		(3.918)
Yardage	0.00495	0.00458
	(0.788)	(0.658)
% Carts Required	49.369	48.399
	(5.875)	(5.218)
Cartpaths Only	12.204	17.101
	(1.562)	(2.042)
Income	-0.0912	0.0537
	(-0.631)	(0.341)
Adjusted r-squared	.727	.673
n	46	46

As Eq. (3.1) shows, the demand curve is downward sloping. The coefficient of the price variable is -3.564 which means that for each increase in cart price of $1, the percentage of golfers renting carts falls by about 3.6 percentage points. Since the average cart usage is about 49.7%, and since the average cart price is about $9.48, the regression figure means that if cart price were to increase by $1 to $10.48, the average cart usage would fall to about 46.1%.

The estimate of the coefficient of the Hilliness variable is also statistically and economically significant. Holding price constant, for an increase in the measurement of a golf course's hilliness of one point, say from the average of 2.50 to a somewhat steeper 3.50, the cart usage increases by 12.39 percentage points.

The estimate of the coefficient of the % Carts Required variable is also meaningful. The estimate is 49.37. If carts are required 100% of the time, as opposed to not at all, cart usage goes up by almost 50%. Should this figure be 100%? The answer is no because, remember, carts are already used 49.7% of the time on average in the whole sample which is dominated by courses that do not require carts. This means that about half the time carts are taken anyway. Making carts mandatory increases the percentage of golfers who rent them by roughly 50 percentage points from 50% to 100%.

Since the t-statistics for Yardage, Cartpaths Only, and Income indicate that the estimates are not significantly different from zero in the statistical sense, we will not spend any time on the specific results. One cannot conclude that these factors, as measured here, are important determinants of demand. Whether the problem lies in the measurement of the variables or in the prior supposition that these variables should matter is left undetermined.

We can, however, also use the results to diagram a demand curve and highlight changes in demand and quantity demanded as illustrated in Fig. 3.3. Demand curve D_1 shows the demand curve as it would look for the "average" golf course. That is, consider a golf course that had a Hilliness rating of 2.5, required carts to be taken 13% of the time, required carts to stay on the cart paths 14% of the time, had golfers whose income averaged $59,380, and measured 6574 yards from the back tees. Point A on D_1 corresponds to the average price of $9.48, and the average cart rental rate of 49.7%. As calculated above, suppose the price on this course were to increase to $10.48, then the quantity demanded would fall to 46.1%. This is shown by the movement along the demand curve from point A to point B, and is an example of a decrease in quantity demanded due to an increase in price.

Now suppose that starting from point A we hold price constant at $9.48 but increase the hilliness of the course from a level of 2.5 to 3.5 on the subjective Hilliness measure. According to the regression equation, the demand for carts increases, that is, shifts to the right, by 12.39 percentage points to 62.09%. This is illustrated in the diagram by point C on the demand curve labeled D_2. This is called an increase in demand and is depicted by the movement of the whole demand curve to the right.

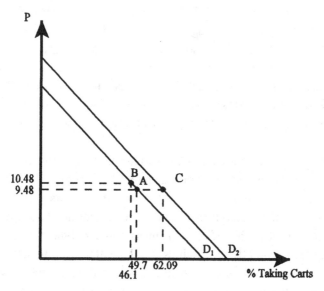

Fig. 3.3 Demand curves from estimation of Eq. (3.1).

3.3 Golf Cart Economics

Using the demand curve we have just estimated we can comment on golf course policy with respect to the pricing of cart rentals. The first step is to calculate the elasticity of demand that is implied by the above estimation. Recall from Chapter 2 that an elasticity is a ratio of percentage changes. With respect to quantity demanded and price, economists divide the percentage change in quantity by the percentage change in price and call it the "price elasticity of demand" or the "demand elasticity with respect to price," or even simply the "elasticity of demand" as given by the following equation:

$$\text{elasticity} = (\% \text{ change in quantity})/(\% \text{ change in price}) \quad . \quad (3.3)$$

It is customary to evaluate the percentage changes at the averages in the data. In this case the price change of $1 is divided by the starting price of $9.48 to equal .105 which corresponds to a 10.5% change in price. This 10.5% change in price causes a negative 3.6 percentage point change in quantity. Since the average cart rental rate in the data is 49.7%, the change of 3.6 percentage points corresponds to a 7.2% decrease in quantity (that is, 3.6/49.7 = .072). Calculating the ratio of percentage changes, -7.2/10.5 = -.686, we find that the demand elasticity implied by the data is -.686. Since the elasticity is less than one in absolute value, the demand is called inelastic.

Economists will immediately recognize the finding of an inelastic demand as a signal that prices are too low. A quick numerical example is calculated to illustrate why. Suppose that the golf course sells 200 rounds of golf per day. Actually, any number will do because the effects that we will calculate will be proportionate. The course has average characteristics and is pricing carts at $9.48 and renting them to 49.7% of the golfers for a total of (rounding up) 100 cart rentals. Its revenues are $948 on cart rentals. If the golf course were to raise cart prices by roughly 10.5% to $10.48, the quantity demanded would fall to 46.1% of the golfers or (rounding down) to about 92 cart rentals. The course now earns (92 times $10.48 equals) $964.16. Even though I rounded up in the first case and down in the second, the course earns more revenue from cart rentals with the higher price. This will always be the case for an inelastic demand because the price is changing by a larger percentage than the quantity. When price is increased, quantity falls, but the price effect is the larger of the two. Furthermore, costs will be lower for maintenance and fuel and/or electricity for battery recharging, because fewer carts are being used. The effect on profits should be automatic, revenues up, costs down, profits up.

An economic consultant armed with these figures would encourage golf courses to raise the cart rental fees. Perhaps golf courses have recognized this by themselves since the data was collected in 1994, because cart rental prices have increased since then. In the year 2000, the average cart rental price for these same courses[4] increased to $10.60 and the median price increased from $10 to $12. However, green fees, gasoline, golf balls, and

---

[4]One of the 46 original courses is now closed so the new averages are taken over 45 golf course facilities. Since 2000 cart prices have continued their steady rise.

many other prices have increased by roughly the same percentages over the same time period so the carts may still carry a price below the profit maximizing level.

Before jumping to conclusions about golf cart pricing, however, let me suggest a few possible reasons why these results do not necessarily mean that golf cart prices are too low. First, the difference in revenues as calculated in the numerical example is not terribly large. The change in price of $1 increased revenue by roughly $16 per day and saved the cost associated with about 8 cart rentals per day. These amounts will hardly make or break the bottom line even when aggregated over the course of a year.

Second, the elasticity is actually underestimated to a slight degree if the increase in cart price causes the total number of golfers to fall. Not only do a smaller percentage of golfers take carts due to the increase in price, but there are fewer golfers to begin with. If this effect is important, then cart prices may already be at the correct level. The effect does not have to be large. In the above example with 200 golfers, 100 of them took carts at $9.48 but only 92 took carts at the higher price. The example assumes that the 8 golfers no longer taking carts are still paying green fees and walking the course instead of riding. If even one of those golfers decided to drop out completely, (and that is only 1% of the original cart-riding golfers) the course loses the green fee which could easily wipe out the $16 of extra revenue and the cost savings associated with the decrease in quantity from 100 to 92.[5]

Finally, perhaps the conclusion is correct and golf courses could earn higher profits with higher cart prices. Notwithstanding this fact, the golf course could knowingly set the cart price below the profit maximizing level if the golf course is not trying to maximize profits in the first place. Indeed, many of the golf courses in the sample are municipal facilities that are managed so as to provide the most benefit to residents at the lowest possible prices as long as costs can be covered. As long as cart fees cover the costs of the carts, there will be no political consensus in the community to raise cart prices even further. In Chapter 5 the hypothesis that municipal courses set prices in ways that do not maximize profit is explored in more detail.

---

[5]Remember, we are actually dealing with half cart rentals. When golfers ride two to a cart, 8 riders could mean as few as four trips around the golf course for the actual cart itself.

An even more finely nuanced version of the argument in the preceding paragraph is possible. It seems quite likely that the cart rental portion of a golf course's operations is already a significant profit center. This is so because it is not unheard of for some avid golfers who always play the same course and always ride in a golf cart to own their own golf carts. Sometimes, these golfers will even pay a small "trail fee" to be allowed to use their own carts. So if owning one's own cart and paying a trail fee is still cheaper than renting a cart, there is likely to be a substantial profit margin built into the cart pricing. It may seem embarrassing to golf course managers to raise cart prices to obtain an even higher profit margin. To avoid the appearance of gouging its cart riding customers, the golf course keeps cart prices low, perhaps raising other prices such as green fees or refreshments.

Also keep in mind that the implication that golf cart prices are too low was derived from a calculation of the elasticity made at the average of the data. For a golf course facility with a cart price above the average, and this would be a majority of the courses since the median price of $10 was above the average price of $9.48, the price might already be high enough. On the other side of this coin, however, is the almost certain conclusion that a golf course charging a cart price of zero has set price too low.

The policy of a cart-inclusive price, "but you can walk if you want to," seems hard to justify. This is an economic riddle that begs for a coherent explanation. The golf course is encouraging cart usage for someone who gets only marginal benefit from the cart, but the cart use still imposes costs on the golf facility in terms of fuel and wear and tear. The straightforward economic view is that at the very minimum, the golf course should charge a price equal to the marginal or extra costs incurred in the use of the cart. The riddle is brought into sharper focus by considering the policy of mandatory cart usage. If some golfers do not want to ride in a cart, making them do so imposes a cost on them. At the same time, the use of the cart imposes a cost on the golf course facility. Why adopt a policy that imposes costs on both the buyer and the seller? There must be some benefit that is being overlooked that will offset the costs just described.

This author always makes a point of attempting to find out why carts are mandatory and very rarely gets a coherent response. Several of the responses I have heard follow.

Once in a while a golf course is designed to require very long distances between the green of one hole and the tee of the next. In these cases, the carts-required policy is making up for unfortunate golf course design.[6] This is perhaps the best reason I have heard, but not a completely compelling one since the golf course could use some of its volunteer marshals to ferry walkers along particularly long stretches if it cared to cater to walkers. Indeed, one of the golf courses in the sample now does this.

A reason which I find less compelling is that the golf course uses cart rental as a policing mechanism to help distinguish paying from non-paying customers. This particular course could not use the "long distance between holes" argument because it also had a policy of allowing members to walk but making daily fee players take a cart. The course felt compelled to justify its policy and perhaps felt awkward about admitting that it was a pricing scheme designed to raise profit. Prior to making carts mandatory for visitors, it was alleged that non-paying golfers were sneaking between houses onto the course and playing for free. Presumably, the course marshals knew all the members personally, therefore if all visitors had to ride, then the marshal could spot any walker that was not a member and know that that walker was a nonpayer. However, if nonmembers were allowed to walk, the marshall would be placed in the awkward position of having to ask all walkers who were not members to produce their receipts to show that they had paid the daily green fee. While logically the justification makes sense, it relies on two very suspect assumptions; first, that the marshals can recognize and distinguish members who have the right to walk from nonpaying interlopers, and second, that there is a serious problem with nonpayers in the first place. On the whole I find this reason to be unpersuasive.

A third reason that is commonly given is that requiring carts helps speed the pace of play. There is no question that, on average, a foursome will reach their tee shots more quickly by riding a cart than by walking. Even in cases of a wayward shot when walking would be faster, if two golfers are

---

[6]I say unfortunate instead of bad because in some cases land acquisition costs and environmental concerns require the awkward routing of the holes. The choice is between an awkward golf course and none at all. But this is still unfortunate and these courses will never win design awards.

sharing a cart, then they have the ability to split up allowing one to ride and one to walk along a particular part of the course. Notwithstanding the quicker "travel time" there are several reasons why riding in a cart may not speed play overall. The simplest reason is that arriving at one's tee shot quickly, only to wait for the group in front to clear the green saves no time at all. Another reason comes into play if carts are required to stay on cartpaths. In these cases, any travel time advantage may be negated by the time it takes to walk back and forth from the ball to the cart. Furthermore, the pace of play argument cannot be used by those courses that require carts only some of the time, that require carts only for nonmembers, that allow caddies in lieu of carts, or that allow golfers to walk but require the cart fee to be paid.

Most walkers will insist that taking carts does not speed the pace of play. Most of those making money from cart rental will insist that they do. Cart use and other issues of slow play are examined in great depth in Chapter 8. For now, to the question of mandatory cart use being justified by speeding the pace of play, I will answer with a resounding, "Maybe."

Some golf course personnel are not afraid of being brutally honest, as they see it. Since courses earn a profit margin on cart rental, requiring such rental raises the profits of the golf course. Any other justifications that might be given are simply window dressing hiding this true intent of the course. But this argument also has its weaknesses. First of all, why should a golf course be embarrassed about its intent to earn profit? In this vein it is significant that mandatory cart usage, although not unheard of, is relatively rare on municipal golf courses compared to for-profit, daily fee courses.

The second weakness with the mandatory-carts-increases-profits argument, is that if it is transparently true that the reason for mandatory carts is simply to raise profit, then the window dressing has no effect and there might be a more efficient way to raise profits without the pretense or subterfuge. Indeed, why use a policy that imposes an extra cost on those golfers who would rather walk while at the same time imposing a cost on the golf course in terms of fuel and wear and tear on the carts? Why not instead, lower the cart price to the level of cost and allow carts to be optional, while simultaneously raising the green fee by an amount equal to the decrease in the cart price? With this policy, the golf course makes the same amount of profit and no golfers who value cart usage at an amount lower than the true cost are forced to use them. The following numerical example will help make the point.

Consider a golf course with a green fee of $35, a (shared) cart fee of $10, a cost to the golf course of renting a cart of $7, and a mandatory cart policy. Golfers willing to pay $45 or more while taking a cart will make up the customer base. The course earns a net cash flow of $38 from each golfer, $35 is the green fee, and $3 is the net revenue or profit from the cart. If walking were allowed, then the course would lose the $3 of extra profit from each walking customer. Presumably, this is what people who insist that mandatory carts raise profits have in mind. But by raising the green fee to $38, lowering the cart fee to $7 and making carts optional, the course does not lose any profit. The course still earns $38 dollars of cash flow from each golfer, riders pay $45 as before and walkers get a price break equal to the cost savings of the course due to the fuel savings and the reduction in wear and tear on the carts. Furthermore, the course might get an increase in quantity from the policy. For example, I might be willing to pay only $40 to play the golf course whether or not I take a cart. In fact, I might be willing to pay even more if walking is allowed. For these numbers I will not play given the mandatory cart policy but I would play given the alternative prices of $38 and $7 with carts optional.

If the mandatory cart policy increases profits, it must have something to do with a reason why the golf course does not want to give a price break to walkers. One such reason may be that those who would desire to walk if carts were optional are actually those who are willing to pay more for the whole golf experience on average. The golf course charges them more and implicitly gives riders a relative price break.[7] Another reason may be that walkers have demand curves that are more inelastic than riders and, as was shown above for the inelastic demand for carts in general, inelastic demands cry out for price increases. In such a setting the golf course does not want to give walkers a price reduction. These more sophisticated explanations rest on assumptions about walkers relative to riders that may or may not be true.

---

[7]This is precisely and directly what is happening on those courses with a cart-inclusive price where walking is allowed but you have to pay for the cart anyway. Such a policy more obviously signals that the golf course is trying to extract extra profits from walkers but, nevertheless, avoids the inefficient use of carts when they are unwanted.

A more complete analysis of these issues brings us to the topic of price discrimination, covered in Chapter 5.

As a final note to golf cart economics, it should be recognized that golf carts have for the most part outcompeted and made obsolete their main competition, caddies. Golf carts and caddies are substitute methods for a golfer who wants to play golf without having to carry his or her clubs. Of course, they are not perfect substitutes; a golf cart can also carry the golfer, which some (but not this author) see as an advantage, while a caddie can give advice, entertain, rake bunkers, and tend the flag stick. But at minimum wages, and including a modest tip, a caddie can easily be three or more times as costly as a cart, even before the golf course earns any profit.

The days of casual youth summer employment as a caddie are gone. There are professional caddies who make a living at certain high-end private courses and at some resort courses, but even at most private golf courses, carrying one's own bag or taking a cart are the usual methods. For a young caddie earning minimum wage, the four to five hour round of golf would cost between $20 and $30, before tip, and that would leave no profits for the golf course itself. From the point of view of the golf course owner the switch from caddies to carts is a no-brainer. The golf course can rent carts to customers for far less than the golfer would pay for a caddie, and the cart price would still include some profits. Unless the desire by golfers to walk becomes overwhelmingly strong (and even casual observation indicates that there is little desire, given the number of clearly able-bodied youthful golfers who rent carts), there is no way that the clock can be turned back to the days before golf carts became ubiquitous, to the days when walking was part and parcel of the game.[8]

---

[8]Do I sound bitter? It is probably because carts often require cartpaths and I cannot forget the bet I lost partly because an approach shot of perfect distance (but a little off line) that would have otherwise ended up in a fine position, hit the cart path and bounced high and long. In my view, the greater the distance from the cart path to the green, the better, but catering to my desire would increase the walking and the time spent walking for cart-riding golfers, thus impinging on the alleged ability of carts to speed the pace of play.

Chapter 4

Bad Mood Bias[1]

The previous chapter focused on measuring the demand to rent golf carts. One of the important factors was the hilliness of the course in question. As explained in that chapter, measuring the hilliness by taking objective measurements of elevation changes on the golf course is not as good as simply asking the golfers how hilly they think the course is. This chapter explains the subjective measurement of other golf course characteristics, most importantly, golf course condition and golf course beauty, with an eye toward determining whether the interview method is a useful way of measuring these subjective characteristics.

Several interesting results arise from this analysis. Would you like to know what the prettiest or best-conditioned golf courses are? Top-ten lists are developed based on the golfers' opinions of the courses they play. How can we be sure that these opinions are to be trusted? Correlations of the opinions with other objective information can shed light on this question. Can the golfer's opinions supply useful input to golf course managers about the golf course? The answer to this question is, "Yes," as is explained later in this chapter and in upcoming chapters, but we are getting ahead of ourselves. This chapter first explains some of the generic problems with interview data and how my interviews were designed to mitigate the problems. The chapter then presents some tests to see whether the results are biased in identifiable ways. Finally, the chapter presents several "top-ten"

---

[1]Parts of this chapter were originally published as, Shmanske, Stephen, "Subjective Measurement and 'Bad-Mood' Bias," *Briefing Notes in Economics*, 35 (July 1998) pp. 1-4.

lists using the golfers' opinions of golf course characteristics as the source of the data.

4.1 Surveys: Problems and Solutions

Economists usually shy away from survey data. There are several reasons for this. The first is the difficulty of obtaining an appropriate sample from which to draw opinions. People can be canvassed randomly but not all who are asked will agree to be interviewed. This opens the possibility that only those with a particular interest in the topic will take part, and their opinions might be skewed.

A second difficulty is assuring that the respondent's answers are serious. If the person being interviewed has little or no stake in the outcome or topic of the survey, then he or she may put little effort into crafting a response. Alternatively, if the person being interviewed can determine how the interview might be used to influence a policy decision, and has a stake in such a decision, then he or she may answer strategically in an attempt to skew the outcome of the survey in a particular direction.

A third difficulty is in assuring that the interviewer is not consciously or sub-consciously skewing the results, or spinning the interpretation to suit prior opinions. Many times the problem is in a vague wording of the question. For example, after giving a free sample of a piece of cake, the cafe's survey asks, "Would you buy this cake?" Some people will answer yes or no without knowing the price, implicitly assuming that some "normal" price will be charged. But each subject might have in mind a different "normal" price and the interviewer has no way of knowing what that price is. Better formulations of the question would be, "Would you buy this cake for $2.00?," or "How often would you buy this cake for $2.00?," or "How much would you pay for this cake?" Another example is a survey that asks participants whether they would prefer an expansion of freeway capacity or an expansion of light rail service without giving the corresponding costs and tax burdens of each plan. It is often unclear how to interpret the results of such surveys. It is easily possible for those attempting to shape public opinion to spin the results in a desired direction, which may be why such surveys are used. For the same reason, however, it is also possible to discount or ignore the results.

To mitigate these concerns, the interview must be designed and carried out carefully and the results must be subjected to further examination. In turn I discuss the issues of sample selection bias, strategic responding, and researcher bias.

4.1.1 *Sampling*

A true random sample of the opinions of golfers could be achieved by asking questions of randomly chosen golfers on randomly chosen golf courses on randomly chosen days. It is definitely not the case, for example, that one could simply put a questionnaire on the windshield of all cars in a golf course's parking lot. If the latter attempt were chosen, only those with very strong feelings, or a lot of time on their hands, would respond. The response rate would be low and the results possibly biased. Unfortunately, the cost of obtaining true randomness eliminates that choice from the realm of possibility. The researcher, therefore, must trade off true randomness for workability in what is more of an intuitive balancing act than a scientific prescription. The following description of my interview process shows both where I was successful and where I was unsuccessful in this endeavor.

My research started with a desire to measure the demand for and pricing of public-access golf courses. Price will affect quantity demanded and the demand itself will be affected by the size of the population and the quality of the golfing experience. To obtain these quality characteristics necessitates eliciting subjective opinions from the golfers themselves. How beautiful is a particular golf course? I decided to ask the golfers.

In 1993 there were 48 public-access golf courses with at least 18 holes, with a par of at least 68, and within a one-hour drive of San Francisco. I got permission to interview golfers and staff members at 46 of these courses. The goal was to obtain opinions on as many of these courses as possible, not just a random sample of them, so I arranged for a time to visit each of the golf courses for a day during which I would gather data from staff and customers. The golf courses themselves were not chosen randomly, rather the sample was chosen to include as many observations as possible. It would have been preferable to use all 48 courses in the data but 46 out of 48 is not bad.

The owners of the two golf courses that denied permission did so because they thought the process would be intrusive to the golfing customers while providing little or no value. While several other owners were skeptical about the value, they foresaw no major intrusion to the golfers or other operations and were glad to help me obtain the data. I was offered a complimentary round of golf at two of the 46 golf courses. I gratefully accepted the offers without fear of losing objectivity because my opinions are not included in the study in any case. Interestingly, one golf course manager who was skeptical about the value of any such statistical analysis went out of his way to assure me that under no circumstances would I receive a complimentary round. Evidently, he had some previous experience with other "researchers" doing "studies" for the sole purpose of finagling some free golf.

The visits themselves were more or less randomly determined by mutual convenience of myself and the key staff member of whom I would ask questions about revenues and other data. This eliminated weekends when staff members were either off or too busy. Thus, during weekdays in the latter half of 1994 I was able to spend a day at each of the 46 golf courses.[2]

After interviewing the staff member in the morning, I waited by the 18th green at each course to interview one member of each of 20 groups as they finished playing. The 20 interview target was reached at over 90% of the courses. The times missed were due to poor weather which limited the number of golfers on the day of the interviews. The procedure was to ask for a volunteer from each group of golfers. The golfers were told that the interview would last about one minute. This procedure was successful for over 99% of the groups asked.

---

[2]The elimination of weekend golfers is a serious concern in some respects but not in others. For example, the demographic profile of weekend golfers is much different from that of the weekday crowd, particularly in including more fully employed persons and fewer retirees. On the one hand, this will be very important when correlating the demand to play golf at the course with age and income variables that capture only the weekday crowd. In fact, in the previous chapter we saw how the potentially mismeasured income variable was not an important determinant of the demand to rent carts. On the other hand, there is not a compelling reason to think that opinions about hilliness, or beauty, or golf course condition depend on income or employment status.

Conducting the interviews was very enjoyable, perhaps the most enjoyable thing (short of playing) that I could think of doing on a golf course. I was usually able to observe the approach shots and putts of the golfers. I can even claim, unscientifically, that watching missed and made putts from all angles has helped in my own reading of at least the eighteenth green on these courses. When I was not reading the greens, I was usually reading a magazine or newspaper or doing some calculations based on the information gleaned from that morning's interview with the staff. I could usually find a shady spot to set up my beach chair. Sometimes the shade was not preferred if the day was on the cold side, or if it was late in the afternoon and I was trying to get the last interviews in before dark. On several occasions a golf course staff member would come out to see how I was faring, or to offer a cup of coffee.

The golfers themselves were glad to participate, forthcoming with their opinions, and curious about my study. Many times all four golfers would listen to the interview, interjecting their opinions along with those of the official respondent. I do not think these kibitzers skewed anyone's answers, but the whole experience probably made for some interesting discussion at the nineteenth hole. Several of the golfers expressed an interest in the publication schedule for this book and seemed disappointed when I told them that it would be a long process.

No coin tosses were made to "randomly" choose which golfer of a foursome would be chosen. The sample errs on the side of choosing the first golfer that approached me on the way from the green to the clubhouse. I was rarely rejected. When more than one golfer approached simultaneously, usually the most gregarious or the most outspoken golfer would be the first to respond to my plea, "I am an economics professor and I am doing research on the economics of golf, could I ask you for some of your opinions about this golf course? It will take about one minute," and the first to respond would be the one chosen. I do not consider this to be a serious departure from random selection, I simply note it here as a possibility. But I have no reason to believe that the golfers who walk more slowly or talk more slowly have systematically different opinions about the condition of the golf course.

One other factor about the makeup of the sample also encouraged me to believe that my sampling gave me a representative cross section of opinions from a variety of golfers. Men and women, old and young, course regulars and visitors, low and high handicappers, tournament players and casual players, riders and walkers: all were in my sample. Although I was not surprised to see such diversity, in fact I even expected it, it was nice to have my expectations confirmed. If only 70-year old, white, retired men were canvassed, a distorted impression of a golf course's characteristics would quite possibly be the result.

Later in this chapter I present my attempts to determine whether any systematic relationships between the demographic profile of the opinion giver and the opinions themselves, could be uncovered. For example, will older golfers think that the golf course is hillier than it actually is? Or, (and finally, since the reader is probably wondering about the chapter title) will a golfer who has just finished a poorly played round of golf take out his or her frustration by giving harsh, negative opinions about the golf course because of being in a "bad mood." After all, golfers are notorious for inventing excuses for their sloppy play; and muddy conditions, bumpy greens, and unkempt bunkers are as good as any. If such a psychological "bad mood" bias exists, then a sampling bias can be a problem if only happy smiling golfers are interviewed (or if only frustrated, disappointed golfers are chosen as interview subjects).

To sum up the sample selection issues, I would say that I was encouraged because I was rarely rejected when I approached a golfer for information, and because I was able to obtain a large enough number of opinions from a diverse set of golfers. I remain guardedly cautious about using only weekday golfers.

4.1.2 *Strategic responses*

With respect to the issue of non-serious or strategic responses from the golfers, I do not believe there is a problem. After all, the interviews were short and just when the interview subject seemed to be getting bored with the background demographic questions, I had finished and moved on to asking for opinions. The interviews went as follows: I asked: (1) Which course he/she considered to be his/her home course; (2) Handicap index or usual score range; (3) The score for today's round; (4) The travel time to the course; (5) The waiting time to tee off; (6) The time the round actually started; (7) Income; (8) Age; (9) Employment status; and, (10) The price paid for the round. Additionally, I observed and recorded: (1) Gender; (2) The time the round was finished; and, (3) Whether a cart was rented.

Many people balked at answering the income question. Most ladies simply gave a sly smile to the age question. And it was after these questions that, I suppose, the golfers were getting a little uncomfortable about being in what looked more like a marketing survey than academic research. Nevertheless, the remaining questions brought the interview back to the golf course and seemed to capture the interest and curiosity of the golfers.

To obtain the desired information about the subjectively measured variables, I asked each golfer to rate the hilliness, aesthetic beauty, course condition, and customer service on 1-to-5 scales. For hilliness, "1" corresponded to flat, "3" to rolling, and "5" to steep. For aesthetic beauty, "1" corresponded to plain, "3" to average, and "5" to beautiful. For course condition and customer service, "1" corresponded to poor, "3" to average, and "5" to excellent. In the cases where the golfer was not playing his/her home course, the golfer was also asked to rate his/her home course if it was one of the other 46 courses in the study. Whole numbers from 1 to 5 and the inclusive "half-points," that is, 1.5, 2.5, 3.5, and 4.5, were allowed as valid ratings. Although there were no dimpled chads to worry about, some of the more impassioned respondents gave answers of "zero" or "six." These were scaled to one or five as appropriate.

My original plan was to ask only about hilliness, beauty, and condition, but Paul Henderson, the manager at my home course, Tilden Park Golf Course, which happened to be the first course where interviews were conducted, suggested that I also ask about customer service. I had explained that I was trying to correlate demand to the subjectively measured quality variables, beauty and condition, and Paul, proud of the efforts that Tilden Park was putting into customer service, convinced me to include it in my interviews. Ultimately, however, I was unable to discover any significant effect that the customer service rating had on any of the demand or pricing variables. Of all the top-ten lists at the end of the chapter, I have the least confidence in the one for customer service.

Because of the interest of the golfers, and the high response rate, it is unlikely that haphazard, non-serious replies are a problem. Strategic replies may be a problem but I do not think so. A golfer might harshly rate the condition of his/her home course in the hopes that management might use the results to justify greater expenditure on maintenance. But keep in mind, the management was not using the survey for this purpose and the golfers were told as much. Only a small number of golfers seemed to question my motivation, doubting whether any interesting academic research questions could be addressed by interviewing golfers.

There is, however, one area in which golfer opinions may be biased. Might not the mood of the golfer, based on how well he/she played, bias the responses given? Several of the golf course managers who were skeptical about the legitimacy of my study stressed this possibility. "If you ask golfers about the quality of the course, you are just going to find out whether they played well or poorly," was a sentiment that I heard from several golf course managers and superintendents. I had the same response for each of them, namely, that I could try to find out whether they played well or poorly and identify and control for any bias that did exist, and that doing so would be another interesting research paper which was the whole point. That research paper became, "Subjective Measurement and 'Bad-Mood' Bias" which was published in *Briefing Notes in Economics*. The results of that paper are presented and extended below.

4.1.3 *Researcher bias*

Other researchers conducting opinion polls may be biased but I, most certainly, am not. Trust me. No? Okay, let me start over. What I mean to say is that while researchers will always insist that they are impartial in developing survey data, such claims must be taken with a grain of salt. There are, however, a number of things that researchers can do to doublecheck their own procedures and to help instill confidence in the readers of their research.

The first thing a researcher can do is to attempt to highlight and uncover any sampling biases or other irregularities that occurred. Above, I have detailed my interview process and below, I report on my statistical attempts to find a bias. Owing to space limitations, a magazine or newspaper editor will often report the results of a survey with a story about the subject matter but without reporting the (boring) underlying methods or procedures. Such opinion polls are not as persuasive as they would be if the authors could convince the reader of their objectivity.

Another thing that survey and opinion poll researchers can do is to develop a history of accuracy. If inaccurate, self-serving, or otherwise distorted survey information is acted upon with poor results, the next survey reported by the same author or company is less likely to carry as much weight. An objective reputation on the part of the poll/opinion-survey research firm is a valuable part of such a firm's good-will capital. Instantly developing such a history is impossible for me. There is a first time for everything. But there is something that can be done.

The other, and perhaps more important thing, that can be done is to show how the survey results can be usefully applied in another setting, thus lending credence to their accuracy. I will accomplish this in later chapters but the argument can be foreshadowed here with the following example. It is one thing to ask golfers to rate a golf course's beauty on a 1-to-5 scale and then report the rankings thus received. At least to the extent of reporting several top-ten lists I do as much in this chapter. It is something much more if the resulting rankings also correlate appropriately with other independent measures. For example, if my listing of the ten most beautiful courses identified golf courses that no one wanted to play even if they had low prices and were conveniently located, one would have to question the legitimacy of my survey. "The proof of the pudding is in the eating," they usually say. For subjective quality rankings this translates to, the proof of the rating system is in its effective statistical application. Likewise, for someone recommending a top-ten list of mutual funds to you, you would like to know his/her last year's list of funds, and whether they ended up with impressive, average, or below average performance. If a rating scale can be developed and used effectively in further research, it will be much more believable than a rating scale which is simply developed and presented off the cuff.

The fact that my ratings of golf course beauty, condition, and hilliness are important variables in demand, cost, and pricing studies lends credence to the care with which they were calculated. Alternatively, because the customer service rating did not prove to be useful in further research, perhaps the rankings of customer service should be discounted. If too much bias or error in sample selection or on the part of the researcher existed, then the resulting variables would not measure what they were supposed to with any degree of accuracy. Consequently, they would turn out to be useless in further analysis.

4.2 Looking for a Bad-Mood Bias

Whether a bad-mood bias exists can be verified in a multiple regression of the individual golfer's subjective assessment of the golf course on the golfer's personal characteristics and on a measure of how well the golfer played on the day of the interview. If the estimated coefficient of the measure of how well the golfer played is significantly different from zero, then there is support for the suggestion that subjective measurements of golf course characteristics are biased.

Let us first consider the golfer's assessment of the aesthetic beauty of the golf course. Let BEAUTY, measured on the 1-to-5 scale, be the dependent variable in the first regression, given in Eq. (4.1). Summary statistics for BEAUTY and for all the variables used in this chapter appear in Table 4.1. The variables themselves are explained below.

$$\text{BEAUTY} = b_0 + b_1\text{SUNDERHC} + b_2\text{SLOWPLAY} +$$
$$b_3\text{WAIT} + b_4\text{AGE} + b_5\text{HOME} + b_6\text{GENDER} + \quad (4.1)$$
$$b_7\text{EMPLOYED} + b_8\text{INCOME} + b_9\text{AVEBEAUTY} \quad .$$

The regression equation will contain roughly 20 observations from each of 46 different golf courses so a proxy for the beauty of each particular course must be included because golfers will rate courses that are more beautiful with higher numbers. Remember that the goal here is not to obtain a prediction equation to find out what makes a course beautiful; rather, the goal here is to determine whether any systematic biases exist in measuring beauty through a survey of golfer opinions. For this proxy, AVEBEAUTY, the average of all of the subjective ratings for the course being played by the golfer in question, is used as an explanatory variable. AVEBEAUTY contains more information than simply the average of all the BEAUTY ratings for those observations used in the regression. AVEBEAUTY contains opinions of a golfer's home course when the golfer was actually interviewed on a day when he or she was playing an away course. AVEBEAUTY also contains the opinions of golfers who may be excluded from the regressions because of other missing information, most often AGE or INCOME.

As an alternative to BEAUTY, regressions were also run with DELTABEAUTY as the dependent variable, as specified in Eq. (4.2).

$$\text{DELTABEAUTY} = b_0 + b_1\text{SUNDERHC} + b_2\text{SLOWPLAY} +$$
$$b_3\text{WAIT} + b_4\text{AGE} + b_5\text{HOME} + b_6\text{GENDER} + \quad\quad (4.2)$$
$$b_7\text{EMPLOYED} + b_8\text{INCOME} .$$

Table 4.1 Summary statistics.

Variable	Mean	Std. Dev.	Minimum	Maximum	N
BEAUTY	3.610	1.065	1	5	1022
CONDITION	3.530	0.928	1	5	1022
HILLY	2.500	1.193	1	5	1022
HANDICAP	18.72	8.342	0	48	1016
SUNDERHC	-4.200	5.067	-36.9	14.0	850
WAIT	2.739	11.04	0	120	869
SLOWPLAY	256.1	29.18	128.0	368.0	846
INCOME	59.86	45.00	0	501.0	589
EMPLOYED	0.441	0.497	0	1	1022
AGE	56.56	14.90	15	89	1000
GENDER	0.871	0.336	0	1	1022
HOME	0.702	0.458	0	1	1022
AVEBEAUTY	3.607	0.626	2.455	4.609	1022
AVECOND	3.533	0.450	2.262	4.525	1022
AVEHILLY	2.501	0.981	1.040	4.542	1022
DELTABEAUTY	0.0030	0.873	-3.480	2.545	1022
DELTACOND	-0.0023	0.817	-2.667	2.738	1022
DELTAHILLY	-0.0014	0.696	-1.773	2.850	1022

Notes: BEAUTY, CONDITION, HILLY, AVEBEAUTY, AVECOND, AVEHILLY, DELTABEAUTY, DELTACOND, and DELTAHILLY are measured in rating points. HANDICAP and SUNDERHC are measured in strokes. WAIT and SLOWPLAY are measured in minutes. INCOME is measured in thousands of 1994 dollars. EMPLOYED, GENDER, and HOME are dummy variables with 1's for employed, male, and home course respectively. AGE is measured in years.

DELTABEAUTY is the difference between a golfer's rating of the golf course's beauty and the average rating of beauty for that course, that is, BEAUTY - AVEBEAUTY. For example if a golfer rates a course as a 4 on the 1-to-5 beauty scale, but AVEBEAUTY is 3.7, then this golfer has rated the course more highly than average, and gets a value for DELTABEAUTY of 0.3. Although BEAUTY and AVEBEAUTY are measured on the 1-to-5 scale, an individual's ranking of BEAUTY might be below AVEBEAUTY, therefore giving a negative value for DELTABEAUTY. Note that when DELTABEAUTY is the dependent variable, we are trying to determine whether the difference between a golfer's opinion and the average opinion is systematically related to anything about the golfer. Also note that we go from Eq. (4.1) to Eq. (4.2) essentially by restricting the coefficient of AVEBEAUTY to equal one and by subtracting AVEBEAUTY from each side of the equation. Therefore, with BEAUTY as the dependent variable and AVEBEAUTY included on the right hand side, Eq. (4.1) is essentially an unrestricted version of Eq. (4.2). Notably, in the unrestricted version, the hypothesis that the coefficient of AVEBEAUTY is equal to one is not rejected.

Regressions are also performed for condition and hilliness. The same relationships that exist among BEAUTY, AVEBEAUTY, and DELTABEAUTY exist for the hilliness (HILLY, AVEHILLY, and DELTAHILLY) and course condition variables (CONDITION, AVECOND, and DELTACOND). The results for all these regressions are listed in Tables 4.2, 4.3, and 4.4 below. However, before moving to the results, let us examine the other right hand side variables.

Let SUNDERHC (strokes under handicap) be a measure of how well the golfer played on the day in question relative to how well that golfer might be expected to play. By using the golfer's handicap index, or the golfer's usual score range, and information about the difficulty of each particular golf course, an anticipated score can be calculated for any golfer on any golf course. The person's actual score is subtracted from the anticipated score to measure how well the golfer played. An example can highlight the calculation. Suppose a golfer has a handicap index of 10. If the golf course has a difficulty rating of 71, then this particular golfer would take an average of 81 strokes to complete the round.[3] If on the day in question, the golfer took only 78 shots, then the value of SUNDERHC for this observation would be 3. Therefore the lower the score, the higher the value for SUNDERHC. Low (high) golf scores and high (low) values of SUNDERHC may mean that the golfer will be in a good (bad) mood. Table 4.1 shows the range of this variable to be from -36.9 to 14. The -36.9 figure means that the golfer was almost 37 strokes above his usual score; talk about a bad day. I do recollect that the individual reporting a score 14 shots better than his handicap was beaming happiness. If this mood influences the golfer's subjective rating of the course characteristics, then the coefficient of SUNDERHC will be positive.

WAIT is the number of minutes the golfer had to wait before starting to play. Golfers may have had to wait if they did not have reservations, or if the golf course was overbooked so that the reservations could not be honored. Having waited a long time to tee off may have added to a golfer's frustrations and had a detrimental effect on his or her mood. If this effect is translated into harsh ratings, then the coefficient of WAIT will be negative.

SLOWPLAY is the number of minutes it took the golfer to complete the round. Slow play is often cited as a problem at public golf courses. Table 4.1 shows that the average length of time for a round of golf was 4 hours and 16 minutes. This length would not upset too many golfers, but remember, it is only an average. Perhaps it is the variance or the unexpected delays that upset golfers. One golfer actually finished playing in just over two hours. One group took what must have been an agonizing six hours and eight minutes to finish their round. Similar to WAIT, a negative coefficient of SLOWPLAY indicates that the golfer has taken out his/her frustrations in the subjective rating of the course.

The demographic factors that are also included as control variables are defined as follows. INCOME is the golfer's yearly income measured in thousands of dollars. EMPLOYED is a dummy variable equal to one if the

---

[3]This is not precisely true because the calculation of a golfer's handicap is slightly more complicated. The two most important complications are that high scores on individual holes are "adjusted" downward, and that only the best ten of the last twenty scores are used. Each of these factors will lower the calculated handicap, thereby raising the golfer's expected score a few strokes above the sum of the course rating and the handicap. Indeed, the sample mean of -4.1 for SUNDERHC confirms this tendency.

golfer is employed. AGE is the golfer's age in years. GENDER is a dummy variable equal to one if the golfer is male. Finally, HOME is a dummy variable equal to one if the golfer is playing on his/her home course. Table 4.1 indicates that the "average" golfer in the survey is a 56 and one-half year old, partially-employed male with income of almost $60,000, playing his home course. This person, of course, does not exist. But the table does indicate that more than half of the respondents are not employed (mostly retired), that about 13% of the sample was female, and that over 40% of the sample refused to answer the income question.

4.3 Results

The results of estimating Eqs. (4.1) and (4.2) are listed in Table 4.2. The equations are reestimated using the CONDITION and HILLINESS variables as the dependent variable and these results appear in Tables 4.3 and 4.4. Each of these tables contains four equations, namely, Eq. (4.1) with and without INCOME, and Eq. (4.2) with and without INCOME. When INCOME is omitted the sample size increases from 465 to 812. Missing observations on variables other than INCOME account for the reduction of the sample size to 812 usable observations.

Consider the results of the BEAUTY equations in Table 4.2. In the first two columns BEAUTY is the dependent variable and, as expected, the coefficient of AVEBEAUTY is close to one. This simply means that golf courses which are highly rated on average are highly rated by individuals. Without controlling for the average beauty of the golf course either by including AVEBEAUTY on the right hand side, or by subtracting it from the dependent variable, as in the second two columns, there would be no way of comparing opinions across the 46 different golf courses represented here.

So we turn our attention to the coefficients and t-statistics of the other variables to determine whether any significant correlations exist between a golfer's rating of beauty and the demographic control variables or the mood variables. We find at once that how a golfer played on the day of the interview had no influence on his/her BEAUTY rating. Across the board the SUNDERHC variable is not statistically significant. There is no identifiable bad-mood bias coming from a golfer's poor play in this data. This is a result that may come as a surprise to the golf course insiders who warned of such a possibility.

Table 4.2 Regression coefficients (t-statistics).

Dep. variable	BEAUTY	BEAUTY	DELTABEAUTY	DELTABEAUTY
Variable				
Constant	0.7902	0.1275	0.6593	0.2282
	(1.546)	(0.328)	(1.420)	(0.635)
SUNDERHC	-0.00526	0.00231	-0.00501	0.00215
	(-0.663)	(0.391)	(-0.633)	(0.363)
WAIT	-0.000482	-0.000957	-0.000239	-0.001124
	(-0.149)	(-0.348)	(-0.075)	(-0.410)
SLOWPLAY	-0.00390	-0.00221	-0.00397	-0.00211
	(-2.803)	(-2.068)	(-2.865)	(-1.995)
GENDER	-0.2077	-0.2030	-0.2088	-0.2057
	(-1.686)	(-2.194)	(-1.696)	(-2.226)
AGE	0.0104	0.00843	0.01055	0.00831
	(2.935)	(2.896)	(2.996)	(2.863)
HOME	0.1754	0.1682	0.1756	0.1700
	(2.035)	(2.517)	(2.039)	(2.547)
EMPLOYED	-0.1609	-0.0991	-0.1667	-0.0932
	(-1.461)	(-1.131)	(-1.520)	(-1.069)
INCOME	-0.0000483		-0.0001139	
	(-0.054)		(-0.129)	
AVEBEAUTY	0.9595	1.0333		
	(14.515)	(21.345)		
Adjusted R^2	.330	.374	.100	.059
n	465	812	465	812

Neither is there an effect of waiting to tee off on golfer opinions of the course beauty. Again, across the board the low t-statistics on WAIT show that there is no systematic relationship. This is not too surprising because, in this data set, the average wait was less than three minutes and most golfers reported that they teed off on time or even ahead of schedule. Although one golfer waited two hours, this observation was extraordinary. Furthermore, a long wait for a golfer who shows up without a reservation may be fully expected by the golfer. Sufficiently armed with reading matter and/or a practice routine, such a golfer's mood need not be a bad one. Although waiting to tee off might not be a problem, there is some evidence that slow play is. In each of the four equations in Table 4.2, SLOWPLAY is a statistically significant negative factor. Rounding, the estimates range from -0.002 to -0.004. Let us put these estimates in perspective. Consider a round of golf that took one hour longer than average. Multiplying 60 minutes by these estimates yields an effect on the beauty rating of between -0.120 and -0.240 rating points. The average beauty rating overall was 3.610, so an hour of delay could cause the beauty rating of the average course to fall to 3.490 or 3.370. This is a decline on the order of 3.3% to 6.6%. Evidently the effect is an inelastic one because the hour of extra delay is about 23% of the average time of four hours and sixteen minutes that it takes to finish a round of golf. I conclude that there is a small, inelastic, negative effect of slow play on a golfer's rating of the golf course's beauty.

That spending five hours in beautiful surroundings instead of four could cause a negative result probably seems paradoxical, especially to non-golfers. Nevertheless, it is naive to ignore the fact that golfers have time commitments and appointments like anyone else. Unless a golfer has budgeted the whole day exclusively for golf, he/she may become annoyed at the slow pace of play. Too much time on a golf course is not necessarily a good thing.

Turning from the mood variables to the demographic variables, we see from the low t-statistics that employment status and income are not significant factors. The GENDER dummy variable is statistically significant and negative, meaning that males are somewhat harsher in their ratings than females. I simply note the result here, leaving the gender psychologists and sociologists to mull it over.

There are consistently significant positive effects on the BEAUTY rating due to age and playing one's home course. Older golfers rate beauty more highly by about 0.008 to 0.01 per year. This is not a large effect but it is systematic. A group of golfers who were ten years older than average would rate the beauty of the average course at a 3.7 instead of a 3.6. The home course effect is also positive, and measured consistently across all four specifications at about 0.17 rating points. Golfers playing their home course rate its beauty about 0.17 points higher than average.

I can think of two possibilities for the home-course effect. The first is a type of home-course pride or chauvinism, which may be an offshoot of the golfer's selection of a home course. After all, travel distance to the golf course and price aside, a golfer would not want to claim as a home course one that he/she did not find aesthetically appealing. It is not surprising that golfers think their home course is beautiful, that is one reason why it is their home course. Nevertheless, many golfers have little geographic choice especially when their home course is the local municipal golf course with special rates for residents, so this explanation is not totally satisfactory.

A second possibility can work in conjunction with the first effect. Aesthetic beauty may be something that it takes more than one or a few rounds to appreciate. A visitor will be able to take in the large picture, the scenic vista, but it will take continued play on the same course to appreciate the subtler details of its beauty. Playing a course during different seasons, under different weather conditions, and at different times of the day will confront the golfer with the full range of a course's beauty including different light patterns, seasonal flora, blossoms, and foliage color, and a variety of wildlife such as deer, foxes, hawks, eagles, migrating waterfowl, wild turkeys, and even mountain lions. The fact that something must be experienced over and over again to truly appreciate it may also help to explain the age effect covered above.

If it takes multiple rounds of golf on a course to really experience its beauty, the potential for a marketing angle presents itself. Assuming that golfers like to play beautiful golf courses, those who are new to a course will place a lower value on playing it than course regulars who do not systematically underrate its beauty. Those who have played the course often will have higher demand curves. In such a situation, the golf course should be able to profit by targeting special promotions to golfers who are unfamiliar with the course. This can be accomplished, for example, with half price or two-for-one coupons distributed outside of the golf course's usual geographic market area. As always in such a market segmentation scheme, the trick is to keep the regulars, who most appreciate the beauty and are willing to pay full price, from also using the coupons.

Table 4.3 Regression coefficients (t-statistics).

Dep. variable	COND	COND	DELTACOND	DELTACOND
Variable				
Constant	-0.08415 (-0.160)	-0.2272 (-0.567)	-0.1153 (-0.264)	-0.0914 (-0.268)
SUNDERHC	0.006611 (0.884)	0.006555 (1.165)	0.006664 (0.894)	0.006398 (1.139)
WAIT	0.001538 (0.509)	0.001003 (0.384)	0.001557 (0.516)	0.000894 (0.343)
SLOWPLAY	-0.00002 (-0.016)	0.000009 (0.009)	-0.000025 (-0.019)	0.000051 (0.051)
GENDER	0.09677 (0.833)	0.01806 (0.205)	0.09745 (0.841)	0.01754 (0.200)
AGE	0.00256 (0.771)	0.001095 (0.396)	0.002578 (0.778)	0.001039 (0.377)
HOME	0.1100 (1.353)	0.0999 (1.570)	0.1105 (1.363)	0.0969 (1.527)
EMPLOYED	-0.1783 (-1.725)	-0.0847 (-1.020)	-0.1786 (-1.730)	-0.0817 (-0.985)
INCOME	-0.000594 (-0.710)		-0.000602 (-0.725)	
AVECOND	0.9912 (11.880)	1.0404 (16.684)		
Adjusted R^2	.230	.251	.024	.004
n	465	812	465	812

One way to implement such a pricing scheme is when a golf course management company that owns or manages several golf courses in different areas distributes to its members a booklet of discount coupons with one coupon for each course. Presumably the golfer will use the coupon for his home course, thus costing the company whatever the discount amounts to because the golfer would play his home course anyway. The upside for the company, however, is that the golfer might use five or six of the other coupons to play at courses that he/she would ordinarily not consider. So to

Table 4.4 Regression coefficients (t-statistics).

Dep. variable	HILLY	HILLY	DELTAHILLY	DELTAHILLY
Variable				
Constant	0.7438	0.2222	0.5919	0.1782
	(1.916)	(0.738)	(1.588)	(0.588)
SUNDERHC	-0.00134	-0.003708	-0.001263	-0.003629
	(-0.211)	(-0.778)	(-0.199)	(-0.762)
WAIT	0.00289	0.002824	0.003442	0.002995
	(1.113)	(1.269)	(1.338)	(1.356)
SLOWPLAY	-0.00167	-0.000680	-0.001635	-0.000687
	(-1.498)	(-0.798)	(-1.469)	(-0.806)
GENDER	-0.2084	-0.1182	-0.2087	-0.1165
	(-2.110)	(-1.585)	(-2.111)	(-1.563)
AGE	0.00016	0.00169	0.000671	0.001884
	(0.057)	(0.716)	(0.237)	(0.805)
HOME	0.06295	-0.01799	0.06974	-0.01546
	(0.909)	(-0.333)	(1.008)	(-0.287)
EMPLOYED	-0.09458	-0.01798	-0.1055	-0.02136
	(-1.071)	(-0.255)	(-1.198)	(-0.304)
INCOME	0.0000747		0.00001306	
	(0.105)		(0.018)	
AVEHILLY	0.9539	0.9840		
	(28.701)	(38.905)		
Adjusted R^2	.656	.671	.012	.000
n	465	812	465	812

obtain five or six discounted rounds from visitors who otherwise would not play, the golf course has to allow the discount on one round that would have been played for full price. Depending on the size of the discount, and the number of coupons used by visitors, this could easily be a profitable strategy. Note that single golf courses might be at a disadvantage when it comes to such marketing schemes. The full discussion of pricing practices is the subject of the next chapter.

We can wrap up this section with a quick look at Tables 4.3 and 4.4 which list results for the regressions with condition and hilliness as the dependent variables. As a perusal of the tables indicates, significant effects are hard to find. Obviously, AVECOND and AVEHILLY, respectively, must be significant when CONDITION and HILLY are the dependent variables. Beyond that, however, only GENDER is statistically significant and only in two of the four hilliness regressions in Table 4.4. Men rate courses as less hilly than women do by about one or two-tenths of a rating point. There appears to be no obvious bad-mood or demographically linked biases in golfer's subjective opinions about golf course condition or golf course hilliness. If golfers played poorly on the day of the interview, they did not use the hilliness or the condition as an excuse. This result is slightly eyebrow-raising. Personally, I have often been tempted to blame poor bunker play on inconsistent sand and unraked bunkers, at least, that is, until I remember that I almost never practice.

4.4 Top-Ten Lists

The remainder of this chapter includes the top-ten lists of most beautiful, most hilly, best conditioned, and best at provision of customer service golf courses among the 46 golf courses in the study. Course ownership and course management policies have undoubtedly changed for some of these courses since the surveys were done in 1994. Some changes have been for the better, and some for the worse. Several courses have been opened, refurbished, or expanded since the survey, and two have closed and since reopened. The lists, therefore, might be worth more as a historical reference rather than as a current guide as to where to play golf in the San Francisco area. Nevertheless, to those of us who were here at the time and who have played (or have missed out on playing) these courses over the years, the lists provide interesting feedback to supplement our own impressions.

Also keep in mind that course hilliness and course beauty are less changeable than course condition and customer service. Hilliness will almost never change and the rankings will be affected only by the addition or removal of courses from the list. Beauty, especially to the extent that it depends on views will change only very slowly by the growth or removal of trees, or by the construction of housing developments on what used to be open space. The cumulative effect of housing development over several years can be large. Condition is susceptible to change over a period of months based on the effort and resources devoted to golf course maintenance. Chapter 6 examines and quantifies the relationships between maintenance expenditure and beauty, and between maintenance expenditure and golf course condition. Customer service could change most rapidly, depending on management priorities in hiring and training employees.

Table 4.5 Most beautiful golf courses.

RANK	GOLF COURSE	CITY	RATING
1.	Lincoln Park Golf Course,	San Francisco	4.609
2.	Oakhurst Country Club,	Clayton	4.575
3.	Half Moon Bay Golf Links,	Half Moon Bay	4.500
4.	Indian Valley Golf Course,	Novato	4.480
5.	Willow Park Golf Course,	Castro Valley	4.479
6.	Oakmont Golf Course,	Santa Rosa	4.432
7.	Lake Chabot Golf Course,	Oakland	4.333
8.	Crystal Springs Golf Course,	Burlingame	4.325
9.	Fountaingrove Resort & Country Club,	Santa Rosa	4.286
10.	Tilden Park Golf Course,	Berkeley	4.271

Table 4.6 Best conditioned golf courses.

RANK	GOLF COURSE	CITY	RATING
1.	Oakhurst Country Club,	Clayton	4.525
2.	Bennett Valley Golf Course,	Santa Rosa	4.420
3.	Santa Teresa Golf Course,	San Jose	4.167
4.	Sonoma Golf Course,	Sonoma	4.146
5.	Half Moon Bay Golf Links,	Half Moon Bay	4.143
6.	Lone Tree Golf Course,	Antioch	4.019
T7.	Paradise Valley Golf Course,	Fairfield	4.000
T7.	Willow Park Golf Course,	Castro Valley	4.000
9.	Palo Alto Golf Course,	Palo Alto	3.885
10.	Rancho Solano Golf Course,	Fairfield	3.825

Table 4.7 Hilliest golf courses.

RANK	GOLF COURSE	CITY	RATING
1.	Lake Chabot Golf Course,	Oakland	4.542
2.	Pittsburg's Delta View Golf Course	Pittsburg	4.325
3.	Indian Valley Golf Course,	Novato	4.260
4.	Tilden Park Golf Course,	Berkeley	4.188
5.	Summitpointe Golf Course,	Milpitas	4.119
6.	Fountaingrove Resort & Country Club,	Santa Rosa	3.714
7.	Oakhurst Country Club,	Clayton	3.650
8.	Crystal Springs Golf Course,	Burlingame	3.525
9.	Blue Rock Springs Golf Course,	Vallejo	3.475
10.	Rancho Solano Golf Course,	Fairfield	3.250

Table 4.8 Best customer service golf courses.

RANK	GOLF COURSE	CITY	RATING
1.	Bennett Valley Golf Course,	Santa Rosa	4.720
2.	Oakhurst Country Club,	Clayton	4.650
3.	Spring Valley Golf Course,	Milpitas	4.571
T4.	Oakmont Golf Course,	Santa Rosa	4.545
T4.	Sunol Valley Golf Club,	Sunol	4.545
6.	Santa Clara Golf & Tennis Club,	Santa Clara	4.520
7.	Las Positas Golf Course,	Livermore	4.458
8.	Adobe Creek Golf Course,	Petaluma	4.364
9.	Sunnyvale Golf Course,	Sunnyvale	4.333
10.	Lone Tree Golf Course,	Antioch	4.308

Chapter 5

Price Discrimination

At some golf facilities the complexity of the pricing scheme has even the clerks baffled. "No, not $6.50," said one customer. "I live in the original "A" subdivision, and I'm a senior, and this is Tuesday morning before 10:00 AM, so including the 10% surcharge for the new bridge on 16, my price is $4.28." The variety of different pricing schemes employed by public access golf courses includes weekday/weekend differentials, twilight rates, early-bird discounts, resident discounts, senior discounts, junior discounts, tournament surcharges, monthly passes, multi-play cards, quantity discounts, two-for-one promotions, and on and on. Does this variety add to profits, or is it simply a source of unneeded complexity? To address this question this chapter draws on my published research describing golf course pricing.[1]

The descriptions of the pricing schemes are only part of the story. The economic analysis of complex pricing is also fascinating. Economists have habitually used a simple measure of price (perhaps the manufacturer's list price) in statistical work. Though inadequate, it is usually the best that researchers can hope for given the difficulty of obtaining the more detailed, and often proprietary, information required to keep track of multiple-price strategies. My work on golf course pricing shows that it is possible to carry out the more detailed analysis, and highlights the payoff in terms of better results and a more complete understanding of the industry. In particular, this

---

[1]Shmanske, Stephen, "Price Discrimination at the Links," *Contemporary Economic Policy*, Vol. 16, No. 3, (July 1998), pp. 368-378. Adapted with permission of Western Economic Association International.

chapter shows for golf course pricing that some types of complex pricing are designed to enhance the profitability of the seller, while other types are designed to distribute what could be profits preferentially among different groups of citizens.

This chapter proceeds by presenting a simple numerical model to illustrate the differences between competition and monopoly and between simple pricing and complex pricing. Several different types of pricing are discussed, each with a specific pattern that leads to different implications in a statistical model. Following the basic numerical model are the results of the search for a useful statistical approach to complex pricing. Finally, basic differences in ownership structure are shown to influence the choice of pricing structures in predictable ways.

5.1 Competition and Monopoly with Uniform Pricing

With the exception of supply and demand, the most important distinction that economists make is between competition and monopoly. Whether markets are competitive or monopolistic affects prices, quantities, revenues, and profits. The economist's policy prescriptions favoring competition stem mostly from the effect on quantity, although this point is largely obscure to non-economists who focus first on prices and profits. Because of this obscurity it will now be helpful to review, briefly, the economist's argument.

Competitive markets allow greater quantities to be produced than in monopoly markets, thus enhancing consumer well-being. The greater quantities will be sold at lower prices, but the net gain to society comes from the greater quantity, not from the lower prices. This is because the lower prices (and profits) represent a gain to consumers that is equally offset by a loss to sellers. If you pay a dollar less, then the seller earns a dollar less. While you are a dollar richer, the seller is a dollar poorer, and there is no unambiguous way to evaluate this purely distributional effect. At the level of society, we are all consumers and sellers, and the purely distributional effect is a wash. Consumers do, however, still end up with a greater quantity of goods and services in competitive markets.

Unfortunately, the economist's standard prescription is based on an incomplete analysis. The prescription stems from an unrealistic, truncated model that, for reasons of computational ease, considers only simple, or uniform, pricing. Uniform pricing is an extra assumption, added for convenience, requiring that all units of a seller's good be sold for the same price. While this assumption makes the arithmetic easier, casual observation is all that is required to see that there is no seller that sells every unit it produces for the same price.

Complex pricing schemes, also known as price discrimination and/or non-linear pricing, are the norm and must be considered. Despite this imperative, textbooks largely bury the discussion of complex pricing as a special, advanced case, while focusing attention on simple pricing. This emphasis is backwards. Furthermore, and again for computational ease, statistical demand studies ignore complex pricing and consider only simple pricing. Even many advanced theoretical studies of market behavior and interaction between firms use uniform pricing as a simplifying assumption, while purporting to derive policy-relevant implications for industrial structure and antitrust policy. Policy analysis of this sort may be completely irrelevant--but we are getting ahead of ourselves.

Our immediate purpose is to develop a simple model that illustrates competitive and monopolistic uniform pricing as well as several notions of complex pricing. Let there be two individuals with different, downward sloping demand curves for a product. Mr. N (N for nine) places a value of nine on his first unit of consumption, seven on his second, five on his third, three on his fourth, one on his fifth, and zero thereafter. Mr. E (E for eight) places a value of eight on his first unit of consumption, six on his second, four on his third, two on his fourth, and zero thereafter. The individual demand curves and the aggregate, or market, demand curve are pictured as step functions in Fig. 5.1.

The values of nine, seven, and so on for Mr. N are sometimes called marginal values, but in this case are more properly called incremental values, or demand prices. By adding up these incremental values we can derive the total value that Mr. N places on this good. In this case Mr. N's total value for five units of the good is $9 + 7 + 5 + 3 + 1 = 25$. Mr. E's total value for four units is 20. The total value for the market, denoted TV, is the sum of the individual total values and in this example is equal to 45.

The emphasis in this chapter is on pricing schemes, therefore the cost structure will be kept very simple. Let the cost of each unit produced be equal to two.

A table like Table 5.1 is included in virtually every principles of economics textbook. The numbers in Table 5.1 help us to clearly separate the competitive equilibrium from the monopoly equilibrium. The first column, P, lists the individual prices that might be charged for this good. The second column, Q, lists the amount that will be sold corresponding to the price in the P column. For example, at a price of five, five units will be sold, three to Mr. N and two to Mr. E. By convention, Mr. N buys the third unit which is worth five to him for a price of five and just breaks even on that unit. Mr. E, of course, does not buy a third unit for a price of five because it is only worth four to him.

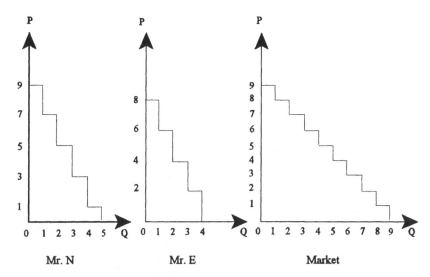

Mr. N   Mr. E   Market

Fig. 5.1 Individual and aggregate demand curves.

The third column, labelled TR, stands for total revenue and is simply the price times the quantity.

Skipping over the fourth and fifth columns for the moment, the sixth column, TC, stands for total cost, which in this case is simply two times the quantity listed in column Q.

By subtracting TC from TR we obtain the profit to the seller, denoted π. The simplest way of looking at the monopoly equilibrium is that the monopolist will choose the solution that maximizes profit. In this case a price of six and a quantity of four yields the highest possible profit of 16.

Note that the quantity that maximizes profit, in this case, four, is not the same as the quantity that maximizes TR, in this case, five. By contrast, the simplest way of looking at the competitive equilibrium, is that open market competition will bid the price down until the profits disappear. In this case, price will be competed down to two and quantity will increase to eight.

Table 5.1 Revenue, expenditure, and value with uniform pricing.

P	Q	TR	IV	TV	TC	π	CS	SW
9	1	9	9	9	2	7	0	7
8	2	16	8	17	4	12	1	13
7	3	21	7	24	6	15	3	18
6	4	24	6	30	8	16	6	22
5	5	25	5	35	10	15	10	25
4	6	24	4	39	12	12	15	27
3	7	21	3	42	14	7	21	28
2	8	16	2	44	16	0	28	28
1	9	9	1	45	18	-9	36	27

The economist's policy conclusion that competition is preferred to monopoly stems from the remaining four columns of Table 5.1. The column headed IV, is the incremental valuation associated with the market demand curve in Fig. 5.1, that is, nine for the first unit (Mr. N), eight for the second unit (Mr. E's first unit) and so on. The column headed TV is the total valuation as discussed above. The column headed CS, which stands for consumer surplus, is the difference between the value of the good to the consumers and what they have to pay to get it. This is the measure of the net benefit to consumers of any particular amount of the good. In this table CS is maximized with a quantity of nine at the loss-making price of one.[2]

While consumer advocacy groups typically lobby for low prices, economists stress the need to consider the producer interests as well. As the table shows, consumer surplus always increases as price decreases. However, after a point, profits start to decrease as price decreases and, for prices below cost, profits become negative. Naive attempts to keep prices low for the benefit of consumers have, time and time again, ruined individual

---

[2]Consumer surplus would be even higher with a price of zero, but sellers will not volunteer to make such losses.

markets (rent control, gasoline price controls, crowded freeways, California power) and thwarted growth in whole economies by taking away the incentive to produce the product in the first place.

Considering both profits and consumer surplus by adding them together, the last column of Table 5.1 lists what economists sometimes call "social welfare" denoted, SW. Social welfare is maximized at a quantity of eight (or seven), which happens to correspond to the zero-profit, competitive equilibrium. Alternatively, the uniform price monopolist maximizes profit at a price of six, produces only four units, and social welfare is only 22.

5.2 Complex Pricing

5.2.1 *Model A*

It is unfortunate that many students of economics never advance beyond this point because dramatic changes to these calculations follow once the uniform pricing assumption is relaxed. Consider first the type of pricing known as quantity discounting, multipart pricing, or declining block pricing. Instead of charging six for each unit, the seller could charge seven for the first unit to each person, and five for each succeeding unit. A "$2 off next purchase" coupon attached to each unit sold will easily accomplish such a pricing scheme. What would be the result?

Mr. N will now buy three units of the good, the first is worth nine and Mr. N pays seven, the second is worth seven and Mr. N pays five, and the third is worth five and Mr. N pays five, just breaking even on the third unit. The total value that Mr. N places on three units is $9 + 7 + 5 = 21$, and Mr. N pays $7 + 5 + 5 = 17$ and retains a consumer surplus of $21 - 17 = 4$. Mr. E buys two units, worth eight and six, for prices of seven and five, and retains consumer surplus of $(8 + 6) - (7 + 5) = 2$. The total revenue to the seller is 29 which is up from 24 in the monopoly case. Output is also up from four in the monopoly case to five in the case with quantity discounts. Average revenue, which is simply the total revenue divided by the quantity is down slightly from six to 5.8. The seller's reason for establishing the quantity discount is that profits increase from 16 in the simple monopoly case to $29 - 10 = 19$.

Because profits have gone up by three, and consumer surplus has remained the same at six, four for Mr. N and two for Mr. E, it follows that social welfare goes up by three from 22 to 25. Essentially, the first two units together cost the same as before to each customer, namely 12, but the seller gains by being able to expand the market and collect revenue of five on the third unit to Mr. N, a unit which only costs two to produce.

The seller can do even better than the prices of seven and five. If the seller charges eight for the first unit and then lowers price to five, Mr. N will buy three units paying a total of 18 and Mr. E will buy two units paying a total of 13 for a total revenue of 31, total cost of 10, and profit of 21. The seller has turned two more dollars worth of consumer surplus into profit by raising the price of the first unit to eight for each customer. Profits, output, and total revenue are all up compared to the uniform price case. Average revenue, 31/5 = 6.2, is increased slightly.[3]

Now suppose that three prices could be used. Keeping the assumption from the previous footnote that no single unit be sold for more than its demand price, the best pricing scheme is eight for the first unit, six for the second unit, and four thereafter. Mr. N and Mr. E each buy three units, and each pay 8 + 6 + 4 = 18 for a total revenue of 36. Mr. N gets consumer surplus of three and Mr. E gets zero. Total cost equals 12 and profits equal 24. Output and total revenue have gone up compared to the two-price case. Average revenue is once again equal to six.

The numerical example presented here is just one example but these results can be generalized. As the number of different prices in the quantity discount scheme increases, total revenue increases, quantity increases, and average revenue stays about the same. These predictions of the model are summarized in the model A row of Table 5.2.

---

[3]The best two-price scheme is to charge 12 for the first unit and then lower price to three. Mr. N buys four units for a total of 21, getting consumer surplus of 3. Mr. E buys three units for a total of 18, and retains no consumer surplus. Profits equal 21 + 18 - 14 = 25. This scheme, however, requires both consumers to "overpay" for the first unit hoping to make up the difference on the increased number of low price purchases. A high "up-front" price like this is similar to a membership fee which is considered below in the discussion of "two-part" pricing, called "model C." For the current section, I consider only cases where each unit individually will be purchased without requiring the simultaneous expectation of future lower price purchases.

5.2.2 *Model B*

The characteristic of Model A is that different prices may be charged for different units, but the same pricing scheme must be offered to each individual. Model B, called third degree price discrimination, or interpersonal price discrimination, by economists, and market segmentation by those in marketing, involves separating the market and charging a different, uniform price to each consumer. Thus, selling to Mr. N, the best single price that could be charged is seven. Mr. N buys two units which cost a total of four to produce, and pays 14, leaving a profit of 10. Selling to Mr. E, the best single price is six. Mr. E buys two units, pays 12, and the seller earns a profit of eight. Combining the segments, the seller collects revenues of 26, incurs costs of eight, and earns a profit of 18. Comparing this to the simple monopoly equilibrium in Table 5.1, we see that output remains the same, while total and average revenue both increase.

Table 5.2 Predicted effects of price discrimination on the dependent variable.

	Quantity	Average Revenue	Total Revenue
Model A	+	0	+
Model B	0	+	+
Model C	+	-	+
Model D	0	-	-
Model E	+	-	-

This example generally captures the flavor of third degree price discrimination. More complex examples can be constructed in which quantity can go up or down in the market as a whole, therefore, the quantity effect must be considered ambiguous. In general, however, both average revenue and total revenue would be expected to increase from an increase in this type of price discrimination. This pattern of predictions is listed in Table 5.2 in the row for Model B.

Is it difficult to segment markets? Not at all. At golf courses for example, if people like Mr. N tend to play on weekends while people like Mr. E tend to play on weekdays, then a simple weekday/weekend price differential will do the trick. The market segmentation does not have to be complete to increase profits. Different prices on different days, or at different times of the same day as in twilight or early bird discounts, will work as long as not too many of those targeted for the high price switch over into the low price market segment. Those who have the flexibility to switch over and play early in the morning on weekdays will benefit from price discrimination, while the remaining weekend players pay the price. Complete separation of the markets can be made if golfers do not misrepresent themselves, when the low price segment is composed of senior citizens, juniors, or residents who are entitled to discounts.

5.2.3 *Model C*

Two-part pricing is the name economists give to a variety of pricing schemes that consist in one form or another of an up-front, lump sum, membership fee, that entitles the member to consume the good at a discounted price. The lump sum fee could be yearly or monthly. The discounted price will usually be set close to the per-unit production cost. The idea is that the seller is attempting to turn what would be consumer surplus at the low per unit price, into revenue through the membership fee. The seller, however, must avoid setting the membership fee too high, for fear of losing the customer altogether.

Consider, then, our numerical example. If the per unit price were set equal to two, then both Mr. N and Mr. E would buy four units of the good, paying eight at the point of purchase. Mr. N values his four units at $9 + 7 + 5 + 3 = 24$, and, therefore, would earn consumer surplus of 16. Mr. E values his four units at $8 + 6 + 4 + 2 = 20$, and, therefore, would earn consumer surplus of 12. The seller could set the lump sum no higher than 12 without losing Mr. E. The result is that total revenue is 40, $(12 + 2 + 2 + 2 + 2 = 20$ from each), total cost is 16 and profit is 24.

The seller can actually do a little better by raising the per unit price slightly to three and lowering the membership fee to nine. Mr. N still values his four units at 24, and subtracting four times the per unit price of three, would be willing to pay a maximum of 12 to become a member. But Mr. E, will now only buy three units, which are worth $8 + 6 + 4 = 18$ to him. Subtracting the per unit payments which equal nine, the most Mr. E will pay to join is nine. With this pricing scheme, seven units are sold and total revenue is $9 + 9 + 21 = 39$. The seven units cost 14, so the profit is 25.

Compared to simple monopoly pricing, both quantity and total revenue increase but average revenue decreases. Remember that average revenue was equal to six for the uniform price monopolist; here, average revenue is $39/7 = 5.57$. These results also generalize to other examples, and the resulting pattern of effects is listed in the Model C row of Table 5.2.

The three models of price discrimination just presented comprise the basic themes in the economics of non-linear pricing. But the variations on these themes are almost endless. For example, there is nothing to stop a seller from combining aspects of the different models. Model B and Model C can be combined by offering different membership plans to different groups. A full membership plan may be available for the highest membership fee and carry with it the most expansive benefits. Simultaneously, an auxiliary membership plan with fewer benefits (perhaps golf only on weekdays) is available for a lower price to a possibly circumscribed portion of the market. Alternatively, at the same time that some golfers are enjoying unlimited play on a monthly ticket, others are paying different green fees for each round depending on time of day, day of week, and senior or resident status. Whether any of the patterns in Models A, B, or C can be disentangled is the empirical question to be addressed later in the chapter.

First, however, there are two additional patterns of coefficients which are motivated by the possibility that the municipal golf courses may not have profit maximization as a goal.

5.2.4 *Model D*

The first of these patterns, motivated by public finance theory, is that the municipal golf courses willingly subsidize consumption for the residents of the municipality. As noted, many courses segment their markets charging a lower price to residents. But residents have fewer closely available substitutes to their local course, and lower travel costs to their own municipality's golf course. Residents are, in a sense, the captive market of consumers with higher demand prices and thus would be charged higher prices in profit maximizing third degree discrimination. A system of resident discounts seems to be price discrimination in the "wrong" direction.[4] This may have an ambiguous effect on quantity, but the greater the degree of resident discounts, the lower the average and total revenue.

For example, suppose Mr. N is the local golfer and receives a discounted price of 5. Mr. E, from out of town is charged 7. Mr. N now buys three units, which have a total value of 9 + 7 + 5 = 21, pays a total of 15, and retains consumer surplus of six. This level of consumer surplus for Mr. N is higher than in the simple monopoly case or any of the models A, B, or C. Mr. E buys one unit and pays seven. Output is the same as the simple monopoly case, four, but total revenue, average revenue, and profits have fallen to 22, 5.5, and 14 respectively. This pattern of results is labeled Model D in Table 5.2.

5.2.5 *Model E*

The last pattern of results is motivated by a quirk that often exists in the contract that becomes necessary when the golf course is owned and managed by separate entities. Suppose, for example, that a municipality wants to hire a golf course management company to run its golf course. There are several ways such a contract could be drawn up.

First, the city could pay the management company a fixed fee for a specified list of services like collecting the green fees, cutting the grass, and so on. The city collects all the revenue and hopes to collect more than the fixed fee. In such a plan, the management company has almost no incentive to do a good job; they will collect the fee without any extra effort as long as

---

[4]Such a policy is not necessarily ill-advised if the subsidized (for, and by, the residents) municipal golf course is an amenity that increases property values and tax collections. An even more global measure of price discrimination involving estimation of an hedonic housing price function is required. A Quang Do and Gary Grudnitski have recently estimated such a model. See Do, A Quang and Gary Grudnitski, "Golf Courses and Residential House Prices: An Empirical Examination," *The Journal of Real Estate Finance and Economics*, Vol. 10, Issue 3 (1995) pp. 261-270. After considering 717 sales transactions they conclude that abutting a golf course adds 7.6% to a house's value. Regardless, the narrow price discrimination at the course still goes in the wrong direction.

they fulfill the minimum obligations specified in the contract.[5] The only extra incentive that the management company does have comes from the city's ability to choose another company at the end of the contract. In such cases, short term contracts will be the norm. To assure that the golf course is being maintained properly, or at least that the letter of the contract is being followed, the city itself will have to monitor the conditions at the golf course and the performance of the manager anyway. This defeats the whole purpose of hiring the outside manager in the first place. Some municipalities end up managing and maintaining their own golf courses with city employees. It is often the case that these courses lack the correct incentives, and their quality suffers accordingly.

Second, the management company could pay the city a fee for the right to manage the golf course and keep all the revenues produced by it. Now, the management company has the incentive to most efficiently operate the facility, at least in the short run. Near the end of such a contract, however, the management company could skimp on maintenance efforts without causing a rapid deterioration of the golf course. Longer term damage will be the problem of the next management company to take over. Economists call this "the last period problem."[6] This problem can be partially avoided by limiting the number of last periods, that is, by granting longer term contracts in the first place.

However, granting longer term contracts makes a different problem worse, namely, the setting of the fee at the right level. The longer the term of the contract, the more uncertainty there is about demand, costs, pricing, and potential profits. In a fixed fee contract, if the demand is higher than

---

[5]No matter how specific the contract is, it is impossible to specify everything. The contract may be as explicit as to require daily mowing of the greens, twice yearly aeration, fertilization, and reseeding of the fairways, and maintenance of a required minimum number of working golf carts, but can never be so explicit as to require smiling and being friendly to customers.

[6]Another example of this, with which we are all familiar, happens whenever a new administration takes over a political office. The cost of maintenance to prevent potholes can be avoided and the pothole problem worsens only a little in the short term. The problem only becomes severe in the long run when a different administration may be in office. Meanwhile, the money saved from skimping on the maintenance can be applied to salaries, staff, pet projects, or other vote-buying schemes.

expected, the management company keeps the unexpected profits and the city loses out on the bonanza. Alternatively, if there is an unexpected demand shortfall, perhaps due to unusually inclement weather, the city's revenues are protected but the management company loses out. Management contracts typically specify that revenues be shared between the owner and the manager according to some formula in order the share the risk of fluctuating demand.

The quirk in the contract between the city and the golf course management company is that it is often the case that green fee revenue is shared at a higher percentage than other revenue items. For example, suppose the management company has to share the revenue from green fees, but gets to keep all the revenue from the cart rentals, restaurant sales, and merchandise sales. Such a management company could be expected to set low green fees to maximize the number of customers, which will increase the demand for these other revenue items. The numerical example with Mr. N and Mr. E is not rich enough to capture this effect but the result is clear. If one is attempting to maximize the number of rounds played, then any price discrimination scheme that is used will be expected to increase quantity, even if average and total revenue (from green fees) are reduced. This is Model E, and the resulting pattern of coefficients is summarized in Table 5.2.

5.3 Measures of Price Discrimination

The preceding sections have shown that complex pricing can take a variety of forms, with varying effects on quantity, average revenue, and total revenue. There are many ways, statistically, that complex pricing could be captured, and in this section, I explore several. Some of these measures can, and should be, applied generically to demand studies of any industry. Other measures are specifically motivated by the institutions of the golf course industry.

First, is the generic measure motivated by the multipart pricing in Model A, that is, n, the number of different prices charged by a seller. The summary statistics for this measure and all of the variables used in the statistical regressions are listed in Table 5.3. As the table shows, the number of different prices charged by golf courses ranges from four to 20, with an average of over eight. Every golf course in the sample used at least four different prices: weekday, weekday twilight, weekend, and weekend twilight.

Resident discounts, senior discounts, and membership plans were the other most common pricing variations used.

Table 5.3 Summary statistics.

Variable	mean	std. deviation	minimum	maximum
ROUNDS	86,790	34,541	34,000	210,000
CAPACITY	.3261	.4740	0	1
AVEREV	19.302	11.878	8.473	62.43
TOTREV	1,449,200	495,420	548,500	3,230,000
HOLES	20.957	6.5793	18	45
RATING	70.672	1.9649	64.4	74.9
HILLINESS	2.5014	.97023	1.04	4.542
BEAUTY	3.614	.6347	2.455	4.609
WATER	7.103	3.937	0	16
CARTPATH	.1413	.3442	0	1
REGPRICE	23.565	12.024	12	70
ADJPOP10	375,920	252,370	45,090	966,300
ADJPOP10/#	94,273	71,030	28,240	398,300
ADJPOPCLOSE	105,900	96,286	13,670	416,300
n	8.6522	2.8614	4	20
SIGMA	8.7922	4.7825	3.684	25.71
WKEND-REG	9.0109	5.8949	3	25
2PART%	.15428	.18725	0	.697
RESIDENT	3.1424	4.4115	0	22.55
MUNI	.54348	.50361	0	1
2PARTMUNI	.055478	.10823	0	.495
2PARTMUNINO	.098804	.18590	0	.697

Notes: Raw population data are from 1990 US Census maps. Author's calculations are the source for all data.

A couple of problems arise when simply counting the number of different prices. First, doing so does not capture the importance of each of the prices in the pricing scheme. For example, the golf course might have a special lower price for juniors during twilight hours, but that price might only be used once or twice per week. Second, counting the number of prices does not capture how different the prices are. For example, a resident discount of over $20 will have a very different effect than a resident discount of a dollar or two, but both will be counted the same if simply the number of prices is used.

The second measure of price discrimination, namely, the statistical standard deviation of the actual prices charged, solves both of the above problems with the number of prices. The standard deviation takes into account the level of each price and number of times it is charged. Another benefit of the standard deviation is that, unlike some of the measures discussed below, it is a generic statistical measure that can be applied in any industry. The downfall of using the standard deviation is the level of detail and the computations required to derive it, as shown in the appendix to this chapter. However, as the results show, the standard deviation can capture some of the effects of price discrimination.

Table 5.3 shows that the standard deviation, called SIGMA, ranges from a low of 3.684 to a high of 25.71 with an average of 8.792. The higher is SIGMA, the more variation there is in the pricing structure.

SIGMA, the standard deviation, or n, the number of prices, might be able to capture the effects of Models A or B, but will probably not be very useful in capturing two-part pricing. Therefore, a third measure is examined, namely, the percentage of total quantity that is accounted for by people using two-part pricing, hereafter called, 2PART%. Both yearly and monthly membership plans are counted in this measure, as long as there is a lump sum fee and a marginal price (which in most cases equals zero). If the argument in Model C is correct, this measure should be positively related to output and total revenue, but negatively related to average revenue. As shown in Table 5.3, there is significant usage of two-part pricing in the sample. The average usage of two-part pricing in the sample is about 15%. While some courses do not use any sort of two-part pricing, one course sells almost 70% of its rounds using yearly or monthly membership plans.

Any of the above measures could be applied generically in any industry. But when looking specifically at the golf course industry, there are several other measures motivated by the institutions therein. These other measures also have the advantage that they might be simpler to calculate.

For example, a measure attempting to capture third degree price discrimination is the difference between the regular weekday price and the regular weekend price. All of the golf courses use a weekend/weekday differential, so this measure is available for all the courses. A golf course that does not discriminate very much will only show a small difference between these prices, while another course which was able to more profitably exploit this type of price discrimination will have a large difference. As Table 5.3 shows, this differential, called WKEND-REG, averages about $9 and ranges from a low of $3 to a high of $25. If Model B is correct, WKEND-REG should be positively related to average revenue and total revenue, and exert no strong effect on quantity. As shown below, this is precisely what happens.

Finally, two attempts were made to separate the possible differential effect between municipal courses and daily fee courses. The first attempt highlights the suspect resident discount. The maximum resident discount offered by a course for any of its categories is chosen to capture this effect. In a sense, this variable is the opposite of the weekend minus weekday price variable. Both measure the extent of third degree price discrimination, but the resident discount seems to be price discrimination in the wrong direction. One would expect this variable to mimic the pattern of coefficients in Model D.

Table 5.3 shows that the resident discount averages a little over $3. The maximum resident discount in the sample was $22.55. Interestingly, and consistent with economic theory, the only courses to use resident discounts were municipal golf courses. Presumably, city councils require the use of resident discounts even though doing so does not maximize the profits of the golf course facility. City residents and taxpayers who are not golfers end up subsidizing those who are. Perhaps the nongolfers acquiesce, thinking that, through logrolling, they obtain the benefits of other amenities purchased with tax dollars. The smallest resident discount, that is, zero, is used by every one of the for-profit, daily fee golf courses.

The last attempt involved separating the variable capturing the percentage of rounds sold with two-part pricing into two separate variables, one capturing two-part pricing by municipal golf courses (and expected to show the pattern in Model E), and one capturing two-part pricing at non-municipal golf courses (expected to show the pattern in Model C). A comparison of the coefficients of these variables sheds light on whether municipal golf courses and daily fee courses use membership plans differently.

Once again, refer to Table 5.3. The variable MUNI is a dummy variable set equal to one if the golf course is a municipal golf course. Multiplying MUNI by 2PART% gives us the variable, 2PARTMUNI, which is a vector containing the percentage of rounds sold through membership plans at municipal courses only.   2PARTMUNINO is the complement to 2PARTMUNI, containing the percentage of rounds sold through membership plans at daily fee golf courses. MUNI indicates that slightly over one-half of the golf courses in the sample are municipal facilities. A comparison of 2PARTMUNI and 2PARTMUNINO indicates that municipal courses use membership plans less than for profit courses (an average of about 5.5% of total rounds at municipal courses to almost 10% of rounds sold at daily fee courses). Also, the most intensive use of two-part pricing, almost 70% of total rounds, was made by a daily fee course, although there was one municipal facility that sold almost one-half of its total rounds using two-part pricing.

5.4 The Statistical Model

The following three equations were estimated.[7]

$$\text{ROUNDS} \ = \ a_0 + A_1 Z_1 + a_2 P + a_3 X \ .\qquad\qquad (5.1)$$

$$\text{AVEREV} \ = \ b_0 + B_1 Z_2 + b_2 Q + b_3 X \ .\qquad\qquad (5.2)$$

$$\text{TOTREV} \ = \ c_0 + C_1 Z_3 \qquad\quad + c_3 X \ .\qquad\qquad (5.3)$$

In these equations, the dependent variables are measures of quantity, average revenue, and total revenue, P is a measure of price, Q is a measure of quantity, X is the measure of price discrimination, Z_i represents three, possibly different, vectors of demographic and demand shift variables, and the a's, b's, and c's are the coefficients to be estimated.

The estimates of a_3, b_3, and c_3 are of interest for comparison with the predictions in Table 5.2. Eq. (5.1), for example, estimates a_3, which is the marginal effect of an increase in a measure of price discrimination, X, on

---

[7]The equations were estimated separately with ordinary least squares. Experimentation with multiple equation models was not fruitful. Given the sample size, there are simply too many coefficients to reliably estimate in a large structural model.

quantity, ROUNDS, controlling for price, P, and other important demand shift variables, Z. Eqs. (5.2) and (5.3) are interpreted similarly.

The coefficients of the various Z vectors are of interest as far as the economics of golf is concerned and will be discussed briefly below. It is not necessarily the case that the same control variables appear in each equation.

The research plan was to find the set of explanatory variables that best captures the relevant demographic and demand shift effects for each of Eqs. (5.1)-(5.3). Then, each price discrimination variable was separately added to the equation to test for sign, statistical significance, and economic significance. Through this procedure, we find out which of the several measures of price discrimination can capture the effects of the varieties of price discrimination presented in Models A-E.

The price discrimination variables are the main focus of our attention, however, some discussion of the variables in the Z vectors is required to put the demand for golf in perspective. The demand to play at any particular course will be a function of the physical attributes of the course and the management policies of the course. Physical attributes would include the number of sand traps, the extent of water hazards, and the size of the greens. Policies would include whether carts must remain on paved cart paths and whether carts are mandatory. Some of these factors are objectively measurable, while others such as the aesthetic beauty of the golf course are only subjectively measurable as discussed in Chapter 4.

There are a few factors which deserve special attention. First, and obvious for any demand study, is the population from which a golf course draws its golfers. All else equal, higher population should lead to higher demand. There are several ways to measure the relevant population, none of which seems preferred on purely theoretical grounds. Various measures were used including: the population of the city in which the golf course is located divided by the number of golf courses in that city; the population within a ten-mile radius of the golf course; the population within a ten-mile radius divided by the number of other competing courses within a ten-mile radius; and the population that is closer to the particular course of interest than to any other course.[8]

---

[8]The complete discussion of the population figures is taken up in Chapter 7 in order to avoid being distracted here.

An additional adjustment is made to the population figures based on the National Golf Foundation's *Golf Consumer Profile*. The population of potential golfers is systematically related to the demographics of the underlying population, especially age and income. Youths do not golf very much, and senior citizens golf roughly twice as much as those in middle age. While golf and income are positively related, many of the wealthy golfers will belong to private courses, and are not really customers of public access courses. At the other end of the income spectrum, those below the poverty level are substantially out of the market. The adjusted population figures used in this chapter delete those below the poverty level, delete those under the age of 18, and give twice the weight to those over the age of 60. The adjusted population figures perform uniformly better than the raw figures.

A second important factor to golfers is the difficulty of the course. Although some beginner golfers and some senior citizens prefer to play on an "easy" golf course, most golfers seem to prefer more difficulty. There are many ways to measure the course's difficulty. The number of water hazards or bunkers are possible direct measures that are objectively countable. The overall length of the course measured in yards is also a possibility, since short courses are typically easier to play. Additionally, local and national golf associations have developed rating systems of course difficulty (higher ratings mean a more difficult golf course). Golfers are very interested in the difficulty rating, and golf course managers know it; some even highlight their high difficulty ratings in advertisements.[9]

Another factor that many in the golf industry feel is very important is the pace of play. Human nature is such that waiting is not enjoyable, so most suspect that slow play will negatively effect the demand on a particular course. Unfortunately, there is no easy way to measure the pace of play. Early in the morning at most courses the pace is swift, however, once a slower group is on the course, all the groups behind will have to wait. Short of clocking every round at every course over a period of time (which some

---

[9]There are two quantitative difficulty rating systems in use; the older is called the course rating and the newer is called the slope rating. Both measures were tried; the results are reported for the course rating, called RATING, which worked better. Although the slope rating system has some theoretical advantages for the average golfer, it probably measures difficulty with a larger error because it contains more subjective components and because, as of the 1994 data, experience with it was still in its infancy.

of the courses have started to do), there is no direct way to measure this effect. However, some other variables may be correlated to slow play. For example, a course in poor condition will typically take longer to play as golfers search for lost golf balls imbedded in soggy turf or unkempt weeds. Also, the restriction of golf carts to cart paths will require more time walking back and forth from the cart to the ball.[10]

One final factor to control for is the capacity of the golf course facility. Regardless the type of golf course, the typical round of golf consists of play on 18 holes, and takes an average of 4.5 hours to complete, or 15 minutes per hole. Traditionally, golfers play in groups of four, and there can be two groups on each hole. This pattern implies that foursomes can start no faster than every 7.5 minutes. Scheduling 8 foursomes every hour from slightly before sunrise to 4.5 hours before dusk, say roughly 6:00 AM until 2:00 PM on average, leads to a capacity for an 18-hole course of 93,440 (8x4x8x365) rounds per year. Additional partial rounds are played by golfers who play the "back nine" early in the morning or by golfers who start after 4.5 hours before dusk, knowing that they may not finish the full 18 holes. These partial rounds raise the capacity of the golf course. Indeed, some of the 18-hole golf courses sell over 100,000 rounds per year. Increasing the capacity over 100,000 rounds by a substantial amount requires additional holes which several of the golf course complexes have added. As Table 5.3 indicates, one facility in particular has 45 holes and provided 210,000 rounds.

The issue of capacity is potentially an important one for the estimations in this chapter. Suppose a golf course could improve its quality to increase demand. Typically, a golf course that is not at capacity would raise both price and quantity in response to an increase in demand while a course at capacity could only raise price. This suggests that there will be a difference in the parameter estimation between a sample with courses at capacity and a sample with courses below capacity. For this chapter, a dummy variable is used to distinguish between these effects.[11]

---

[10]A full discussion and economic model of golf course pace of play is covered in Chapter 8.

[11]The dummy variable (CAPACITY = 1 if the number of rounds per 18 holes is over 90,000) is a crude but useful first approximation. Splitting the sample based on capacity led to small sample size and large standard errors. There is nothing obvious about the

As implied by the above discussion, explanatory variables in demand and revenue equations may include measures of all or some of the following variables: the relevant population; whether a course is at capacity; the number of holes that a course has, the yardage or rating of the course, the hilliness, the course condition, the aesthetic beauty, the size of the greens, the length of time it takes to play a round, the acres of lakes, the number of holes with water hazards, the number of bunkers, the course's advertising, whether carts are mandatory or optional, and whether carts are restricted to cart paths.

5.5 Results

Arguably, the most natural generic measure of price dispersion is SIGMA, the standard deviation of the prices charged. To get the flavor of the results, and to illustrate the influence of the demographic and demand shift variables in Z, Table 5.4 lists the results for Eqs. (5.1)-(5.3), estimated with and without SIGMA.

The first two columns of Table 5.4 present the results for Eq. (5.1). All the variables have the predicted sign. Population, holes, price, and the dummy for constrained capacity are clearly important in explanatory power. And, the two included subjectively measured variables, hilliness and beauty, are statistically significant and economically meaningful in their magnitudes.

Let us examine the specific implications of some of the point estimates in the first column. For example, the estimated coefficient of HOLES is 3,725. Multiplying this by 18 yields 67,050. Therefore, courses with 18 more holes sell about 67,000 more rounds of golf per year. Note that this statistical correlation does not prove causation. If population were low, and there was no demand to play golf, then adding another 18 holes would not automatically lead to 67,000 more customers. The result simply means that those courses with more holes sell more rounds. It is probably the fact that

relationship between capacity and price discrimination. A very simple model might suggest that once at capacity a firm can dispense with price discrimination and just sell all its units at the highest price. For golf courses, however, there is a daily (indeed hourly) capacity, as well as a yearly capacity and it might be that the successful market segmentation and two-part pricing is what allows the course to reach capacity in the first place.

there is the demand to play golf that causes the facility to build more holes in the first place.

Table 5.4 O.L.S. estimation of Eqs. (5.1)-(5.3) with and without SIGMA
(t-statistics in parentheses).

	Dependent Variable					
	ROUNDS		AVEREV		TOTREV	
CONSTANT	1431	3651	-159	-148	-8,932,800	-7,560,500
	(.111)	(.267)	(-3.16)	(-2.99)	(-3.32)	(-2.74)
CAPACITY	23,985	23,750	4.685	3.699	-298,849	-194,796
	(4.95)	(4.84)	(1.08)	(.860)	(-1.75)	(-1.09)
HOLES	3,725	3,726			22,036	22,026
	(13.3)	(13.2)			(2.15)	(2.20)
RATING			2.795	2.506	128,745	107,547
			(4.19)	(3.71)	(3.57)	(2.88)
HILLINESS	-7,322	-6,877	-2.658	-2.710	-167,139	-180,680
	(-2.65)	(-2.36)	(-1.53)	(-1.60)	(-1.83)	(-2.02)
BEAUTY	7,227	6,542	4.731	4.294	297,968	274,083
	(1.84)	(1.57)	(1.92)	(1.77)	(2.33)	(2.18)
WATER	-854	-809				
	(-1.77)	(-1.63)				
CARTPATH	-9,987	-8,341				
	(-1.69)	(-1.24)				
REGPRICE	-368	-300				
	(-2.14)	(-1.38)				
ADJPOP10	.0208	.0204				
	(2.48)	(2.40)				
ADJPOP10/#			.0000436	.0000427		
			(2.13)	(2.14)		
ADJPOPCLOSE					2.453	2.369
					(2.94)	(2.90)
ROUNDS/18			-.000476	-.000382		
			(-4.43)	(-3.21)		
SIGMA		-321		.5572		25,233
		(-.521)		(1.67)		(1.68)
adj. R²	.89	.89	.55	.57	.31	.34

According to the coefficient of WATER, adding another water hazard will decrease play by 854 rounds per year. Whether this is because it makes the golf course more difficult, or because it makes a round of golf longer, or because of something else, is not determinable from this equation. Regardless, the effect is small, amounting to less than three rounds per day.

According to the coefficient of CARTPATH, -9,987, restricting carts to cart paths only will decrease play by almost 10,000 rounds per year. This effect is probably due to two factors. First, many players who take carts do so because they do not want to do the extra walking. These players will go elsewhere, thus depressing the demand at courses with the restrictive policy. Second, limiting carts to cart paths only slows the pace of play limiting both the capacity of the golf course and the demand to play on it.

Of particular interest are the coefficients of the subjectively measured characteristics. An additional rating point on the one-to-five scale for hilliness will cost about 7,000 rounds of golf, while an additional point on the beauty scale will increase rounds played by roughly 7,000 rounds per year. Both of these effects are in the expected direction, and both are statistically significant, although not overwhelmingly so. The ability of these subjectively measured variables to capture the intended effects is an affirmation of the value of the procedures explained in Chapter 4.

The population variable indicates that an additional 10,000 in adjusted population in a 10-mile radius from the course will increase rounds played by about 200. While this effect may seem small, remember that there may be more than one course located in that radius and this coefficient indicates that demand will go up by 200 rounds per year for each of them.

Finally, the price coefficient, -368, implies an elasticity of -0.1 when evaluated at the mean price and quantity, 23.565 and 86,790 respectively.[12] For example, raising all prices, including the regular price, by one dollar, means that green fee revenue would go up by $86,790 if quantity did not fall. Quantity does fall, however, but only by about 368, so the golf course no longer gets 368 times the original price of $23.565 which equals $8,672. Therefore, the net effect on revenues is a whopping gain of $78,118. According to these estimates, golf course profits would increase following an

---

[12]The percentage change in quantity is -0.42% (-368/86,790 = -0.0042) and the percentage change in price is 4.2% (1/23.565 = 0.042).

increase in price. Therefore, the low elasticity as implied by the data is inconsistent with profit maximization. This is an important piece of evidence in support of the suspicion that municipal courses, which make up over half of the sample, may not be maximizing profit.

Turning to the price discrimination variable, in this case SIGMA, the second column indicates that the price discrimination variable seems to make no difference to the number of rounds played. The low t-statistic indicates that the estimate is a statistical zero. This is not necessarily a bad result. Indeed, both Models B and D from Table 5.2 indicate that increasing the extent of price discrimination will have no effect on the number of rounds played.

To distinguish between Models B and D requires that we examine the effect of price discrimination on AVEREV and TOTREV. Turn, first, to the middle two columns in Table 5.4 which present the estimates for Eq. (5.2). A slightly different set of explanatory variables was significant in these equations. Again, all the regressors have the anticipated sign. It is not necessary to belabor each coefficient but, note in particular, that: an increase of one point on the course beauty scale increases average revenue by more than $4. Beauty had a positive effect on rounds played in Eq. (5.1) and had a positive effect on average revenue per round in Eq. (5.2). Golfers appreciate beauty, play more rounds at more beautiful venues, and are willing to pay higher prices to do so. While it is hardly surprising that this is so, these equations quantify the effect for the benefit of golf course managers. By combining the revenue effects here with the costs of supplying a more beautiful golf course, to be examined in the next chapter, useful implications are derived for golf course management.

With respect to price discrimination, SIGMA is significant (p-value = .10)[13], and indicates that an increase of $1 in the standard deviation of the pricing structure, leads to a $.56 increase in average revenue. This is consistent with Model B. Adding more variety in the pricing structure leads

---

[13]The t-statistic on SIGMA is 1.67, which corresponds to a p-value of .1. Roughly, this means that there is less than a 10% chance that the value of the coefficient, .5572, could be that far away from zero simply by random variations in the data. When the t-statistic is two or greater, the p-value decreases to .01, meaning that there is less than a 1% chance that the results are nothing more than random fluctuations.

to an increase in average revenue. Furthermore, this is a quantitatively important effect. If the average golf course sells over 86,000 rounds per year, an increase of over $0.50 per round on average yields over $43,000 in extra revenue per year.

The last two columns of Table 5.4 present the results of Eq. (5.3) and confirm the previous result. More holes, more difficulty, less hilliness, more beauty, higher population, and more price discrimination as proxied by SIGMA all lead to more total revenue. An additional 18 holes is worth about $397,000 in revenue, an additional stroke in the difficulty rating is worth over $100,000, and an additional point on the subjective beauty scale brings in close to $300,000 per year. The coefficient of SIGMA is positive and significant, fitting the predictions of Models A, B, and C.

Taking all three equations into account, the measurement of price discrimination as the standard deviation of the prices charged supports the pattern of effects that are associated with third-degree price discrimination as presented in Model B. Thus, capturing the statistical effect of price discrimination by including the standard deviation variable is possible. Furthermore, although golf course facilities may be simultaneously attempting to use more than one type of price discrimination, the dominant one, at least in terms of how it shows through the use of the standard deviation, is the market segmentation or third-degree price discrimination variety.

It is possible that other measures of price discrimination will pick up other types of price discrimination. In lieu of rehashing all the coefficients of the golf and demographic variables for each case, only the coefficients of the price discrimination variable are reported for the other potential measures. These are presented in Table 5.5. The model of price discrimination from Table 5.2 that most closely corresponds to the pattern of coefficients is indicated in the last column of Table 5.5.

The first three measures reported in Table 5.5 are the generic measures that could be applied in any industry. As the table shows, there is some support for Model B in the standard deviation measure, but no support whatsoever for Models A or C. The regression estimates are more consistent with the non profit maximization cases as indicated in Models D or E. For example, when the number of different prices, n, is used, there are significant negative effects on average revenue and total revenue but no significant effect on quantity. This pattern of coefficients matches Model D, the price-discrimination-in-the-wrong-direction case. Unfortunately, n was not supposed to capture Model D; it was supposed to capture Model A.[14] The effects using the 2PART% measure are statistically weaker, again providing no support for Model C. A golf course's desire to expand quantity as in Model E or subsidize residents as in Model D, is hiding any profitable price discrimination that might be taking place.

Table 5.5 Coefficient estimates of the price discrimination variable (t-statistics in parentheses).

	Dependent Variable			Inference*
	ROUNDS	AVEREV	TOTREV	Supports Model
SIGMA	-321	.5572	25,233	B*
	(-.521)	(1.67)	(1.68)	
n	-208	-.9872	-38,741	D*
	(-.275)	(-2.44)	(-1.65)	
2PART%	10,157	-10.13	-345,413	D or E
	(.980)	(-1.46)	(-.957)	
WKEND-REG	-82.84	.7098	40,486	B*
	(-.172)	(2.85)	(3.46)	
RESIDENT	525	-.2896	-13,689	D or E
	(1.26)	(-1.03)	(-.898)	
2PARTMUNI	18,498	-22.70	-864,883	D* or E*
	(.871)	(-1.78)	(-1.19)	
2PARTMUNINO	8,595	-6.936	-234,113	
	(.779)	(-.973)	(-.606)	

Notes: An asterisk (*) next to the letter signifying which model is supported indicates strong support for that model. The letter by itself corresponds to somewhat weaker support.

[14]Some of the golf courses that have high values of n do so because they have separate resident discounts in multiple categories. For example, all courses use weekday and weekend, regular and twilight, which makes four price categories. If each of these categories has a resident discount there are now eight different prices. In this sense, n is capturing multiple applications of the "wrong-way" price discrimination of Model D.

The main problem, however, with trying to capture price discrimination with a single generic measure is that more than one form of price discrimination may be in effect simultaneously. To address this difficulty, let us examine the measures specifically designed to capture only a single type of effect.

For example, WKEND-REG is designed to highlight the weekend/weekday price differential as an example of third-degree price discrimination. As Table 5.5 shows this measure does obtain the pattern of coefficients expected in Model B. There are significant positive effects on average revenue and total revenue, and no significant effect on quantity.

RESIDENT, which captures the maximum size of the resident discount, is expected to show profit-losing price discrimination, that is, Model D. The effects on average revenue and total revenue are negative, and the effect on quantity is positive, but none of the effects are statistically significant. Thus, although there is some support for Models D or E, it must be considered weak.

There does not seem to be a measure which can satisfactorily capture Model A. The number of different prices seems to be more closely related to market segmentation than to declining block or multi-part pricing. There are a few direct instances of quantity discounting by golf courses, such as 10-play cards, 4-for-3 pricing and so on, but in the aggregate, there are not enough of these schemes to form a separate variable. However, since it has been shown for very general settings, that any declining block pricing schedule can be implemented through the proper choice of a set of two-part prices, perhaps more attention should be directed to two-part pricing.[15]

The 2PART% variable which is designed to capture Model C (and perhaps also Model A) yielded only weak results, and those in support of Models D and E. The problem here is that the municipal courses may not be using two-part pricing in a profit maximizing manner. The variables 2PARTMUNI and 2PARTMUNINO, separate the 2PART% variable into two variables, the percentage of rounds sold with two-part pricing by,

---

[15] See, Goldman, M. B., H. E. Leland, and D. S. Sibley, "Optimal Nonuniform Prices," *Review of Economic Studies*, 51: 1984, 305-319, and Maskin, E. and J. Riley, "Monopoly with Incomplete Information," *Rand Journal of Economics*, 15: 1984, 171-196.

respectively, municipal and daily fee courses. As the last two rows of Table 5.5 indicate, the separation worked. 2PARTMUNI now strongly, in terms of the pattern of signs and the levels of significance, shows support for Model D.

This chapter intertwines a variety of conclusions for people coming to golf course pricing from a variety of perspectives. For golf course managers, the analysis clearly shows that complex pricing can be used to increase revenues. Overall, adding more variation to the pricing schedule, as measured by the standard deviation of prices charged, is profitable. However, not just any type of variation will do. Weekday discounts (or weekend price increases) work, but resident discounts seem to be price discrimination in the wrong direction. Perhaps golf course managers already implicitly know this. All courses use weekday discounts, and none use resident discounts unless forced to by their municipalities.

For golfers, the lessons are also clear. Profitable operation of a golf course entails the use of price discrimination. Many golfers can save money by choosing to play where or when they qualify for discounts. Golfers who do not qualify for discounts end up in higher priced segments of the market. These golfers would gain from the movement to a more uniform price structure.

For nongolfers there is also a lesson. Resident discounts on a municipal golf course are actually subsidies from nonresident golfers and from the community's taxpayers. Unfortunately for these groups, nonresidents do not have a voice in the making of municipal golf course policy. Taxpaying, nongolfing residents have a voice, but it is not as coordinated or concentrated as the lobbying pressure brought to bear by the golfers who are the direct beneficiaries of the subsidy.

Finally, for economists and statisticians, the chapter illustrates how complex pricing can be captured in a demand model. Generic measures like the standard deviation of prices should be included in regression models. Furthermore, more focused, industry-specific measures can distinguish several types of price discrimination.

Appendix to Chapter 5

This appendix illustrates, for a simple example, the conversion of the raw data into usable data.

Suppose that interviews revealed the following information. The course has five price categories: regular ($15); early morning and twilight ($11); weekend and holiday ($22); weekend and holiday early morning and twilight ($13); and a monthly pass allowing free play on weekdays ($70). The total rounds played per year was about 95,000, and the total green fee revenues were about $1,400,000. Further questioning revealed that 25 passes were sold each month and that each of those golfers played about 3 times per week. Also, there were about 100 rounds per day in the early morning and twilight categories. Finally, it was about 4% busier on weekends and holidays. (If there were more price categories than just five, then more questions were asked to obtain sufficient information about the course's price/quantity profile).

The first step was to determine the number of rounds played per day. Assuming 104 weekend days and 14 holidays per year, and using the 4% busier figure, the number of rounds on an average weekday is given by x in the following formula:

$$247x + 118(1.04)x = 95,000 . \qquad (5.A1)$$

Rounding to whole numbers, this yields 257 rounds per day on weekdays and 267 rounds per day on weekends and holidays.

The monthly passes account for about 75 rounds per week which comes out to about 15 rounds per weekday.

Given these figures and the 100 discounted rounds per day figures, the following table can be filled out.

Table 5.A1 Pattern of play.

type of day	weekday			weekend/holiday	
price category	regular	twilight	monthly	regular	twilight
price	15	11	0	23	13
rounds per day	142	100	15	167	100
rounds per year	35074	24700	3705	19706	11800
$ per year	526,110	271,200	21,000*	433,532	153,400

* $21,000/year = (12 months/year)(25 passes/month)($70/pass)

One more issue remains in the calculation of the variance of prices, namely, how to account for the two-part pricing scheme charged to monthly pass holders. There are two possibilities. One can either not count the revenues from the monthly passes and count the rounds as being played for a (marginal) price of zero (as in column A below), or one can count the membership fees and count the rounds as being played for a price equal to the average cost of such rounds (as in column B). The former construction, which is used in the chapter, will yield slightly larger variances.

It is now straightforward to calculate the following:

Table 5.A2 Calculation of standard deviation.

		A	B
number of rounds	=	94,985	94,985
revenues	=	1,384,242	1,405,242
average revenue	=	14.57	14.79
average revenue squared	=	212.28	218.74
imputed price for members	=	0	5.67
variance	=	23.68	18.47
standard deviation	=	4.87	4.30

Chapter 6

Replace Your Divots, and Please Don't Eat the Daisies[1]

All else equal, golfers prefer to play on beautiful, well-conditioned golf courses. Therefore, a golf course's managers know that by making their golf course more beautiful, or by maintaining it in better condition, they can increase the demand for their course and, thereby, increase their revenues. But golf course maintenance is expensive, so golf course managers have important decisions to make about how much maintenance they can afford to do, and about how beautifully maintained or well-groomed they can make their course.

The basic economics of what are essentially quality decisions such as beauty and condition is not difficult. Simply, the extra cost of improving the condition of the golf course, called the "marginal cost of condition," must be compared to the extra revenue that the improvement in condition leads to, called the "marginal revenue of condition." The same applies to beauty. If the marginal revenue is more than the marginal cost, then the expenditures should be made; the condition will improve, and the profits will go up. Alternatively, if the extra revenue is less than the extra cost, then improving the condition of the course will cost more than it is worth. The golf course attempting to maximize profit should pursue all of the improvements that

---

[1]This chapter is adapted from, Shmanske, Stephen, "The Economics of Golf Course Condition and Beauty," *Atlantic Economic Journal*, Vol. 27, No. 3, (Sept. 1999) pp. 301-313. The divots and the daisies in the rather goofy title of this chapter refer to golf course condition and golf course beauty, respectively.

increase revenues more than costs, and none of the improvements that increase costs more than revenues. After completing all the projects that increase revenues more than costs, the best of the remaining projects will increase revenues by an amount, at most, equal to the increase in cost. Of course, undertaking a project for which revenues and costs rise by the same amount leaves the bottom line profit unchanged. Economists economize on the use of words by coining the following jargon to describe the above reasoning: "Profit maximization is obtained when marginal revenue equals marginal cost."

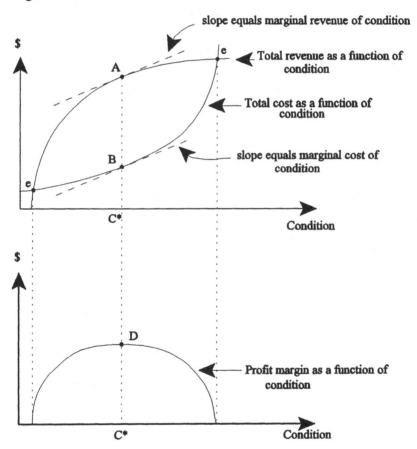

Fig. 6.1 Revenue, cost, and profit as functions of condition.

Economists also use a simple diagram to present the same idea. In the top part of Fig. 6.1 are representations of functions that relate total revenues and total costs to course condition. A similar diagram would exist for beauty. As condition improves (rightward movements in the diagram), the total revenues increase though probably at a decreasing rate as shown in the curve labeled eAe. The curve labeled eBe shows that costs increase at an increasing rate. The vertical distance between the two curves represents the profit margin, and is plotted in the bottom part of Fig. 6.1. Note that at the points labeled "e" the total revenue equals the total cost so that the profit margin is zero. At the level of condition labeled "C*," there is the maximum distance between the total revenue, point A, and the total cost, point B, in the top diagram, while in the bottom diagram, the profit margin function has flattened out and reached its maximum at point D. Also note that the slopes of the revenue and cost functions represent the marginal revenue of condition and the marginal cost of condition. At points to the left of C*, the revenue function is steeper than the cost function which means that the marginal revenue is greater than the marginal cost, and profits will increase if the condition is improved. At the maximum profit, at points A and B, the slopes are equal.

None of this is meant to imply that measurement of the marginal costs and revenues is easy. But, by the same token, exact forecasts of the marginal costs and revenues are not necessary; indeed, they may not even be possible, before a decision has to be made. All that is required for the implementation of any policy that improves quality is the belief that doing so will increase revenues more than costs. Surely mistakes will happen. But if the managers of a firm systematically make poor decisions, decisions that increase costs more than revenues, then that firm will have a hard time staying in business. Ultimately, the firms that do stay in business must have made decisions good enough to avoid bankruptcy.[2]

This chapter measures and compares the marginal cost and the marginal revenue of two separate golf course quality variables: the beauty of the golf course, and the condition of the golf course. Ultimately, the measures turn

---

[2]For the original exposition of this line of reasoning see, Alchian, Armen A., "Uncertainty, Evolution, and Economic Theory," *Journal of Political Economy*, Vol. 58, No. 3, (June 1950), pp. 211-221.

out to be reasonable both in terms of their relative magnitudes and in terms of their statistical properties. As such, this material supplies valuable information to golf course professionals struggling with decisions about maintenance budgets. It also supplies a nice illustration of economics and statistical economics in action. Furthermore, the nice results here confirm that the subjective measurements described in Chapter 4 usefully capture the notions of beauty and condition as quality dimensions of the golf course.

The chapter proceeds by reviewing the subjective beauty and condition measures and by explaining how they should differentially affect the costs and revenues of a golf course. Following this, the chapter introduces several other independent variables that are used as control variables in the statistical analysis. Then, the results for condition and beauty are presented in separate sections.

6.1 The Economics of Golf Course Condition and Beauty

Golf course condition refers to the length, uniformity, and plushness of the turf on different areas of the golf course, the absence of weeds and bare areas, the absence of soggy or muddy turf, the condition of the trees, the condition of the sand in the bunkers, and many other similar facets of the golf course. Although there is no convenient objective measure of condition, it is possible to obtain a subjective measure by asking golfers their opinions. I asked golfers to rate the condition of the golf course they had just played on a 1-to-5 scale with 1 being "poor" and 5 being "excellent."[3] Using over 900 interviews at 46 public access golf courses in the San Francisco area, I was able to obtain a measure of condition for the 46 golf courses. Table 6.1 lists the summary statistics for this variable, called CONDITION, and for all the variables used in this chapter. As the table shows, condition ranged from a high of 4.525 at Oakhurst Country Club in Clayton, to a low of 2.262, and averaged 3.539 for the 46 courses.[4]

---

[3]Chapter 4 fully explains the interview process that led to the measurement of condition and beauty.

[4]Also see Table 4.6 in Chapter 4 for a list of the top ten best-conditioned golf courses.

Golf course beauty also has many determinants. The topography of the land is an obvious factor, affecting the views of the golf course itself and of the surrounding areas. Lakes, rivers, mountains, reservoirs, trees, oceans, houses, airports, railroad tracks, and factories are just some of the things visible from the 46 golf courses in the sample. In terms of fauna; deer, mountain lions, snakes, hawks, eagles, rabbits, bullfrogs, canada geese, etc., are all present somewhere on these golf courses. As was the case for golf course condition, there is no one objective measure which can capture the beauty of a golf course. Indeed, even whether an individual item like railroad tracks, houses, snakes, or canada geese is a positive or a negative influence can differ from individual to individual. I again resorted to the interview method, asking golfers to rate the beauty of the golf course on a 1-to-5 scale

Table 6.1 Summary statistics.

Variable	mean	std. deviation	minimum	maximum
MAINTEXP	766	319	335	1,900
REVENUE	1,449	495	548	3,230
πMARGIN	694	489	-231	2,498
CONDITION	3.5392	.46125	2.262	4.525
BEAUTY	3.614	.6347	2.455	4.609
LANDFILL	.196	.401	0	1
GREENSIZE	5,914	1,778	3,000	14,520
ROUNDS	86,790	34,541	34,000	210,000
ACREAGE	161	53	85	305
RATING	70.672	1.9649	64.4	74.9
POPULATION	124,240	109,530	17,000	462,100

Notes: Raw population data are from 1990 US Census maps. Author's calculations are the source for all data.

with 1 being "plain" and 5 being "beautiful." Table 6.1 lists the summary statistics for this variable, called, BEAUTY. BEAUTY ranged from 4.609 for the most beautiful golf course in the sample, Lincoln Park Golf Course in San Francisco, to a low of 2.455, with an average of 3.614.[5] Lincoln Park Golf Course is the shortest golf course in the sample with only 5146 yards and a par of 68. It owes its beauty to its location in hilly parkland at the

---

[5]See Table 4.5 in Chapter 4 for a list of the top ten most beautiful golf courses.

northwest corner of San Francisco, encircling several monuments and the art museum housed in the Palace of the Legion of Honor, and to its views of the downtown skyline, the Golden Gate Bridge from the ocean side, and the ocean, beach, and rocky shores from bluffs overlooking the Pacific Ocean.

Even though condition and beauty are measured on similar 1-to-5 scales, and have similar distributions, and even though they are positively correlated with a simple correlation coefficient of .4, and even though they are both demand-enhancing quality factors expected to have a positive effect on revenues, there is an important theoretical difference in how these measures should relate to costs. Verifying this difference with statistical analysis will provide strong evidence that the interview method of developing measures of condition and beauty is both reasonable and useful.

But first, consider the revenue side. The demand to golf at a particular golf course is a function of its price, its location, the relevant population, and several quality characteristics including the difficulty, condition, and beauty of the golf course. The subjectively measured quality variables, CONDITION and BEAUTY are the focus of our attention here. Both CONDITION and BEAUTY are attributes that, holding other relevant factors constant, are expected to correlate positively to golf course revenues. As is explained below, however, BEAUTY and CONDITION differ in their relationship to cost, and in how optimizing decisions are made with respect to them.

Golfers generally prefer to play on golf courses that are in top condition. This implies that, holding other factors constant, demand will be higher on those courses that are in better condition. This higher demand will lead either to higher price or higher quantity (or both) and, regardless of which, will definitely lead to higher total revenue. Therefore, there is, in effect, a marginal revenue of golf course condition.

It is not necessarily the case that marginal revenue of condition is positive. Consider Harding Park Golf Course in San Francisco, which is a challenging, 6,743 yard golf course with course and slope ratings of 72.1 and 124 respectively. It has hosted PGA tournaments in the past, and is now a potential site for the PGA TOUR championship if the condition of the golf course can be improved. With its great layout and its modest regular green fee of $24 in 1993, Harding Park was busy all the time, selling over 100,000 rounds of golf, with long daily waiting lists. It is clear that Harding Park

Golf Course could have raised its prices and still remained at capacity, but the prices were set in political markets by the recreation and parks department and approved by the city council. The golf course revenues supplied the funds for the maintenance budget with money left over that went to subsidize the rest of the recreation and parks system. The prices were kept low ostensibly to benefit the golfers, and the maintenance expenditures were kept low to allow the maximum amount of cross-subsidization. This system, however, works to the golfer's disadvantage because there is no incentive to improve or maintain the condition of the golf course.[6] The superintendent and the green-keeping crew do an admirable job given their resources, but the fact remains that since neither price nor quantity will go up if the course is improved, extra expenditure on maintenance simply takes away from the net cash flow of the golf course that is used to subsidize the other city parks. Given the political constraints, the marginal revenue of condition for this course is zero.[7]

The analysis of the marginal revenue of beauty is similar to that of the marginal revenue of condition. All else equal, golfers will prefer to play in beautiful surroundings. Therefore, a more beautiful setting will attract more customers, or command higher prices, or both, as long as price is not fixed and quantity is not already at capacity. If either price or quantity increases, revenues will also increase.

Now consider the cost side and the optimization decision of the golf course, starting with golf course condition. The golf course superintendent has responsibility for the budget and for overseeing the employees that tend to these so-called "green" areas of the golf course. Among other things, these workers mow, water, and fertilize the grass, care for the trees and other live shrubbery, and rake and weed the sand traps. These tasks must be continued on a daily basis because, if effort and expenditure in these areas is

---

[6]There are other unintended negative consequences of keeping prices of publicly supplied goods low and rationing the scarce amount with waiting lists instead of raising prices. See, Shmanske, Stephen, "Contestability, Queues, and Governmental Entry Deterrence," *Public Choice*, vol. 86, (1996), pp. 1-15.

[7]In 2002-2003, Harding Park went through a $16 million, 15-month restoration, with a commitment from the city council to properly maintain the course. Some are now touting Harding Park as one of the best municipal courses in the nation.

shortchanged, the condition of the golf course will suffer. This implies that there will be a positive relationship between the condition of the golf course and the ongoing, yearly expenditure on golf course maintenance. There is, in effect, a marginal cost of golf course condition.

Optimization with respect to golf course condition requires that marginal revenue equal marginal cost in this dimension. Expenditures on golf course condition will increase profits as long as the marginal revenue of golf course condition is higher than the marginal cost. In the optimum, the marginal effect of increases in the condition of the golf course on profit is zero, because costs and revenues go up by the same amount. The estimation of the marginal cost of condition, the marginal revenue of condition, and the marginal effect of condition on profit is undertaken later in the chapter.

The analysis of the golf course's optimization with respect to beauty differs from that outlined above for condition. Golf course beauty has less to do with continuing variable expenditures than it does with the overhead expenditure on the design and placement of the golf course to begin with. A golf course with magnificent ocean vistas, or a golf course that winds through a majestic forest can be a beautiful golf course regardless of continuing yearly expenditures on golf course maintenance. Indeed, the aforementioned Lincoln Park Golf Course, which was ranked first in beauty, was (mis)managed similarly to Harding Park Golf Course, and ranked only 40th out of 46 in terms of condition. Granted, some maintenance expenditures on trimming hedges or tending flower beds can enhance a golf course's beauty, but these effects are minor compared to the beauty inherent in the view from a seaside bluff over pounding surf below. On the other side of the coin, extra yearly maintenance expenditures will do little to beautify a flat course that winds its way among houses in a development. Simply put, skimping on maintenance will not detract from the views of the oceanside course, and lavish expenditures will not make the flat municipal course next to the runway and/or the railroad tracks into a course with picture-postcard beauty. Because of this, one should not expect a tight connection between yearly maintenance expenditures and the beauty of the golf course.

Most of the cost of a golf course's beauty comes from the original purchase of the land and the routing and the construction of the golf course. These costs are what the business community calls overhead costs, sunk costs, or non-recurring costs. Because most of the costs of beauty are overhead in nature, the (yearly) marginal cost of beauty is close to zero. That is, there should be no systematic relationship between golf course beauty and the yearly expenditure on golf course maintenance.

There will, of course, still be a marginal revenue of beauty as long as golfers prefer to play on more beautiful golf courses. But there will not be a connection between the yearly marginal revenue and yearly marginal cost of beauty as there was for golf course condition. So how does optimization in the beauty dimension occur? Since expenditures enhancing beauty take the form of once and for all overhead cost of land acquisition and golf course design, these expenditures are a capital investment that will pay off over time. Therefore, the original investment cost must be compared to the continuing stream of extra revenues that are attributable to the extra beauty that comes from the original extra expenditure. At the time of the original investment, the stream of extra future revenues must be estimated since the future is uncertain, and must be discounted to its present value as in any standard investment decision involving an up front expenditure and a future expected earnings profile.

I do not venture to test for the optimality of the investment decision. The data requirements are such that the likelihood of any such test being performed is doubtful. There is, however, an interesting test that can be run on the 1993 year data alone. That is, the statistics should show that there is a marginal revenue of beauty, but that there is no (yearly) marginal cost of beauty. The regressions for beauty are designed to parallel the regressions for condition, but we should expect different results. The marginal revenue of condition should be positive and equal to the marginal cost of condition. Meanwhile, the marginal revenue of beauty should be positive but there should be no relationship between beauty and maintenance cost. The results for beauty are reported below, after the regressions for condition.

6.2 The Data, the Model, and the Control Variables

For most statistical economic propositions the economist insists on holding "all else equal." For example, below, I test propositions like the following: All else equal, golf course facilities that maintain a higher standard of golf course condition will have to spend more on golf course maintenance; and, all else equal, golf courses that maintain a higher standard of golf course condition will earn more revenue. However, we cannot just look at a simple linear regression of costs or revenues on condition because other systematic factors will also affect costs and revenues. Therefore, in a multiple regression setting, other independent variables are added to control for these other influences on costs and revenues. The variables are introduced below. Again refer to Table 6.1 for the summary statistics on all the variables used in this chapter.

I again call on the data collected from 46 San Francisco Bay area golf courses. Spending one weekday at each of the courses, I interviewed the course manager, the superintendent, and one golfer each from 20 groups as they finished play on the 18th hole.

From the golf course employees, information was obtained on the measurable aspects of the course, the patterns of play, and selected financial and operating statistics. Information was purposefully not sought on several types of bottom line profit figures, or on separately franchised operations like the restaurant or the merchandise sales in the pro shop. In most cases, permission would not have been granted if it appeared that a profitability study or new course feasibility study was the goal of the information gathering. Golf course operators are understandably wary about tipping their hands to potential new competition, or in some cases about having to justify their city-subsidized land use in an area of high land values and scarce buildable space.

Cost data were collected for all costs specifically having to do with the maintenance of the golf course. These costs are dominated by the labor costs for the golf course maintenance crew. Additional costs involve water, materials such as fertilizers, and maintenance of the equipment like tractors, mowers, and sprinkler systems. Costs of staffing the restaurant or pro shop, costs of goods sold in the pro shop, and special occasional costs for items like new roofs or a new parking lot are not included. The maintenance costs are captured in the variable MAINTEXP which is the dependent variable in the equations that yield the estimates of the marginal cost of condition and the marginal cost of beauty. MAINTEXP ranges from a low of $335,000, to a high of $1,900,000 for the 45-hole municipal Chuck Corica golf complex, around an average of $766,000. On a per 18 holes basis, the highest expenditure on maintenance was by the Palo Alto Municipal Golf Course which spent $1,482,000.

Information was also collected on regular revenues (called "green fees"), membership revenues, cart revenues, and practice range revenues. This chapter uses the direct revenues from playing golf as the dependent variable in equations from which the marginal revenue of condition and the marginal revenue of beauty will be estimated. This variable is called REVENUE and consists of the sum of green fees (which are the direct payments for playing golf) and membership revenues (which are essentially the lump sum parts of two-part pricing schemes for playing golf). Revenues range from a low of $548,000 to a high of $3,230,000 for Half Moon Bay Golf Links, with an average of $1,449,000.

The third dependent variable that is used in this chapter, πMARGIN, is the difference between REVENUE and MAINTEXP. This measure is not exactly the profits of the golf course because it leaves out other costs such as interest expense, restaurant and pro shop employees, and other revenues, such as from the driving range and the restaurant. This measure ranges from a low of a loss of $231,000, to a high of $2,498,000, with an average of $694,000.

The main variables of interest are the subjectively measured CONDITION and BEAUTY of the golf course as explained above.

The remaining variables used in this chapter are control variables that attempt to capture other important effects on costs and revenues that differ across the golf courses in the study. Regressors for the cost equation are presented first, followed by those factors expected to influence revenues.

LANDFILL is a dummy variable equal to one if the course is built on a landfill site. This variable is included on the recommendation of many of the golf course superintendents at courses that were built on landfill. Landfill sites pose at least two special problems for golf course maintenance. The first is an uneven settling of the land that makes turf maintenance more difficult. The second is the upward percolation of methane through the soil that can kill the root systems of the turf grasses. Because of these problems, maintaining any given level of golf course condition is likely to be more expensive on a landfill course. It is expected that LANDFILL will have a positive coefficient in a regression with maintenance expenditures as the dependent variable. However, it is not expected that LANDFILL will be significant in the revenue equation.

GREENSIZE is the average size of greens on the golf course measured in square feet. Although it takes a little longer to mow the grass on larger greens, thus raising costs slightly, the main effect of large greens is to spread out the wear and tear caused by golfer's footsteps and by golf balls landing with great force. It was a virtual unanimous view of golf course superintendents that large greens are easier (and cheaper) to care for than small greens. Therefore, holding condition constant, the effect of GREENSIZE on maintenance costs should be negative. The smallest greens are at Tilden Park Golf Course, built in 1937 (one of the older courses in the sample), averaging just 3000 square feet. The largest greens are almost five times as big at 14,520 square feet. They are found at Rancho Solano Golf Course, a relatively young municipal course built in 1990. The relationship between age and green size is very strong, a testimony to the more economical care that large greens afford. The average level of GREENSIZE is 5,914 square feet.

ROUNDS is the number of rounds of golf played during 1993. The more heavily the golf course is played, the more wear and tear on the turf. Holding other factors constant, the effect of ROUNDS on maintenance costs should be positive. The coefficient of ROUNDS is an estimate of the marginal cost an additional golfer imposes on the course. Following McCloskey and Ziliak,[8] in addition to paying attention to the sign and statistical properties of this estimate, we should also pay attention to its magnitude. Theoretically, we know that the optimizing golf course will set marginal cost equal to marginal revenue. Since regular prices go as low as $12 in this sample, since all of the golf courses further lower prices by using a variety of discounts and market segmentation schemes in setting up their nonlinear pricing schedules, and since marginal revenue is less than price in any case[9], we should expect a coefficient significantly below the $12 level.

---

[8]See, McCloskey, D. N. and S. T. Ziliak, "The Standard Error of Regressions," *Journal of Economic Literature*, Vol. 34, (March 1996) pp. 97-114.

[9]The statement, "marginal revenue is less than price," holds whenever price has to be reduced in order to sell an additional unit. For example, if you could sell 10 units for a price of $20 each, total revenue would be $200. Supposing that you had to lower price to $19 to sell 11 units, total revenue would be $209 (that is $19 times 11). The extra or

A good result for this coefficient should be positive, statistically significant in the usual sense, and significantly, also in the statistical sense, lower than $12. The variable itself, ROUNDS, ranges from a low of 34,000 at the privately-owned Chardonnay Golf Club in Napa, to a high of 210,000 at the Chuck Corica Golf Complex in Alameda, around an average of 86,790 rounds.

ACREAGE, the number of acres of golf course property, is the last control variable on the expenditure side. This is expected to have a positive effect on costs since caring for more acres will be more expensive than caring for fewer acres. ACREAGE is also included in the revenue equation. The main effect of acreage on revenue is that golf course facilities with more than 18 holes will have a larger total acreage and will also have a larger capacity. Demand permitting, these multiple course facilities will earn more revenues. ACREAGE ranges from a low of 85 acres at Peacock Gap Golf and Country Club in San Rafael, to a high of 305 acres at the 36-hole Mountain Shadows Golf Courses in Rohnert Park, around an average of 161 acres.

Continuing with the control variables for the revenue equations, RATING is the golf course difficulty rating as established by the Northern California Golf Association (NCGA). The NCGA expends much time and effort to determine the relative difficulty of all the golf courses in its area in order to achieve a fair handicapping system. For example, a golfer who averages five over par on an easy golf course would not be as good as a golfer who averages five over par on a difficult one. Through the use of the rating system, a golfer's handicap is adjusted so that golfers from different courses can compete evenly. Although some beginner golfers and many senior citizens prefer to play on an "easy" golf course (one with a low difficulty rating), most golfers seem to prefer a more difficult test (ie. a course with a higher rating). Golfers are very interested in the difficulty rating of any particular course and golf course managers know it. Some golf courses even highlight their high difficulty ratings in their advertising material. Because of this, RATING is expected to have a positive effect on revenues. The easiest golf course in the sample is the beautiful par 68

---

marginal revenue associated with the increase from 10 units to 11 units is $9 which is less than the price.

Lincoln Park Golf Course with a course rating of 64.4. The toughest was the Sonoma Golf Club with a course rating of 74.9. The average course rating was 70.67.

Finally, the relevant population from which a golf course draws its customers is expected to be an important positive influence on revenue. Simply put, where there are more people, the demand to golf should be higher, leading to higher revenues. There are several ways to measure the relevant population. The following measures were calculated as part of this research: the population of the city in which the golf course is located divided by the number of golf courses in that city; the population within a ten-mile radius of the golf course; and, motivated by spatial competition in a two-dimensional location model, the population that is closer to the particular course of interest than to any other course. This last measure is calculated by plotting the location of each course on county census maps, plotting the lines that spatially separate a course from its neighbors, and assuming that population density is uniform within each jurisdiction for which a population is reported. For the results reported in this chapter, POPULATION is captured by this last measure. Evidently, the extra effort to calculate the spatially motivated population measure pays off. The results using the other possible measurements of population yielded estimates with larger standard errors.[10] POPULATION ranges from a low of 17,000 for the rural Chardonnay Golf Club to a high of 462,100 for the urban Harding Park Golf Course in San Francisco, with an average of 124,240 per course. Note that Harding Park is located in an area with several other golf courses most notably, the Olympic Club, the Lake Merced Golf and Country Club, and the ultra-exclusive San Francisco Golf Club, but these are all private golf courses that are not available to the general public for open play.

6.3 Golf Course Condition

To estimate the marginal cost of condition, the following equation was estimated with ordinary least squares (OLS):

---

[10]Chapter 7 gives a detailed analysis of the statistical adjustments to the population figures.

$$MAINTEXP = b_0 + b_1 CONDITION + b_2 LANDFILL +$$
$$b_3 GREENSIZE + b_4 ROUNDS + b_5 ACREAGE + e . \qquad (6.1)$$

The results are reported in Table 6.2. As the table shows, all of the explanatory variables are the expected sign, and all are statistically significant. Furthermore, each of the estimated coefficients has a plausible economic interpretation.

Table 6.2 Estimates of Eqs. (6.1) - (6.4) (t-statistic in parentheses).

Equation	(6.1)	(6.2)	(6.3)	(6.4)
Dependent variable	MAINTEXP	REVENUE	πMARGIN	REVENUE
Constant	-340.4 (-.984)	-7106 (-2.77)	-6055 (-2.14)	-7149 (-2.67)
CONDITION	194.0 (2.36)	266.4 (1.81)	-25.5 (-.145)	260.5 (1.63)
LANDFILL	303.1 (3.24)		-355.2 (-1.84)	-14.86 (-.082)
GREENSIZE	-.0389 (-1.95)		-.0015 (-.035)	-.0230 (-.563)
ROUNDS	.00296 (2.48)		-.00074 (-.259)	.00040 (.146)
ACREAGE	2.017 (2.71)	3.065 (2.49)	.2147 (.134)	2.993 (1.97)
RATING		97.24 (2.80)	97.22 (2.52)	100.1 (2.74)
POPULATION		.00198 (3.07)	.00064 (.750)	.00179 (2.22)
sample size	45	46	45	46
adjusted R^2	.48	.24	.08	.19

For example, to achieve an extra point on the condition rating costs about $194,000 per year in extra maintenance expenditure. To put this in perspective consider the averages for MAINTEXP and CONDITION. The average maintenance expenditure is $766,000 and the average condition is about 3.54. For a 25% additional expenditure (194,000/766,000 = .253) the average course could raise its condition measure to about 4.54, and be among the leaders in that category. Of course, a 25% increase is a lot to consider, but the magnitude of the estimate seems reasonable. An estimate on the order of $10,000 would surely be too low. This would be less than $1000 per month, not even enough to hire one additional employee, and could hardly have such a major effect on course condition. Meanwhile, an estimate on the order of $1,000,000 would be too high an amount to increase the CONDITION rating by only one point. Golf course superintendents could virtually guarantee pristine, country club conditions for such a major increase in their maintenance budgets.

Holding condition constant, courses built on landfill require extra maintenance expenditure of about $303,000 per year, just to stay even. This is consistent with the comments of those superintendents who were overseeing the maintenance on landfill courses.

Increasing the average size of the greens by one hundred square feet will reduce maintenance costs by almost $3,800 per year. This is also consistent with the unanimous comments of the superintendents that I interviewed. All of them were adamant in their opinions that large greens were easier to care for than small greens. Superintendents now have a number to work with.[11]

Special interest attaches to the coefficient of the rounds variable in that it is the marginal cost of an additional round of golf. Here, this marginal cost of each extra golfer is estimated to be about $2.96. Obviously, there is not much wear and tear that one extra golfer imposes on a golf course. But just as obviously, there must be some. The estimate of $2.96 is an appropriate positive amount, and one that is significantly below the lowest regular price of $12, as it must be in order for the golf course to avoid losing money as play increases.

---

[11]Keep in mind that all the dollar figures in this chapter refer to 1993 dollars.

Finally, extra acreage leads to extra costs on average, at a rate of about $2000 per acre. ACREAGE is also included in the revenue equation, and the significance of this estimate is discussed there.

Several additional right hand side variables that might be expected to influence expenditures were tried, however, they did not significantly effect MAINTEXP. None of the following variables added to the explanatory power of the equation: the acreage of lakes; the number of sand bunkers; whether or not carts are required to stay on the cartpaths; the hilliness of the course; and, the size of the teeing areas.

Moving now to the marginal revenue of condition, the following equation was estimated with OLS:

$$\text{REVENUE} = b_0 + b_1\text{CONDITION} + b_2\text{ACREAGE} +$$
$$b_3\text{RATING} + b_4\text{POPULATION} + e \ . \qquad (6.2)$$

These results also appear in Table 6.2. Each coefficient is statistically significant, has the expected sign, and is economically meaningful.

First, consider the main variable of interest, CONDITION. An extra point on the condition scale yields extra revenue of $266,000 per year. This compares to a marginal cost of condition estimated in Eq. (6.1) of $194,000. Each of these estimates is statistically significant, but their difference is not statistically significant. The inference to be drawn is that there is a positive marginal cost of condition, a positive marginal revenue of condition, and that the hypothesis that golf courses optimize by equating marginal cost and marginal revenue in this dimension cannot be rejected.

With respect to the other explanatory variables in Eq. (6.2), an extra acre of land yields about $3000 in revenues per year, an extra stroke in the course difficulty rating increases revenues by about $97,000 per year, and an extra 10,000 people living closer to this course than any other increases revenues by almost $20,000 per year.

Of particular interest is the estimate of the marginal revenue per acre. Once again, marginal cost should equal marginal revenue if the golf course is optimizing with respect to its total acreage. In Eq. (6.2) the marginal revenue of an additional acre is about $3000. In Eq. (6.1), the marginal *maintenance* cost of an additional acre is about $2000. These values are unequal, and they suggest that if acreage could be obtained for free, then each additional acre would increase revenues by $1000 more than costs. However, the $2000 figure for the cost per acre includes only the maintenance cost, and land is not free. The capital cost or holding cost per acre must be added to the maintenance cost. Although no attempt was made to obtain the private information about original purchase prices of the land, or about rental prices of the land, the difference of $1000 per acre between the costs and revenues measured here does not seem unreasonable. At a 5% capitalization figure, the $1000 cash flow supports a capitalized value of about $20,000 per acre.[12] This figure is probably too low for subdividable suburban land in desirable areas and too high for marginal land under airport flight paths, on landfills, or in outlying rural areas. As an average, these estimates are neither embarrassingly high nor low.

To further test the proposition that decisions with respect to golf course condition are made optimally, the difference between the dependent variables in the first two equations is regressed on the complete set of variables from the first two equations. The equation to be estimated is:

$$\pi MARGIN = b_0 + b_1 CONDITION + b_2 LANDFILL +$$
$$b_3 GREENSIZE + b_4 ROUNDS + b_5 ACREAGE + \qquad (6.3)$$
$$b_6 RATING + b_7 POPULATION + e \ .$$

The results are included in Table 6.2.

To interpret Eq. (6.3), remember that items which are under direct control of the optimizing golf course, and which only affect the yearly maintenance costs and revenues, should not affect this revenue-minus-cost differential on the margin. CONDITION may have been significant in Eqs. (6.1) and (6.2), but its coefficient should not differ from zero in this equation.[13] Only things which cannot be influenced by golf course policy on

---

[12]That is, the golf course would earn a 5% rate of return if it spent $20,000 for an additional acre that increased its cash flow by $1000 per year.

[13]The set of tests in Eqs. (6.1)-(6.3) make a convincing case that the theory is sound, and that the measurements are accurate. In Eqs. (6.1) and (6.2) we have "confirmed" theories in the sense that the null hypothesis that condition does not matter is rejected. But theories can be confirmed spuriously. In Eq. (6.3), using the same data, the theory is given a chance to be rejected in the sense that the theory's prediction that condition does not matter, coincides with the standard null hypothesis. Here, the null hypothesis is not rejected. So

a yearly basis, like LANDFILL, POPULATION, or RATING should have an effect on πMARGIN. The third column in Table 6.2 indicates that this is so. The effects of CONDITION, GREENSIZE, and ROUNDS disappear. The explanatory power is coming mostly from RATING and LANDFILL. The signs on the coefficients of these variables are the expected ones, and the magnitudes are comparable to those from the first two equations. The LANDFILL dummy costs over $355,000 in lost πMARGIN per year (as compared to $303,000 of extra maintenance from Eq. (6.1)). Remarkably, the coefficient of the course difficulty rating variable is the same $97,000 per extra stroke of difficulty as in Eq. (6.2).

Equation (6.3) is slightly less restrictive than Eqs. (6.1) and (6.2). The tests using Eqs. (6.1) and (6.2) require the marginal costs and the marginal revenues to be equal to each other, and equal across courses. For the coefficient of CONDITION to be zero in Eq. (6.3) requires each course to have a flat profit function at the optimum, which in turn requires that the marginal cost of condition be set equal to the marginal revenue of condition at each course, but does not require these marginal costs and revenues to be equal across courses.

As one final indication that the results of the model are not spurious, consider the possibility that it is simply the addition of extra right-hand-side variables that causes CONDITION to be insignificant in Eq. (6.3), and not the theory behind the specification. To illustrate that this is not the case, Eqs. (6.1) and (6.2) were reestimated using all of the explanatory variables. For example, Eq. (6.2) becomes:

$$\text{REVENUE} = b_0 + b_1\text{CONDITION} + b_2\text{LANDFILL} +$$
$$b_3\text{GREENSIZE} + b_4\text{ROUNDS} + b_5\text{ACREAGE} + \qquad (6.4)$$
$$b_6\text{RATING} + b_7\text{POPULATION} + e \ .$$

The results of this regression are listed in the last column of Table 6.2.

in addition to having a "confirmed" theory, we also have a "non-rejected" theory. See Jensen, Keith Christian, Shyam Kamath, and Robert Bennett, "Money in the Production Function: An Alternative Test Procedure," *Eastern Economic Journal*, Vol. 13, No. 3, (July-Sept. 1987), pp. 259-269.

The results of Eq. (6.4) strongly support the validity of the model. The cost variables add nothing to the explanatory power in the revenue equation. The variables other than CONDITION remain significant, while CONDITION itself loses slightly in statistical significance, but does not disappear as it does in Eq. (6.3). The loss of significance comes solely from an increase in the standard error of the coefficient estimate because the parameter estimate itself, 260, is almost identical to the estimate, 266, obtained in Eq. (6.2).

The results of reestimating Eq. (6.1) with all the right-hand-side variables are not included here, but they tell the same story. In fact, the estimated coefficient of CONDITION increases from 194 to 261, and the statistical accuracy actually increases as measured by the t-statistic which improves from 2.36 to 3.25.

6.4 Golf Course Beauty

Equations (6.1)-(6.3) are reestimated with BEAUTY replacing CONDITION on the right hand side.[14] This leads to the following three equations, the results of which are listed in Table 6.3.

$$\text{MAINTEXP} = b_0 + b_1\text{BEAUTY} + b_2\text{LANDFILL} +$$
$$b_3\text{GREENSIZE} + b_4\text{ROUNDS} + b_5\text{ACREAGE} + e \ . \quad (6.1a)$$

$$\text{REVENUE} = b_0 + b_1\text{BEAUTY} + b_2\text{ACREAGE} +$$
$$b_3\text{RATING} + b_4\text{POPULATION} + e \ . \quad (6.2a)$$

$$\pi\text{MARGIN} = b_0 + b_1\text{BEAUTY} + b_2\text{LANDFILL} +$$
$$b_3\text{GREENSIZE} + b_4\text{ROUNDS} + b_5\text{ACREAGE} + \quad (6.3a)$$
$$b_6\text{RATING} + b_7\text{POPULATION} + e \ .$$

[14]When both CONDITION and BEAUTY are included simultaneously in the cost equation, CONDITION remains positive and significant, while BEAUTY is insignificant as predicted by theory. However, in the revenue equation both variables are positive but insignificant, due to their collinearity. The correlation between CONDITION and BEAUTY is .4.

The estimates of the coefficients of all the control variables tell the same story as in the above regressions, and need not be rehashed here. Consider, then, the coefficients of BEAUTY in these three equations. The effect of beauty on continuing maintenance expenditures is not significant. This is the theoretically expected result since the cost of beauty is mostly a one-time overhead expenditure consisting of land purchase and golf course design. BEAUTY does have a positive impact on revenue. An extra point on the

Table 6.3 Estimates of Eqs. (6.1a) - (6.3a) (t-statistic in parentheses).

Equation	(6.1a)	(6.2a)	(6.3a)
Dependent variable	MAINTEXP	REVENUE	πMARGIN
Constant	503.0 (1.53)	-7270 (-2.78)	-7291 (-2.59)
BEAUTY	-32.56 (-.476)	165.5 (1.61)	189.0 (1.48)
LANDFILL	209.7 (1.92)		-197.7 (-.969)
GREENSIZE	-.0355 (-1.66)		.00808 (.191)
ROUNDS	.00276 (2.17)		-.00064 (-.230)
ACREAGE	1.893 (2.39)	2.807 (2.28)	.1373 (.089)
RATING		105.5 (2.99)	102.4 (2.72)
POPULATION		.00173 (2.76)	.00074 (.923)
adjusted R^2	.41	.23	.13
sample size	45	46	45

BEAUTY rating scale increases yearly revenue by over $165,000, but this estimate is not as precise as the above estimates of the marginal revenue of CONDITION. Finally, since BEAUTY does not affect cost, but since it does affect revenue, it should also affect πMARGIN, which it does. An extra point on the BEAUTY rating scale raises yearly profit by $189,000, a point estimate that differs significantly from zero at the 15% level.

6.5 Summary and Discussion

This chapter uses a cross section panel of data on the operations of public-access golf courses in the San Francisco Bay area. The demand to golf depends on many factors including objectively observable ones such as population and golf course difficulty, and subjectively measurable opinions on golf course condition and beauty. This research uses multiple regression analysis to estimate the marginal cost and marginal revenue of golf course condition and golf course beauty.

With respect to the condition of golf courses, the analysis shows that it costs more to maintain a golf course in better condition, and that doing so leads to higher revenues. These results confirm our intuition and prior beliefs about the effects of condition on cost and revenue. They also give ballpark estimates of the magnitude of the effects. Furthermore, the hypothesis that golf courses set the marginal cost of condition equal to the marginal revenue of condition cannot be rejected, either by comparing coefficients from two separate equations, or by confronting the hypothesis implied by optimization (namely, that optimization requires the profit function to flatten out in the condition dimension, as shown in Fig 6.1) with the data.

Even though the BEAUTY variable combines golfer's subjective opinions on the same 1 to 5 scale as the CONDITION variable, and even though the measures are positively correlated, the results with respect to BEAUTY turn out differently from those with respect to CONDITION, as indeed they should. The regressions indicate that there is not a yearly marginal cost of BEAUTY but that there is a marginal revenue of BEAUTY, and a marginal effect of BEAUTY on profit. The optimizing condition for BEAUTY would have equality on the margin between the original overhead cost of producing a beautiful golf course and the present discounted value of the stream of extra revenues that the extra beauty brings about. This condition is not tested because of the lack of appropriate data.

The estimated coefficients of the other control variables are also significant and economically meaningful. Revenue is influenced by the relevant population, the difficulty of the golf course, and the amount of acreage available to the golf course. Maintenance cost is influenced by the size of the greens, the acreage of the golf course, the number of rounds of golf that are played, and whether the golf course is built on a landfill site.

Additional information about golf course costs and revenues comes from the failure of other variables to have significant effects. Several variables that one's prior notions might expect to influence cost or revenues were tested but turned out to be unimportant. The following variables did not influence cost: the size of the teeing areas, whether carts have to stay on cartpaths, the number of holes with water hazards, the hilliness of the course, the acreage of lakes, and the number of bunkers. The following variables might have been expected to influence revenues, but did not do so in this sample: the expenditure on advertising, the size of the greens, and the subjectively measured golfers' rating of the customer service.

The results reported here were obtained using the simplest estimation techniques, in particular, ordinary least squares on single, reduced-form, linearly specified equations. Other techniques were tried but did not alter any of the inferences presented above. For example, other functional forms which would highlight an increasing or decreasing marginal cost or marginal revenue led to insignificant results. Also, estimation of a multiple equation structural model was not fruitful. Unfortunately, the simultaneous estimation of the number of interesting coefficients in a multiple equation model where costs, revenues, condition, and beauty were all endogenous is beyond the capability of this sample size to resolve with appropriate accuracy.

Chapter 7

Location, Location, Location

The joke in marketing is that the three most important concepts for success are location, location, and location. Obviously, being near to your customers, visible to your customers, and convenient for your customers will enhance the sales of your product. For retail outlets, the correct location could mean being on the right side of the boulevard for the maximum foot traffic, being close to parking (or having room to supply parking) for customers with cars, or being on the corner instead of halfway up the block for maximum visibility. These examples put the emphasis of location on proximity to customers. This aspect of location supplies the topic for this chapter.

Lest we begin on the wrong foot, however, it is useful to distinguish between the impact of location on the size of the market and the impact of location on the nature of the good that is sold. For example, location for a restaurant might mean a spot with a scenic vista, and might even be inconvenient to get to. For a resort hotel, location means proximity to a national park or other attraction that brings in customers as opposed to being situated near the homes of the customers. The location of successful ski resorts is important primarily because of the suitability of the terrain and climate for skiing, and not because of a large nearby captive pool of customers.

Of course, both aspects of location are at work simultaneously. If prime skiing terrain is located near a metropolitan population center, so much the better. Golf courses also exhibit this dual nature of location. On the one hand, location determines the character of the golf course itself. Courses located in the hills or in parkland will have a character different from those located on landfill. Each of these types will be different from courses located near the ocean. On the other hand, a golf course's location in terms of proximity to the population base is also an important determinant of demand. The more people living nearby the golf course, the larger is the relevant market to which the golf course will offer its services. Previous chapters have focused attention on golf course beauty, which is largely a function of location, as a determinant of demand. This chapter will focus on the golf course's proximity to the population base. In particular, finding out and illustrating the most useful way to delineate the relevant market and count the relevant population is the topic covered here. Perhaps the chapter should be called, "Population, Population, Population," instead.

That location matters in terms of market size has been studied in formal models going back at least to Harold Hotelling's pathbreaking work in the 1930's.[1] Hotelling looked at a one-dimensional space, a line segment, along which customers and firms were located. The distance between a customer's location and a firm's location represented a delivery, or transportation, cost. If a firm was too far from a customer, the transportation cost would be larger than the possible gains from trade, and the customer would not be included in the firm's market. Another firm might locate between the first firm and the unserved customer in order to exploit its own locational niche in what has become known as the "linear city."

The "spatial" economics literature was born. Theoretical issues such as strategic location, preemptive location, and price discrimination were addressed in the terms of the one-dimensional model. Strategic location issues are concerned with locating one's firm to maximize profit while keeping in mind the fact that competitors are also choosing their locations, or will be choosing their locations in the future. Models of preemptive location deal with an incumbent firm's attempts to expand or establish multiple locations in order to foreclose the market to future competition. Price discrimination issues focus on the ability of spatially separated firms to charge higher prices to a captive market of nearby customers, or, what amounts to the same thing, to offer targeted discounts to customers located nearer to competitors.

---

[1]Hotelling, Harold, "Stability in Competition," *Economic Journal*, Vol. 39, (Mar. 1929), pp. 41-57.

Any of these issues have counterparts in a more realistic two-dimensional model of firm and customer location. A difficult aspect, however, is the jump from the easily measurable population of consumers in the stylized linear city to the complicated real-world measurement of actual consumers in an actual geographic market. In this chapter, I document my attempts to obtain useful real world population measures in a two-dimensional, spatial market setting. I start the next section by defining and examining several ways to measure population in a stylized spatial market showing that the differences among what seem like straightforward measures are not trivial. The chapter ends with the comparison of the different population measures in a demand study based on my sample of 46 public access golf courses in the San Francisco Bay area.

7.1 A Stylized Numerical Example

Consider the geographic area represented in Fig. 7.1. The area is a rectangle fifteen miles from north to south and ten miles from east to west. Outside of the rectangle the population is negligible. It may help to think of the area as an island, or as being surrounded by desert, mountains, or other sparsely populated regions. The area itself is divided into three subjurisdictions which I have labeled city 1, city 2, and city 3, ranked in order of their geographic area. City 1 is the large city with a land area of 75 square miles and a population of 900,000. It is also the most densely populated of the three cities with 12,000 people per square mile. City 2 is a medium size city with 400,000 residents, a land area of 50 square miles and a population density of 8000 people per square mile. Finally, city 3 is a representative suburban locality with a population of 100,000, a land area of 25 square miles, and a population density of 4000 people per square mile.

All locations in this geographic area can be represented as ordered pairs of numbers (x, y) where the "x" value refers to the distance from the western edge of the diagram and the "y" value refers to the distance up from the southern edge of the diagram. Thus, the mathematical origin of the diagram is the southwest corner, denoted, (0, 0), and the "three corners" point where all three cities meet is the point (5, 10).

In Fig. 7.2, six golf courses have been located in a manner that evenly divides the area into six, five mile by five mile squares. In terms of the ordered pair notation, the locations are: (2.5, 12.5), (2.5, 7.5), (2.5, 2.5), (7.5, 12.5), (7.5, 7.5), and (7.5, 2.5). As the diagram shows, three of these courses are in city 1, two in city 2, and one in city 3. A demand study of these six golf courses will have to control for difficulty, hilliness, condition, beauty, etc., and, central to the task of this chapter, population. This seems clear enough, but there are several ways to measure population. The simple

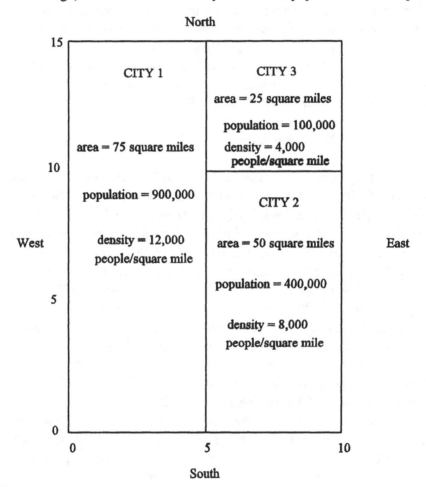

Fig. 7.1 A stylized example.

example here, the next one based on random location, and the statistical measurement at the end of the chapter all show what happens as the measurement of the relevant population becomes more sophisticated.

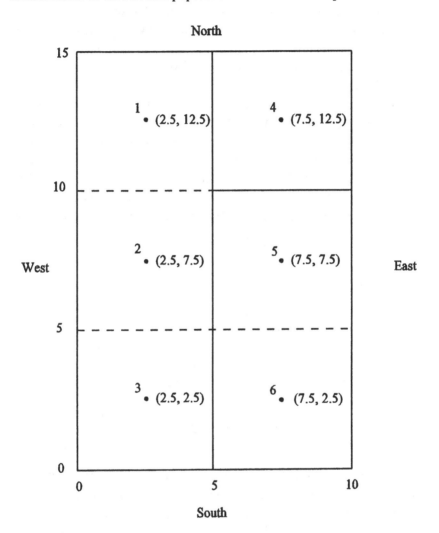

Fig.7.2 A stylized example (continued).

The first population measure one would try is simply the population in the relevant jurisdiction. Indeed, population by city is one of the most basic things collected in every census, and is widely available. Clearly, a city golf course surrounded by many residents will have higher demand than an otherwise identical golf course located in a small town, rural setting. In this case, finding the location of the golf course by city, and using the city's population as the measure of the population for the course clearly distinguishes among three kinds of golf courses. Courses 1, 2, and 3, located in city 1, all get a population measure of 900,000. Courses 5 and 6, located in city 2, each get a population of 400,000. Course 4 in city 3 gets only a population of 100,000. These measurements and the others to be introduced below are all listed in Table 7.1. Also listed in the table are the rankings from largest to smallest. For example, courses 1, 2, and 3 are all ranked T1, that is, tied for first. The big-city courses are clearly distinguished from the others by this population measure which should be a significant positive determinant of golf course demand or revenues.

Table 7.1 Population measures and ranks.

Course	Population,	Rank	Population divided by number of courses,	Rank	Population in 5-mile radius,	Rank	Closest Population,	Rank
1	900,000	T1	300,000	T1	498,520	4	300,000	T1
2	900,000	T1	300,000	T1	689,220	1	300,000	T1
3	900,000	T1	300,000	T1	544,240	2	300,000	T1
4	100,000	6	100,000	6	352,060	6	100,000	6
5	400,000	T4	200,000	T4	521,240	3	200,000	T4
6	400,000	T4	200,000	T4	452.060	5	200,000	T4

The problem with this simple measure is a hidden assumption that there are the same number of golf courses in each city. But what if city 1 actually had nine golf courses? If the 900,000 residents spread out their play over the nine courses, the effect would be as if each course had only 100,000 dedicated to it, much like course 4 in the smaller city 3. But the population variable as measured above would be 900,000 for each course in city 1 and 100,000 for the course in city 3. As such, the simple measurement of citywide population would overstate the effective population for golf courses in cities with multiple golf courses. Therefore, the statistical significance and the economic interpretation of such a variable's coefficient estimate would suffer.

The obvious correction for the above-mentioned problem is to divide the population by the number of competing golf courses in the city. The resulting measure more closely approximates the population per course than the simple population per city. Courses 1, 2, and 3, now have relevant population measures of 300,000 each. Courses 5 and 6 have their populations reduced to 200,000 and course 4 stays at 100,000. In this numerical example, the relative rankings of the courses by population are not changed, but if the numbers were different, they could have been. Again, these measurements and rankings are listed in Table 7.1.

Neither of the above measures, citywide population or citywide population divided by the number of the courses in the city, really capture the essence of location within the city itself. For example, consider courses 1, 2, and 3, each of which is located in city 1, therefore getting the same measurement in the above measures. Upon closer inspection, however, course 2 may have an advantage because it is located closer to the center of the population of the whole geographic area. If any golfers travel between jurisdictions as they surely do in the real world, course 2 is more centrally located than either course 1 or course 3 which are closer to the uninhabited areas to the north and south of our map. Furthermore, between course 1 and course 3, course 3 should have the advantage because of its proximity to city 2 while course 1 is closer to the more lightly populated city 3.

One way of measuring the population to capture the density in the nearby surrounding area is to count all people living within a certain radius of the golf course. For the stylized market here I have chosen a five-mile radius and plotted the overlapping market areas of the six golf courses in Fig. 7.3. The relevant market area for course 1 is highlighted. The area inside each of these portions of a circle is then calculated through the relevant application of a trigonometric integral (the reader will be spared the tedious details). Each area is then multiplied by the relevant population density for that area to obtain the number of people living in that area.

Figure 7.3 shows that course 1 captures an area of 36.43 square miles in city 1, 11.43 square miles in the least dense city 3, and a small corner of city 2 totaling 1.955 square miles. Multiplying each of these areas by the relevant population density and summing, yields a population of 498,520 living within a five-mile radius of course 1.

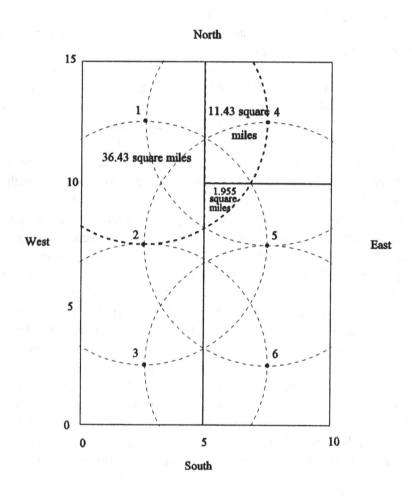

Fig. 7.3 A stylized example (continued).

Looking only at city 1, course 1 and course 3 are symmetrically located. But course 3's five-mile radius spills over into city 2, whereas course 1's five-mile radius spills over only a little into city 2 and mostly into the less dense city 3. Meanwhile, course 2 captures more of city 1 itself by being able to exploit the five-mile radius to both the north and the south, unlike courses 1 and 3 which reach the boundary of the populated area in one direction or the other. Counting the population within a five-mile radius has the ability to capture the specific locational advantages and disadvantages of each course. Table 7.1 verifies that the population counts and the resulting ranks differ for each course.

Conceptually and theoretically, counting the population within an n-mile radius of a golf course is an improvement over measures that treat identically each course within a jurisdiction. It is an improvement mainly because it includes more information. It captures not only the city, but also the location within the city. It uses not only the population density of the city, but also the density of adjacent cities whenever they are close enough. Furthermore, it is consistent with the view that most golfers will play the vast majority of their golf within a reasonable distance of their homes. There are, however, two conceptual difficulties with such a measure, namely, the choice of how large to make the radius around the course, and the effect that other nearby courses will have on the sharing of overlapping markets.

Consider first, the choice of the radius. For the stylized example here I have chosen a radius of five miles.[2] A larger radius suggests that customers can just as easily traverse the extra distance to the golf course implied by the larger radius. A six-mile drive is 20% longer than a five-mile drive but not 20% more expensive because of the fixed costs of unlocking, locking, starting, parking, and so on, that have to be incurred once regardless of the length of the trip. Put another way, the difference between five miles and six miles may be almost completely without consequence for the typical golfer. But being **almost** completely without consequence is not the same as being

---

[2]In the actual statistical work I chose a radius of 10 miles. In the National Golf Foundation survey golfers were asked how far they go to the course they play most frequently. The average distance was 10.4 miles and 58.4% indicated that they went 9 or fewer miles. Golfers would go further, an average of 21.5 miles, to "regularly" play a good course. See, *Golf Consumer Profile 1989 Edition*, National Golf Foundation, Jupiter Florida, August, 1989, pp. 39-40.

completely without consequence. Seven miles is almost the same as six, and eight is almost the same as seven, but the line has to be drawn somewhere. What exactly are the consequences of making the radius larger or smaller?

As the radius increases, the golf courses become less distinguishable on the measure of population because the market areas overlap more and more and count the same people. For our example, if the radius is increased to anything over 14.58 miles, then each of the courses counts the whole population within its market boundaries, and the population variable would do nothing to differentiate the golf courses from one another. In a statistical sense, such a measure would add no information different from the constant term in a regression. Because of this effect, there may be a difference between our intuitive notion of what the market radius should be, and the most useful market radius for the purpose of distinguishing golf courses from one another.

For example, enlarging the radius may better capture our intuitive notion of a relevant market area in terms of acceptable travel time. Additionally, to the extent that these market areas overlap, the radius measure with a large radius concentrates our attention on notions of competition among firms, or even on relevant market delineation for antitrust purposes. Indeed, maybe all six courses in our example should be considered to be in the same market and, therefore, should be given the same population measure. Nevertheless, even though it may be the case that no golfer would consider it an undue burden to travel to any of the six golf courses in our example, the specific location of a course within the one market may still be a relevant factor as long as going one or two miles is less burdensome than going ten or twelve miles. That is, the specific locational advantage of each course that is highlighted when the radius is smaller tends to get blurred when the radius is too large.

Making the radius too small, however, brings us back to another problem. In the limit, one would essentially be capturing the population density of the city in which the course is located. In our example, any radius less than 2.5 miles implies that the course counts only area within its own city, and the resulting population data series is a linear transformation of the first and simplest population series presented above.

Since making the radius too big or too small each presents a different problem, we are in the unfortunate situation of having to choose a radius in an *ad hoc* manner. To make the problem worse, the choice will not only affect the magnitudes of the population measure assigned to each course, but can even affect the rank order of the courses in terms of population. This can be seen even in our simple example. Course 5 in city 2 is ranked tied for fourth and behind course 1 for either of our first two population measures or in a population measure based on a market radius of under 2.5 miles. However, in the population measure based on a five-mile radius, course 5 moves ahead of course 1 into third place as is shown in Table 7.1.[3]

The second conceptual difficulty with the measurement of population within a certain radius is in the treatment of competitor courses which have to share any overlapping market areas. One could think of dividing the resulting population figures by the number of other courses, if any, also located within the same radius. In our example, the closest competitor courses are located just at the limit of the five-mile radius so no adjustment would apply. However, there are reasons to think that such an adjustment will not work as well as one would wish. First of all, the effect of competition between two courses is likely to be stronger when they are located one-half mile apart than when they are located 4.5 miles apart, but simply dividing the population within a certain radius by the courses within the radius lumps the two cases together. That is, the resulting measure would be insensitive to certain locational differences. At the same time, however, the measure is overly sensitive to other slight changes. For example, consider changing the market radius from just under five miles to just over five miles. This will have a small, in the limit, negligible, effect on the numbers just calculated for the five-mile radius case as listed in Table 7.1. But the figures for courses 2 and 5 would be divided by 3 while the numbers for courses 1, 3, 4, and 6 would be divided by only two.

The main problem with dividing any of the radius-based measures by the number of other courses is that it is not the existence per se of other nearby courses that matters, it is their closeness and the extent to which their geographical markets overlap. Referring again to Fig. 7.3, we see that some

---

[3]Course 5 will also move ahead of course 3 as the radius increases further. With a radius of 10.61 miles, the centrally located courses 2 and 5 will cover the whole area and claim the whole population of 1,400,000 and be tied for first in population rank. Course 3 will slip into third place.

consumers live in areas that are within five miles of only one course. The four corners of the diagram contain these "captive" consumers of courses 1, 3, 4, and 6. Other areas are within five miles of two courses; still others within five miles of three or even four courses. One could try to use different weighting factors for the population contained in each of the overlapping market areas. The most obvious weighting scheme comes about by sharing equally any population that is served by multiple courses. We have to divide the population by two in areas served by two courses, by three in areas served by three courses, and so on, and attribute the shares to the appropriate courses. The resulting measure is not calculated here. Conceptually, this measure would take into account the existence and closeness of other competing golf courses. The measure would have the additional property of exactly dividing up the total population among all the courses considered. But, the measure would still suffer from the indeterminacy of the choice of market radius.

The final measure to be considered addresses each of the problems and captures each of the benefits highlighted above. The measure is based on dividing the total area of consumers into separate sets of consumers based on which golf course each consumer lives closest to. This measure exactly divides the total population among the competing golf courses, takes into account the population density in different jurisdictions, takes into account the number and closeness of competing golf courses and does not suffer from any indeterminacy due to an ad hoc choice. Circles, radii, and trigonometry are no longer required. Instead, the position of each course is plotted on the map, and straight lines separating each course from its closest neighbor in each direction are plotted to form the basis of the market division. Lacking the imagination to come up with anything better, I call this the "closest population" measure.

For the simple example considered so far the calculations are trivially easy. The line separating course 1 from course 4 is the line, $x = 5$. This just happens to be the line defining the city limits of city 1. It also is the line separating course 2 from course 5 and course 3 from course 4. The other relevant lines delineating the separate markets are the lines $y = 5$ and $y = 10$. Each course ends up with an exact five mile by five-mile square market fully contained in each course's home city. The resulting populations for each course, and the ranks, are listed in Table 7.1. As the table shows, these figures are the same as the second set of population figures calculated by dividing citywide population by the number of courses located within the city. But this identity is an artifact of the exact placement of the courses to begin with. To illustrate the true nature of this method we must go to a model with a less exacting placement of the six courses.

7.2 A Stylized Example with Randomized Course Location

The previous section defined four methods of counting the population in each golf course's market for a case in which the courses were located in an idealized fashion with each course at the center of a five mile by five mile square land area. Now consider the same geographic area with the same jurisdictional division and the same population densities as above, but this time use the six following locations for the golf courses: (2.50, 14.50), (2.51, 9.25). (3.53, 7.58), (5.24, 14.1), (6.89, 3.98), and (8.73, 3.30).[4] The locations are pictured in Fig. 7.4.

Because there are three courses in city 1, two in city 2, and one in city 3, the first two population measures are the same as calculated above and listed in Table 7.1. Namely, the "population per city" method gives 900,000 each to courses 1, 2, and 3; 400,000 each to courses 5 and 6; and 100,000 to course 4. The "population per city divided by the number of courses per city" method gives 300,000 each to courses 1, 2, and 3; 200,000 to courses 5 and 6; and the same 100,000 to course 4. These measures and the resulting rankings are listed in Table 7.2.

The payoff comes in calculating and comparing the relatively more sophisticated "five-mile radius" and "closest population" methods. The point here is to illustrate that the differences between the methods are not trivial. This will set the stage for the empirical comparisons of the methods in action in the last section of this chapter.

---

[4]The locations were actually chosen from a table of random numbers and just happened to come up with three located in city 1, two in city 2, and one in city 3. The implied ratios of courses per city is the same as the corresponding ratios of land area per city so, in a sense, the location as far as city by city is the modal outcome. It is nice because it makes some of the comparisons with the previous case more straightforward.

As above, I shall spare the reader the details of the trigonometric calculations involved in computing the figures for the five-mile radius method. Circles with five-mile radii were plotted around each of the new locations. The areas encompassed in different arcs were calculated and, then, multiplied by the proper population density figure and summed to

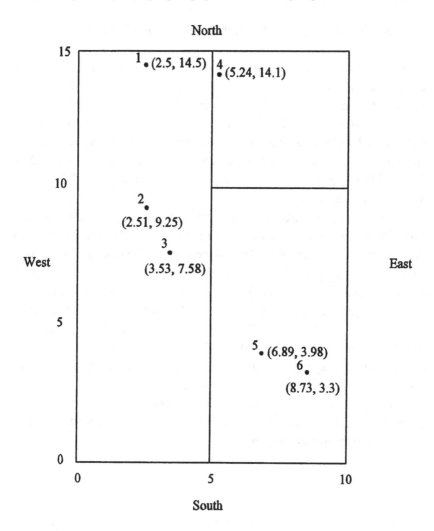

Fig. 7.4 Randomized location.

obtain the population measure for each course. The results appear in Table 7.2.

Table 7.2 Population measures and ranks.

Course	Population, Rank	Population divided by number of courses, Rank	Population in 5-mile radius, Rank	Closest Population, Rank
1	900,000 , T1	300,000 , T1	352,672 , 6	140,472 , 5
2	900,000 , T1	300,000 , T1	674,076 , 2	223,068 , 3
3	900,000 , T1	300,000 , T1	739,876 , 1	370,666 , 2
4	100,000 , 6	100,000 , 6	380,544 , 5	155,293 , 4
5	400,000 , T4	200,000 , T4	473,492 , 3	374,815 , 1
6	400,000 , T4	200,000 , T4	385.704 , 4	135,276 , 6

Course 3 has the largest potential market when ranked according to its population within a five-mile radius. Note in particular how course 1, which is ranked tied for first in either of the first two methods, falls all the way to sixth place owing to its location close to the northern border of the populated area.

To calculate the closest population method requires plotting the course locations and the lines separating the courses from their neighbors. This is illustrated in Fig. 7.5. Finding the lines themselves is straightforward. The almost horizontal line segment in the northwestern part of the diagram marks the delineation between the markets for course 1 and course 2. It is the linear, perpendicular bisector of the line segment (not shown) connecting the locations of course 1 and course 2. Following this line from the western edge of the city across toward city 3, we see that the line bifurcates at the point $(x, y) = (3.5162, 11.8767)$, This point is equidistant from golf course 1, golf course 2, and golf course 4. Shooting off to the north is the line segment of points equidistant from course 1 and course 4, and shooting off to the southeast is the line segment dividing the golfers who live closer to course 2 from those who live closer to course 4.

The rest of the dividing lines are plotted in a similar manner. The result is a segmentation of the total area into six areas, one for each course. The area for each course represents the locations of the homes that are closer to that course than to any other. It is a straightforward, though tedious, matter to divide each of the six areas into triangles or parallelograms for which the numerical value of the area can be calculated. Once each area is found, it is weighted by the appropriate population density and summed to obtain the population number for each course.

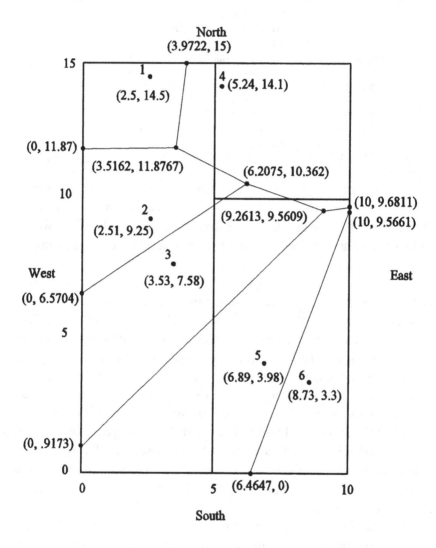

Fig. 7.5 The closest population method.

The results of the "closest population" method are listed in Table 7.2. Comparing these results to those from the five-mile radius method highlights the potential importance of these refinements to the measurement of population. The most obvious difference between the two measures, namely that the numbers are all lower for the closest population method, is not the essential difference. The numbers would have to be higher for the five-mile radius method because of the double, triple, and quadruple counting of the population in the overlapping areas. The important difference is how the ranks change. Indeed, in not even one instance is the rank of a course conserved between these two measures. Course 3 and course 2 are ranked first and second by the five-mile radius method owing to their central locations, followed by course 5. But course 3 and course 2, because of their proximity to each other, must split a large share of the customers who live within five miles, while course 5 enjoys a large geographic area of customers who live closer to course 5 than to any other golf course. In the closest population method, course 5 leapfrogs both course 3 and course 2 to end up with the highest rank.

The stylized examples show how population and location are intertwined as a source of a firm's customers. The examples show how different measurement protocols from simple to complex might be constructed. They also show how the resulting data series can be changed dramatically by the measurement technique. If these measurement differences turn out to be important in a statistical model, then these efforts to include more sophistication in the measurement of population will have paid off. And, if so, it is likely that similar efforts should be made in future statistical applications of spatial competition.

7.3 The Statistical Model

The statistical model requires the computation of population according to each of the four methods discussed above. Data for the first two methods, namely the citywide population and the citywide population divided by the number of courses in the city, are easily obtained from census figures. To develop the data for the other two methods requires the census figures and also requires the actual census maps, the actual locations of the golf courses on those maps, a few simplifying assumptions which are potential sources of measurement error, and a lot of plotting and figuring. The process, which mirrors the discussion above in the stylized example, is outlined below.

The local census population maps exist on a county-by-county basis. Although they do not come in the same scale, copies can be enlarged or compressed until the scales match and the several county maps can be pieced together. Once the map is prepared, the locations of the golf courses are plotted. Then, the procedure is essentially the same for the radius method and the closest population method. Either circles around each course, or dividing lines to spatially separate the courses are plotted to delineate the relevant geographic areas of each course. Typically, the dividing lines will cut across multiple individual cities, each of which has its own population and area figures, therefore, an approximation of the percentage of each city that falls within a course's market area must be made. For example, if a line cuts across the middle of a city, then only 50% of that city's population will be added to the total for the golf course in question. This step necessarily involves a rougher approximation than the precise calculations that were possible in the stylized example from above. This is a cause for concern and a source of measurement error. Keep in mind, however, that if this source of error and all the other possible sources of error accumulate overwhelmingly, then the resulting data series will not work well in the statistical regressions. As we shall see shortly, the measurement errors are not overwhelming, and the resulting data outperform the simpler population measures.

Two other sources of error possibly creep into these calculations. First, once the proportion of the city's land area to be included for a particular golf course is approximated, multiplying that proportion by the city's population assumes that the city's population is spread out evenly over its geographic area. Second, the lines and circles themselves are plotted with all distances measured "as the crow flies." Actual travel distances will vary when roads are not straight, and even if travel distances were exact, travel times would be different depending on road type and the degree of traffic congestion. I have not attempted to control for these sources of error, and it is possible that future research on spatial economics will discover a workable method of so doing. If so, the methods of counting the relevant population that I use may be improved even further.

Summary statistics for the population measures and the other control variables used in the regression equations below are listed in Table 7.3. Focusing first on the population measures, note the difference in magnitudes among the measures. The population within a ten-mile radius has the largest mean value because it involves the most double-counting of the existing population in overlapping market areas. The raw population of the city itself is the next largest because it has some double-counting in those cases where

Table 7.3 Summary statistics.

variable	mean	sad. deviation	minimum	maximum
REVENUE	1,740,300	508,650	765,500	3,230,000
HILLINESS	2.5014	0.97023	1.040	4.542
BEAUTY	3.6140	0.63470	2.455	4.609
CONDITION	3.5392	0.46125	2.262	4.525
MUNICIPAL	0.54348	0.50361	0	1
HOLES	20.957	6.5793	18	45
RATING	71.183	2.0402	64.4	74.9
POPULATION	132,370	207,030	2,115	782,200
POPULATION DIVIDED BY NUMBER OF COURSES	76,428	85,707	2,115	362.000
POPULATION IN 10-MILE RADIUS	445,450	296,320	64,500	1,190,000
CLOSEST POPULATION	124,240	109,530	17,000	462,100

Notes: REVENUE is measured in 1993 dollars. HILLINESS, BEAUTY, and CONDITION are measured on 1-to-5 scales. MUNICIPAL is a dummy equal to one for municipal golf courses. HOLES is the number of holes at each golf facility. RATING is the stroke rating from the most difficult set of tees. All the population figures are measured in number of persons.

several golf courses are located in the same city. The closest population method counts everyone exactly once; and, as such, it gives the purest measure of people per golf course for the whole geographic region. The measure of 124,240 people per golf facility is a useful one through which to compare the degree of golf course availability either through time or across geographic areas.[5] Finally, the smallest of the four measures is the citywide population divided by the number of golf courses in the city. This measure also has no double counting, furthermore, it leaves uncounted anyone living in a city that does not have a golf course.

The essential difference among these measures, however, is not in their magnitude, but in the fact that they are less than perfectly correlated with each other. The differences can be seen in a numerical sense by examining the correlation matrix for the four measures in Table 7.4. The correlations are positive and high, but not perfect. Indeed, the slight differences among the measures form the basis for the improvement in the relative measurement of relevant market size.

Table 7.4 Correlation matrix for population measures.

	POPULATION	POPULATION DIVIDED BY NUMBER OF COURSES	POPULATION IN 10-MILE RADIUS	CLOSEST POPULATION
POPULATION	1.000	0.942	0.653	0.777
POPULATION DIVIDED BY NUMBER OF COURSES	0.942	1.000	0.707	0.838
POPULATION IN 10-MILE RADIUS	0.653	0.707	1.000	0.741
CLOSEST POPULATION	0.777	0.838	0.741	1.000

[5]For example, the National Golf Foundation reported that there were 3917 daily fee and municipal golf facilities that had at least 18 regulation holes in 1989. The nationwide population at the end of 1989 was almost 248 million. These numbers correspond to about one golf course facility for every 63,314 people on average for the whole country. The San Francisco Bay area would seem to be underserved compared to the nationwide average. See *The Economic Impact of Golf Course Operations on Local, Regional, & National Economies*, The National Golf Foundation, Jupiter, Florida, November 1992, pp. 3.

A sense of the differences can also be gleaned from Table 7.5 which lists the top and bottom five for each of the measures. The changes are perhaps not as dramatic as in the stylized example above, but changes in rank order do exist from measure to measure. Three courses are in the top five in each measure. These courses, Harding Park Golf Course and Lincoln Park Golf Course in San Francisco and San Jose Municipal Golf Course in San Jose are centrally located in the largest cities in the geographic area. By any measure, these courses clearly have large markets. At the opposite end of the spectrum, only two golf courses are in the bottom five in each measure. The Island Club Golf Course in Bethel Island and the Sonoma Golf Club in Sonoma clearly have small markets. The Island Club ranks last in three of the measures and next to last in the fourth. Interestingly, the golf course that grabs the smallest market slot in the closest population measure when the Island Club climbs out of the cellar is not even listed on the other three rankings. The Chardonnay Club owes its small market of consumers that are closer to it than to any other golf course to a rural setting in land suitable for vineyards and to being rather closely hemmed in by other courses in all directions.

The following regression equation for golf course revenues was estimated four times, once for each of the population measures along with the other control variables.

$$\text{REVENUE} = b_0 + b_1\text{HILLINESS} + b_2\text{BEAUTY} +$$
$$b_3\text{CONDITION} + b_4\text{MUNICIPAL} + b_5\text{HOLES} + \quad (7.1)$$
$$b_6\text{RATING} + b_7\text{POPULATION} + e \ .$$

In Eq. (7.1) the b's are the unknown coefficients to be estimated, and e stands for the usual random error term. Each of the variables is explained briefly below. Summary statistics are in Table 7.3.

The dependent variable, REVENUE, is the sum of green fees, membership fees, and cart fees. Other ways of capturing the extent of demand are also possible. For example, other chapters have used only the green fees and membership fees, or simply the number of rounds sold as dependent variables. In each of these instances, however, and in other equations estimated but not reported herein, the sophisticated measures based on population within a market radius or population closest to a particular

Table 7.5 Top and bottom ranking courses by population measure.

POPULATION

COURSE	RANK	COURSE	RANK
San Jose Municipal GC	T1	Island Club Golf Course	46
Santa Teresa Golf Club	T1	Sunol Valley Golf Club	45
Harding Park Golf Course	T3	Oakhurst Country Club	44
Lincoln Park Golf Course	T3	Franklin Canyon Golf Course	43
Lake Chabot Golf Course	T5	Sonoma Golf Club	42
Lew F. Galbraith Golf Links	T5		

POPULATION DIVIDED BY NUMBER OF COURSES

COURSE	RANK	COURSE	RANK
Harding Park Golf Course	T1	Island Club Golf Course	46
Lincoln Park Golf Course	T1	Sunol Valley Golf Club	45
San Jose Municipal GC	T3	Oakhurst Country Club	44
Santa Teresa Golf Club	T3	Franklin Canyon Golf Course	43
Lake Chabot Golf Course	T5	Sonoma Golf Club	42
Lew F. Galbraith Golf Links	T5		

POPULATION IN A 10-MILE RADIUS

COURSE	RANK	COURSE	RANK
San Jose Municipal GC	1	Island Club Golf Course	46
Santa Clara Golf &		Sonoma Golf Club	45
Tennis Club	2	Adobe Creek Golf Club	44
Harding Park Golf Course	3	Half Moon Bay Golf Links	43
Lincoln Park Golf Course	4	Peacock Gap Golf and CC	42
Tilden Park Golf Course	5		

CLOSEST POPULATION

COURSE	RANK	COURSE	RANK
Harding Park Golf Course	1	Chardonnay Club	46
Lincoln Park Golf Course	2	Island Club Golf Course	45
Santa Teresa Golf Club	3	Half Moon Bay Golf Links	44
San Jose Municipal GC	4	Windsor Golf Club	43
Santa Clara Golf &		Sonoma Golf Club	42
Tennis Club	5		

course always outperform the simpler measures of citywide population or citywide population divided by the number of courses. REVENUE is chosen here, but it easily could have been one of the other measures of demand. POPULATION refers to any one of the four methods of counting population as explained in this chapter.

HILLINESS, BEAUTY, and CONDITION refer to the subjectively measured quality variables that were introduced in Chapter 4. HILLINESS has a negative effect on the demand to play any particular golf course but it does have a positive effect on the demand to rent a golf cart. Since both green fee revenues and cart revenues are included in REVENUE, the expected direction of the HILLINESS effect is indeterminate. BEAUTY and CONDITION should have positive effects. However, simultaneously including both BEAUTY and CONDITION introduces a multicollinearity problem for the interpretation of their coefficients. Nevertheless, there is no reason to expect the multicollinearity between BEAUTY and CONDITION to influence the interpretation of the POPULATION variable.

MUNICIPAL is a dummy variable equal to one for a municipal, as opposed to a for-profit, daily fee, golf course. Chapter 5 established the fact that municipal courses use price discrimination in a manner different from daily fee courses. In particular, managers at municipal courses may not be trying to maximize revenue or profit to the same extent as are managers at for-profit facilities. Because municipal courses tend to trade off some extra revenues in order to subsidize play by city residents, the expected sign for the coefficient of MUNICIPAL is negative.

HOLES is the number of holes that a golf facility has. All golf facilities in the sample have at least 18 holes but as Table 7.3 clearly shows, many have more. The larger capacity at multiple-course facilities will lead to higher revenues for any facility that would be at capacity otherwise. Furthermore, multiple-course facilities are rarely built unless there is the expectation of enough demand in the first place. Therefore, courses with more holes should earn more revenue, and the expected sign is positive.

RATING is the highest difficulty rating for any of the tees that a golf course facility has. The other chapters have consistently shown that, all else equal, golfers prefer to play at courses with higher difficulty ratings. The expected sign of the coefficient of RATING is positive.

The results are listed in Table 7.6. There are four columns, one for each measure of population. Moving to the right in the table corresponds to using a more sophisticated measure of population. As the table clearly shows, the fit of the equation, as measured by the adjusted R^2, and the precision with which the coefficient is estimated, as measured by the t-statistic, steadily improve as the measurement of population becomes more refined. This is good news because it buttresses our economic intuition about how population should be measured to capture both the relevant markets and the effects of nearby competition in a realistic spatial competition setting. Looking at it another way, it buttresses our faith in the ability of standard multiple

Table 7.6 Regression estimates of Eq. (7.1), (t-statistics).

Dependent Variable	REVENUE	REVENUE	REVENUE	REVENUE
Constant	-3,742,420 (-1.413)	-4,325,390 (-1.613)	-4,700,750 (-1.812)	-5,112,190 (-2.065)
HILLINESS	-91,170 (-0.990)	-86,308 (-0.943)	-98,662 (-1.128)	-51,123 (-0.598)
BEAUTY	125,677 (0.805)	92,746 (0.586)	137,281 (0.935)	94,953 (0.670)
CONDITION	88,651 (0.519)	170,466 (0.945)	223,685 (1.263)	145,757 (0.929)
MUNICIPAL	-356,614 (-2.334)	-422,491 (-2.610)	-338,281 (-2.398)	-415,048 (-2.974)
HOLES	34,035 (3.221)	34,173 (3.263)	32,882 (3.277)	33,277 (3.476)
RATING	60,510 (1.676)	65,460 (1.811)	63,799 (1.845)	74,966 (2.241)
POPULATION	0.877236 (2.301)			
POPULATION DIVIDED BY NUMBER OF COURSES		2.57615 (2.455)		
POPULATION IN 10-MILE RADIUS			0.793338 (3.011)	
CLOSEST POPULATION				2.52159 (3.699)
R-squared	.370	.380	.420	.472
adjusted R-squared	.254	.266	.314	.375
observations	46	46	46	46

regression analysis to capture and illustrate, in a clear fashion, the underlying principles of spatial competition, and how they should be sensitive to measurement issues.

The table also shows which estimates of the other coefficients and which inferences concerning the other variables are changed by improvements in the population variable. Evidently, the measurement errors that are inherent in the less sophisticated population measures are not very strongly correlated with any of the other explanatory variables. The signs of none of the other coefficients are changed. This is also good news because it means that, for certain purposes, a simpler notion of population may suffice.

For example, if one was trying to determine whether municipal ownership leads to lower revenues, one would look at the coefficient of MUNICIPAL and the associated t-statistic. The coefficient itself varies in a relatively small range from negative $338,281 to negative $422,491. Furthermore, each of the estimated coefficients, statistically, is significantly different from zero with at least 95% confidence. It is clear that the for-profit golf courses earn higher revenues than municipal golf courses--about $400,000 higher--no matter how population is measured.

The only difference at all in inferences about the other variables concerns the effect of golf course difficulty on revenues. As was the case for MUNICIPAL, the coefficients of RATING vary in only a very small band from $60,510 per stroke to $74,966 per stroke. Using the best measure of population, the effect of RATING on REVENUE is statistically significant at the 95% level. When the least precise measure is used to control for population, the significance level of the estimate falls to just under the 90% level. One would be marginally more certain that increasing the difficulty rating of a course would increase the revenues of the golf course if one used the more refined population method to control for the relative size of the market.

Regardless of how valuable the improvements in the population measure are to hypothesis testing with respect to other variables, it is clear that the improvements are valuable in the attempt to derive a prediction equation for golf course revenues. The proportion of the variation in golf course revenues explained by the model increases by over ten percentage points (or by about 28%) from almost 37% to just over 47%. This type of improvement will allow current golf course owners and managers to make more precise estimates of the effect of things such as growth or decline of the local population base, entry of new competition, expansion of existing competition, or closure of an existing course. More precise estimates could easily affect negotiations of new leasing arrangements or renewals of existing leases. For example, expectations based on current lease payment and revenue-sharing formulas using recent past experience will be obsolete if a new golf course opens nearby. Both parties would want to use the best possible prediction equation to make suitable adjustments to the lease. Finally, the most precise predictions are obviously desirable to planners and investors considering new course development in any spatial market setting.

Chapter 8

The Economics of Slow Play[1]

When a three and one-half hour round of golf stretches into five or six hours, it's bad for the golfers and bad for the golf course owners. Virtually all golfers and golf course managers know that it is bad, but have been largely unsuccessful in attempts to speed the pace of play. Even serious efforts by the United States Golf Association (USGA) introduced in the *1995 USGA Pace Rating System*[2] have not rid the game of the problem of slow play. Although the USGA's pace rating system makes some strides in the right direction, and offers some good suggestions, it is hampered by an incomplete understanding of the causes of slow play and of the most efficacious ways of dealing with them. This chapter extends our understanding of slow play by employing some insights from production theory as developed in economics and management science. An analogy is drawn between the flow of golfers around a golf course and the flow of partially finished inventory through a factory, explaining how the idea that is variously called Just-In-Time (JIT) production, Zero Inventory Policy (ZIP), or production smoothing, can be applied to help move the maximum number of golfers most comfortably around a golf course.

The remainder of this chapter proceeds as follows. A brief introduction to the relevant issues in production theory is presented first. Following this,

[1]A version of this chapter was presented at the Western Economic Association, International meetings in San Francisco, July, 2001.

[2]*1995 USGA Pace Rating System*, United States Golf Association, Far Hills, New Jersey, 1995.

the similarities between golfers on a golf course and inventory in a factory are developed. Once the analogy is developed, complicating factors, such as the difference between the rate capacity and the volume capacity, will be introduced. This difference, which is not fully appreciated in the *USGA Pace Rating System*, is of crucial importance to understanding and solving the bottleneck problem. After these preliminaries, the bottleneck problem itself is introduced and discussed fully. To further illustrate the bottleneck problem, the chapter develops a stylized, abstract model, comparing three common causes of delays on a golf course and forming the basis for future empirical study. Finally, the abstract model is applied to the bottleneck problem on a par three hole to illustrate how the issues of bottlenecks, production smoothing, and rate and volume capacities interact to produce the optimal flow of golfers around a golf course.

8.1 Just-In-Time Production

A production or assembly plant is typically composed of numerous stations where workers or machines sequentially perform the many discrete steps necessary to produce the product. If the first step can be completed more quickly than the second step, then an inventory will build up. For example, suppose the first step takes 15 minutes (alternatively called a production rate of four per hour) and the second step takes 30 minutes (two per hour). After an hour of production, the station performing the first step has produced a batch of four items, two of which have moved through to completion of the second step, and two of which form an inventory of items finished with step one, but waiting for step two.[3] For the next hour, the station performing the first step can rest, or be employed with another task, while the station performing the second step uses up the inventory. Call this the batch system of production.

There are both costs and benefits of employing a production system like the one described above. The obvious benefit of building up an inventory of items that have completed the first station is that it can be closed for

---

[3]This is not precisely correct if there is no inventory to start with for the second step. In this case the second step is idle for fifteen minutes awaiting the completion of the first unit in the first step.

scheduled or unscheduled repairs or maintenance, or employee absence, without closing the production line. Station two can continue to operate using the inventory that has been built up. The obvious cost of such a system is that money is tied up in partially completed inventory. A less obvious cost is that mistakes being made at the first station may not be caught immediately. A whole batch containing mistakes could be made, temporarily stored in inventory, and eventually moved to the second station, where only then is it discovered that an unacceptable percentage of the batch does not measure within the required tolerances. Perhaps the faulty items could be fixed, adding a cost, or, in the worst case, the items may prove to be pure waste.

In what is now a familiar story to economists and production engineers, the "Japanese-style" production processes as pioneered by Toyota, involve a relentless attempt to reduce inventories throughout the factory. The result is known as production smoothing, ZIP, or JIT. Along a production line, wherever an inventory is seen to build up, that is the signal to employees and managers that the step after the inventory is too slow; it is a "bottleneck" in the production line which is slowing down the rest of the plant. In the example above, station two is the bottleneck. Recognizing the bottleneck, managers know that attempts to speed the completion of step one will have no effect except to build up bigger inventories of possibly defective items. If anything, step one should be slowed down until the items are being finished "just-in-time" for the second station to use them. This would reduce the inventory buildup but do nothing to increase the overall speed. All managerial efforts to increase speed should be targeted at the second station which is the cause of the bottleneck. Once production is "smoothed" between any two adjacent steps, a bottleneck may appear elsewhere along the production line. Management then directs its efforts to obtaining JIT or ZIP at that point in the factory.

Relative to the batch system, the JIT system has the obvious advantage of having less money tied up in inventory, and the less obvious advantage of avoiding waste by catching mistakes sooner. Furthermore, the JIT system has the advantage of fostering continuous improvements in the production process by highlighting bottlenecks and waste as opposed to hiding them with the use of inventories. However, the move from the batch system to a JIT system is not all gain. An extra cost of the JIT system is that whenever an unscheduled breakdown occurs, there is no inventory to tide the factory over until repairs can be made. Because of this, in the Japanese-style plant, the speed of repairs to production machinery is of utmost importance. Japanese workers even practice such speed by having competitive "races" between shifts to see which "team" can more quickly dismantle, troubleshoot, repair, and reassemble the broken machinery. By contrast, maintenance speed is of no importance if a batch of inventory exists.

8.2 JIT on the Golf Course

This very brief overview of JIT, ZIP, and production smoothing contains the insights we need to examine the pace of play on the golf course. The analogy proceeds as follows. The groups of golfers are the units of partially completed inventory. The golf course can be divided into multiple "stations" where the "production" takes place. The stations are the parts of each golf hole where only one group can play at a time. The production is the finishing of the round of golf by successfully completing each station, that is, each part of each hole.

For example, if the first hole is a 400 yard par four, it could be thought of as two stations. The first 250 yards of the hole is the first station. The group of golfers must hit their tee shots, travel to their balls, hit their approach shots and move clear of the first 250 yards at which time their production at the first station is finished and the next group, the second unit of production, can start. The first group then moves to the second station, that is, the last 150 yards of the hole where they must travel to the green, hit their chips, hole their putts and move clear of the green to the next station, the second tee. While the first group is on the green (the second station) the second group is moving up the fairway, that is, moving through the first station.

If the first station takes seven minutes to complete, and the second station takes seven minutes to complete, then the production is "smoothed." The first hole can be completed in 14 minutes. Tee times can be spaced seven minutes apart, and the groups will move through the hole, finishing seven minutes apart. Moreover, if the production is smoothed, the second group finishes the first part of the hole "just-in-time" to start the second part of the hole.

One measure of capacity in a factory is the rate of production, that is, how many units can be produced per unit of time. The rate capacity of the first hole is one group every seven minutes or 8.57 groups per hour. If there are four golfers per group, the rate capacity is about 34.3 golfers per hour. In addition to the rate of production, the total volume of production depends on the total time devoted to production. On a golf course the time is essentially the daylight hours. If a group wanted to finish just the first hole by dusk, they would have to start the first hole no later than 14 minutes before dusk. If there are 18 holes each taking 14 minutes, then the available time to start a round of golf is from daybreak to four hours and 12 minutes (4.2 hours) before dusk. To put this in perspective, consider the equinox and assume that there are exactly 12 hours between dawn and dusk. There are 7.8 useable hours for starting times on such a day. Multiplying this by the estimate of 34.3 golfers per hour, and rounding, yields the volume capacity of the golf course as 267 golfers per day. Obviously, the volume will be higher during the longer summer days and lower in the winter.

We can also talk about inventory, but we must extend the example to a second hole. An inventory of more than one group can never build up in the middle of the first hole because any succeeding groups cannot start the hole until the group in front of them has moved on to the second station, that is, moved up the fairway toward the green. However, groups of golfers can pile up and wait on succeeding tees. Therefore, it is possible to have an inventory of more than one group of golfers who have finished the second station, that is, putted out on the first green, but cannot yet start the third station, that is, hit their tee shots on the second hole.

8.3 Complications

The preceding distinction between where inventories can or cannot pile up on a golf course actually points to a nettlesome complication in pursuing the analogy between the flow of golfers around a golf course and the flow of inventory through a factory. The golf course example points out that some stations in a production process are linked in a more fundamental way than simply being next to each other in sequence. In particular, it is possible for a group of golfers to be in two stations at once.

Consider the group of golfers in the fairway of the first hole waiting to hit their second shots. They are not yet in the second station because the group in front of them is on the green, so the group in the fairway has to wait. While waiting, they are still in the first station and the group on the tee cannot hit their tee shots. Once the group on the green is finished, the group in the fairway can play their approach shots which might take one or two minutes. During this interval, the group in the fairway is simultaneously in station two (using the green as the target for the shots) and in station one (using the part of the fairway that is the target for the tee shots of the next group).

For the example highlighted above, the following slight change in the numbers is necessary. Suppose it takes five minutes to hit tee shots, travel to the balls and line up (but not hit) the next shot. Suppose it takes two minutes to hit the approach shots, replace the divots, and clear away from the tee shot landing area. Finally, suppose it takes five more minutes to travel to the green, hit chips and putts, and clear away from the green. The group would be in station one for a total of seven minutes, and in station two for a total of seven minutes, and production would be smoothed with seven-minute intervals. But the hole takes only twelve minutes to play because for the two minutes required to hit the approach shots, the group is simultaneously in station one and in station two.

Because the first hole now takes only 12 minutes to play instead of 14 minutes, the volume capacity of the golf course increases, even while the rate capacity stays the same. Golfers will still be starting and finishing the first hole at seven minute intervals, so, as above, the rate of production is 34.3 golfers per hour. Because of the shorter time, however, there are now more tee times available within the daylight hours. For example, if the golf course was composed of 18 such holes, the total playing time would be 216 minutes or 3.6 hours. Tee times would then be available from dawn until 3.6 hours before dusk, for a total of 8.4 hours at the equinox. The volume capacity would increase to 288 golfers per day, the rounded product of 8.4 hours per day times 34.3 golfers per hour.

The important insight from this discussion is that the time it takes to play a hole and the rate at which golfers can finish a hole are two separate things. The rate is measured in golfers per hour, and the time is measured in minutes per hole. The two examples considered above have the same rates (that is, one group every seven minutes or 34.3 golfers per hour), but different times, 14 minutes versus 12 minutes.

A naive understanding of the relationship between these two measures can lead to an erroneous calculation. One might mistakenly reason that because par four holes can hold two groups at once, if the hole takes 14 minutes to play, then groups can be spaced at seven-minute intervals. This calculation works for the simple case but not for the case in which the two stations in the first hole overlap. Even though the first hole can be played in twelve minutes, groups cannot be started at six-minute intervals because the first fairway is not clear until the group ahead has played its approach shots.[4]

Unfortunately, it is clear from the *1995 USGA Pace Rating System* that the USGA has not completely understood this relationship. The USGA Pace Rating formula puts all its efforts into computing a "time par," which is the amount of time it should take for a group of four average golfers to complete a hole. The time par takes into account the length of the hole and the difficulty. The time par also factors in items such as restrictions of carts to cartpaths only, and long distances between a green and the next tee. The time par rating formula places no emphasis at all on the time it takes to play each station on each hole, or the time groups spend occupying more than one station. To its credit, the manual mentions in several places the need for correct spacing of golfers on a golf course and suggests ten-minute intervals between tee times. The ten-minute figure, however, is simply picked out of thin air. There is no attempt in the manual to link it to the numerous other time calculations that are made. This is doubly unfortunate for the golf industry because most golf courses use tee intervals that are closer than ten minutes. Many of these courses could benefit from some of the other good suggestions in the manual but management may be afraid to implement them because of the loss of revenue that extra spacing between tee times entails.

---

[4]The calculation might be salvageable if one realizes that the group in the fairway is actually occupying two stations at once, so there cannot always be two groups on each par four hole. For two-sevenths of the time (two minutes out of every seven minutes) there can only be one group on the hole, so on average, there are $(2(5/7) + 1(2/7) = 12/7)$ twelve-sevenths groups on the hole. Dividing twelve minutes per hole by twelve-sevenths groups per hole yields seven minutes per group.

8.4 The Golf Course Bottleneck

By far, however, the most serious complicating factor that is absent so far harkens back to the production smoothing argument. In the above example, the seven-minute intervals could be maintained because the time it took to complete each station was the same, seven minutes. In the first case, the seven minutes were not overlapping and, in the second case, the seven minutes overlapped by two minutes when the golfers were in the fairway hitting their approach shots. But JIT was established at seven-minute intervals.

Now, suppose that for a simple, non-overlapping case, the first station takes six minutes and the second station takes eight minutes. The hole still takes 14 minutes to play and, as such, is indistinguishable from our first example as far as time par and the USGA Pace Rating manual is concerned. Unfortunately, in this case, seven-minute tee time intervals will be disastrous. Suppose the first group tees off at 6:00 AM. At 6:06 AM the group would be clear of the landing area in the first fairway and the second group would be chomping at the bit to begin their round of golf. The starter, a paid or volunteer employee of the golf course who regulates when each successive group of golfers can tee off, will not allow the next group to tee off until 6:07 AM. Six minutes later, at 6:13 AM, the second group could have already hit their approach shots to the green if no one was in front of them. Unfortunately, the green would not have been clear until 6:14 AM, at which time: the first group finishes the second station; the second group begins the second station; and the third group (on the tee) begins the first station.[5]

So far, so good. The third group started right on schedule at 6:14 AM and could have played their approach shots and cleared the fairway by 6:20 AM except for the second group which would still be on the green until 6:22 AM, that is, eight minutes after the previous group has cleared the green. Now the problem starts to manifest itself. The fourth group, with a tee time of 6:21 AM, would find the first fairway not clear until 6:22 AM. Each succeeding group would find its tee time delayed by an additional minute.

---

[5]The simultaneous starts of the second station by the second group, and the first station by the third group, are due to the simplifying non-overlapping assumption.

Unfortunately, on an actual golf course this particular problem would be concealed by a variety of different factors. The first factor is that not all golfers can hit their tee shots 250 yards. For example, a group of ladies, beginners, or senior citizens might not have to wait for the fairway to be clear for 250 yards before playing their tee shots. They could tee off on time with the group in front of them still waiting in the fairway. The group following them might also be able to tee off on time if the short-hitting group plays their second shots short of the green while the group in front of the short-hitting group is still on the green. Sooner or later, however, a group will arrive to tee off and find all the accumulated waiting staring them in the face.

A second factor that can disguise a first-tee bottleneck is when a group shows up to the first tee a minute or two late, and the golfers and the starter might not even notice the delay until the following group. By this time, the starting times might already be four or five minutes behind schedule, and the golfers and the starter would be gazing up the first fairway wondering which group is responsible for the slow play. If one group appears to be playing particularly poorly, or appears to be not ready to hit their shots because of searching for balls in the woods or high grass, then the temptation would be to blame the slow play on the slow group of golfers rather than the "unsmoothed" production timing of the stations on the first hole.

A third disguising factor is that a whole group may fail to show up for their tee time, at which point the golf course can get back on schedule. Note that no-shows are much more common on weekdays than on weekends, and it is on weekends that the problem of slow play is most acute. Also note that some golf courses make it a practice to leave one tee time open each hour. These golf courses will sometimes allow "walk-ons" (golfers without reservations), to tee off in this open spot if the course is not behind schedule. More often than not, the open tee time is skipped over to get the first tee back on schedule. Skipping the open tee time simply converts the seven-minute tee time intervals into realized tee time intervals that are approximately eight minutes apart.[6]

---

[6]Seven-minute tee intervals translate into 8.57 (that is, 60 divided by 7) groups per hour. Consequently, if one time is unfilled, then 7.57 groups per hour translates into 7.93 (that is, 60 divided by 7.57) minutes between groups.

By far, however, the most important disguising factor is that the bottleneck described here might happen on a hole other than the first, say, the fifth hole, out of the direct view of the starters and managers, and after four holes of other random factors that influence the speed of play have occurred. In this case, all groups will have started on time but the backup will occur on the fifth tee. There are many courses that suffer this bottleneck problem somewhere on the golf course. Two or three groups can pile up on a tee and bemoan the slow play, but trade assurances with each other that, "it opens up after this hole." Of course it opens up. Golfers are arriving at the bottleneck station at roughly seven-minute intervals and finishing the bottleneck station at roughly eight-minute intervals. There is no avoiding the resulting backed-up "inventory" of golfers.

Any one of the above factors will disguise what is going on. Some groups seem to be on time and others have to wait long intervals. The first reaction of many golf course managers and marshals would be to bemoan the slow play of those groups directly in front of groups that seem to be waiting the longest. Because the early-morning groups are least effected by the cumulative nature of the backup, they can easily play their rounds within a decent time interval. Afternoon groups are those most slowed down. The fact that some groups meet the time targets while others cannot, reinforces, in the manager's mind, the conclusion that the problem lies with golfers not with the golf course. Thus, the "solution" is to educate and encourage golfers to play faster through a variety of "fast-play" tips, warnings, and incentives, including: keeping up with the group in front of you; playing out of turn (called, "ready golf"); raffles or lotteries for those meeting time targets; and being forced to skip holes to catch up with the group in front of you if you fall behind. Although this last threat is rarely, if ever, carried out, golf course managers must think that it has some efficacy as a signal of the seriousness with which the golf course takes the slow-play problem.[7]

Even the USGA manual does not seem to appreciate the nature of the problem. In a question and answer section near the end of the manual the

---

[7]In this author's view it is unlikely that a golf course would expect its marshals (who are usually elderly, retired gentlemen volunteering their time in return for free golf) to take on the policing and enforcing role of telling a possibly surly, possibly inebriated, and possibly frustrated by their own poor performance, group of golfers to pick up their golf balls and skip the next hole.

following question is posed. "How does the USGA Pace Rating address the common experience that the first groups of the day play at an acceptable pace but later groups take longer and longer to finish their rounds?"[8] The answer given in the manual demonstrates that the USGA does not fully recognize the bottleneck problem even when the pattern of slow play that the bottleneck causes is directly observed. In fact, the answer starts by rephrasing the question into one that is not equivalent.

A. The issue being raised is, "How can a group catch up after it has fallen behind?" First, an awareness of time par allows a group to know how fast it should be playing. Time par takes into account the length and difficulty of the hole and the number of shots it should take a group of four average golfers to reach the green. With time par, golfers have a benchmark time to shoot at on every hole. Because time par assumes a full course, it is a legitimate expectation for golfers on a busy day.[9]

The answer goes on to mention adequate spacing of starting times and sufficient maintenance on difficult holes but without any explanation of how they are connected to the Pace Rating, how they help a slow group catch up, or how they are related to the original question about fast morning rounds and increasingly slow rounds as the day progresses. The proper answer to the question of how the Pace Rating System addresses the longer and longer afternoon rounds is that it does not.

The problem does not lie with any one particular group. The problem lies with the golf course design. To use the language of production theory, production is not smoothed and a bottleneck exists. If tee times are spaced at seven-minute intervals, and if a particular part of the course that only one group can occupy takes eight minutes to play, there is no way around the conclusion that with each successive group, another minute will be lost.

Encouraging faster play by golfers in general would clear the bottleneck if the golfers could take one minute off the completion time for each station

---

[8]*1995 USGA Pace Rating System*, p. 42.

[9]*1995 USGA Pace Rating System*, p. 42.

that they had to move through on the golf course. If what would normally take six, seven, or eight minutes could take only five, six, or seven minutes, then seven-minute tee intervals could be maintained without a problem. The whole round of golf would also be completed in much less time. But, to avoid the bottleneck it is not necessary for the golfers to speed up on every hole. To avoid the bottleneck, the extra speed is needed only at that one step. It is unlikely, however, that golfers can systematically turn on the speed when it is required. Golfers' habits are developed over many rounds of golf and over eighteen holes in each round.

While encouraging a faster pace of play is always a good idea, an immediate fix for the bottleneck is to increase the tee time interval to eight minutes. Indeed, the Pace Rating system manual suggests longer tee time intervals as a way to consistently meet the time par, but it does not say why. Unfortunately, longer tee time intervals can appear to represent a direct loss in revenue to the golf course because they seem to imply fewer tee times each day. For this reason they may not be used.

The quibbling language in the preceding paragraph ("can appear to," "seem to," "may not be") is there for two reasons. First, the loss of tee times may not be real. Golfers will pay full price for a round of golf only if they expect to be able to finish 18 holes before dark. If longer tee-time intervals translate into shorter rounds, golf courses may be able to schedule full price tee times later in the day making up for fewer tee times all day long, and ending up with the same number of tee times. However, if starting-time intervals are too long, then fewer rounds would be scheduled and revenue would fall. The stylized examples later in the chapter will illustrate these effects. As previously mentioned, there is no systematic discussion of how to set the tee-time intervals in the USGA manual.

Second, with respect to the simple economics of this issue the statement that fewer tee times reduce revenue is strictly true only if price is constant. But price could go up for two reasons: (1) the rounds are faster and golfers will pay more because of the reduction in waiting time, and (2) market clearing price is higher when you slide back up the demand curve.

In any case, the better solution is to identify the bottleneck and eliminate it. Production smoothing can occur by slowing all the stations to the speed or capacity of the slowest station, and can offer efficiencies in the form of fewer inventories (in this case fewer golfers waiting in backups on the course) but it can also occur by concentrating efforts to speed up the slowest station, thereby increasing overall capacity. The example in the last part of the chapter, which examines the issue of calling up the next group on a par three hole, nicely illustrates the distinction.

8.5 Three Types of Slow Play

The discussion and explanation of the golf course bottleneck is not meant to deny that there are other causes of slow play and delays on the golf course. For the most part, everyone understands that if one particular group is consistently playing slower than everyone else, then the holes in front of the slow group will be open and the holes behind will be backed up. Everyone also understands that every golfer, including professionals, can hit wayward shots and have to take extra time to find the ball, assess penalties, take relief according to the rules, and finish the hole. A particular part on the golf course might take an average of seven minutes to finish, but because of the game's inherent variability, there will be a deviation around the seven minutes. Will a group that takes a little longer on one hole be able to make it up by playing the next hole a little faster than average? Unfortunately, the answer is no.

The following stylized model illustrates that there are three patterns of delay caused by three different causes: the golf course bottleneck; the slow group; and the variance in completion times. The three patterns set the stage for empirical application to discover which of the three is most important.

Consider the following stylized model of play over four stations. This can also be thought of as any consecutive four stations on an eighteen-hole golf course. Ordinarily, each station takes seven minutes to play, and there is no overlapping of the stations. Golfers arrive at the first station at seven-minute intervals, with the first group arriving at time zero. Each table below tracks the timing of each of four groups through the four stations.

Table 8.1 is the simple benchmark case. The rows refer to groups 1-4. The columns headed by 1-4 indicate the four stations, or holes, on this golf "course." For each group on each hole the table shows an ordered pair representing the time they start and finish each hole. Group 1 starts the first station at time zero, and finishes it at time seven. The stations do not overlap so that at time seven, group 1 simultaneously finishes hole 1 and starts hole

2, while group 2 starts hole 1. In column 4, the second number indicates the time that the indicated group finishes the fourth station. To highlight the total finishing time for all four groups, the last number for group 4 on hole 4 is italicized.

Table 8.1 The benchmark, even-flow case.

#	w	1	w	2	w	3	w	4	interval	total
1		(0, 7)		(7, 14)		(14, 21)		(21, 28)	-	28
2		(7, 14)		(14, 21)		(21, 28)		(28, 35)	7	28
3		(14, 21)		(21, 28)		(28, 35)		(35, 42)	7	28
4		(21, 28)		(28, 35)		(35, 42)		(42, *49*)	7	28

In this case it takes 49 minutes to move the four groups through the four stations. The column labeled "interval" refers to the elapsed time since the preceding group finished. In this case, the groups are always seven minutes apart. The column labeled "total" is the total number of minutes (in this case, 28), it takes each group to play. Finally, the columns headed by w indicate any waiting that takes place on the golf course. In this case the play is "smoothed" and no one waits.

Now, compare Table 8.1 to Table 8.2 which represents what happens if group 2 is slow and takes eight minutes to play each hole. The first group is unaffected since they are ahead of the slow group. The slow group starts on time but falls a minute further behind on each hole. They finish 11 minutes behind the first group and take 32 minutes in total to play. The groups following the slowpokes wait an additional minute on each tee which lengthens their round of golf to 32 minutes also. It now takes 53 minutes for these four groups to play, and if there are only 49 minutes of daylight

Table 8.2 Slow group # 2.

#	w	1	w	2	w	3	w	4	interval	total
1		(0, 7)		(7, 14)		(14, 21)		(21, 28)	-	28
2		(7, 15)		(15, 23)		(23, 31)		(31, 39)	11	32
3	1	(15, 22)	1	(23, 30)	1	(31, 38)	1	(39, 46)	7	32
4	1	(22, 29)	1	(30, 37)	1	(38, 45)	1	(46, *53*)	7	32

available, then the fourth group will not finish. This table highlights the pattern of slow play caused by a slow group. One group can affect all the groups behind it if the course is full.

Would eight-minute tee intervals help in this case? The answer is yes and no. Some of the waiting can be eliminated, but the fast groups would eventually catch the slow group. Furthermore, as Table 8.3 shows, the capacity of the golf course would be reduced even further.

Table 8.3 Slow group # 2 with 8-minute start intervals.

#	w	1	w	2	w	3	w	4	interval	total
1		(0, 7)		(7, 14)		(14, 21)		(21, 28)	-	28
2		(8, 16)		(16, 24)		(24, 32)		(32, 40)	12	32
3		(16, 23)	1	(24, 31)	1	(32, 39)	1	(40, 47)	7	31
4		(24, 31)		(31, 38)	1	(39, 46)	1	(47, 54)	7	30

In Table 8.3 no one has to wait on the first tee. But group 3 would wait a minute on every hole except the first, and group 4 would wait a minute on every hole once they "catch the pack." The waiting is reduced but the capacity of the course shrinks even more because it now takes 54 minutes to get all four groups through, and tee times can only be scheduled until 54 minutes before dusk instead of 53 minutes as in the previous case.

From the first three tables it is clear that a slow group causes a pattern of one long finishing interval after which the golfers are bunched together, finishing at regular intervals. It is usually easy to spot such a delay by noting any big gaps between groups on the golf course.

Now let us see what pattern develops if there is a bottleneck. Suppose that hole 2 takes eight minutes to play. Table 8.4 illustrates the outcome. The groups start out at seven-minute intervals, and end up finishing at eight-minute intervals. This is accomplished by the ever-increasing backup at the second hole bottleneck. Even spacing between finishing groups at an interval longer than the starting time interval, coupled with an increasingly long wait somewhere on the golf course, is the telltale pattern if the problem is a bottleneck. This pattern differs sharply from the pattern that develops when a slow group is on the course. Empirically exploiting this difference can help to determine which type of slow play problem is plaguing a particular golf course.

Table 8.4 Bottleneck hole # 2.

#	w	1	w	2	w	3	w	4	interval	total
1		(0, 7)		(7, 15)		(15, 22)		(22, 29)	-	29
2		(7, 14)	1	(15, 23)		(23, 30)		(30, 37)	8	30
3		(14, 21)	2	(23, 31)		(31, 38)		(38, 45)	8	31
4		(21, 28)	3	(31, 39)		(39, 46)		(46, 53)	8	32

In the case of a hole that takes longer to play, production smoothing by increasing the starting-time interval can eliminate all waiting as is shown in Table 8.5. Instead of waiting on the golf course, the waiting is included in each group's tee reservation. The bottleneck disappears, and production is smoothed at eight-minute intervals but it still takes 53 minutes for the four groups to finish. Thus, increasing the tee-time interval would not reduce capacity for the bottleneck problem, but it would reduce capacity if the problem is a slow group.

Table 8.5 Bottleneck hole # 2 with 8-minute start intervals.

#	w	1	w	2	w	3	w	4	interval	total
1		(0, 7)		(7, 15)		(15, 22)		(22, 29)	-	29
2		(8, 15)		(15, 23)		(23, 30)		(30, 37)	8	29
3		(16, 23)		(23, 31)		(31, 38)		(38, 45)	8	29
4		(24, 31)		(31, 39)		(39, 46)		(46, 53)	8	29

A completely different reason for golf course delays comes from the variability of the time it takes to play each hole, or each station on a hole. In Table 8.1, each group took exactly seven minutes to play each hole. Now consider a very simple type of variation in which the average time is still seven minutes, but sometimes it takes six minutes and sometimes it takes eight minutes. The variability could be by the hole or by the group. Furthermore, the eight-minute time could come before or after the six-minute time. While these variations would balance out if the golf course was not crowded, the tables below show that typically, the variations do not balance out. This, indeed, is a common result in queuing theory. The fast times tend to be wasted, while the slow times cause backups that are not overcome.

First, consider variability by the group. Group 2, instead of playing the four holes in times of (7, 7, 7, 7), plays them with either of the following two patterns, (7, 8, 6, 7) or (7, 6, 8, 7). Table 8.6 tracks the first of these two patterns. The first group is unaffected by the variable play of the second group. Also, group 2 makes up its lost time and finishes in 28 minutes total. Each group afterwards, however, has to wait a minute before starting the second station. Group 3 falls behind by one minute due to no fault of its own. Group 4 is right on the heels of group 3, making it appear as if group 3 is the culprit for slow play when, in fact, it is not.

Table 8.6 Group # 2 variability with pattern (7, 8, 6, 7).

#	w	1	w	2	w	3	w	4	interval	total
1		(0, 7)		(7, 14)		(14, 21)		(21, 28)	-	28
2		(7, 14)		(14, 22)		(22, 28)		(28, 35)	7	28
3		(14, 21)	1	(22, 29)		(29, 36)		(36, 43)	8	29
4		(21, 28)	1	(29, 36)		(36, 43)		(43, *50*)	7	29

Will this problem cease to exist if the fast time comes first? The answer is no, as is shown in Table 8.7. The fast time is wasted as group 2 has to wait to start the third station anyway. Meanwhile, group 2's slow time on the third station will cause every group after group 2 to wait a minute before starting the third station. The main difference between this and the preceding case is that the blameless group 3 will not look like the culprit.

Table 8.7 Group # 2 variability with pattern (7, 6, 8, 7).

#	w	1	w	2	w	3	w	4	interval	total
1		(0, 7)		(7, 14)		(14, 21)		(21, 28)	-	28
2		(7, 14)		(14, 20)	1	(21, 29)		(29, 36)	8	29
3		(14, 21)		(21, 28)	1	(29, 36)		(36, 43)	7	29
4		(21, 28)		(28, 35)	1	(36, 43)		(43, *50*)	7	29

Similar conclusions come if the variability is by station or "hole" rather than by group. Table 8.8 illustrates the case where the second hole is played in eight minutes by group 2 and in six minutes by group 3. Group 2 will fall a minute behind group 1. Group 3 will have to wait a minute to start the second station, which it finishes quickly, only to have to wait again at the third station. Each succeeding group will also have to wait a minute at the beginning of the third station. Unfortunately for golf course managers who are trying to discover the causes of slow play, the problem is well-disguised. The problem is the variability in the playing time of the second hole but it will be manifested by consistent, additional waiting on the third tee. This is the exact counterpart to Table 8.6 where group 2's variability makes it look like group 3 cannot keep pace.

Table 8.8 Hole # 2 variability with pattern (7, 8, 6, 7).

#	w	1	w	2	w	3	w	4	interval	total
1		(0, 7)		(7, 14)		(14, 21)		(21, 28)	-	28
2		(7, 14)		(14, 22)		(22, 29)		(29, 36)	8	29
3		(14, 21)	1	(22, 28)	1	(29, 36)		(36, 43)	7	29
4		(21, 28)		(28, 35)	1	(36, 43)		(43, 50)	7	29

A delay problem still occurs if the quick playing time at station 2 comes first. Table 8.9 covers the case where the playing times for the second hole are (7, 6, 8, 7). Again there is a delay. Group 2 plays the second hole quickly only to have to wait on the third tee. Group 3 would not have to wait, but every group after it would have to wait a minute to start the second station.

Table 8.9 Hole # 2 variability with pattern (7, 6, 8, 7).

#	w	1	w	2	w	3	w	4	interval	total
1		(0, 7)		(7, 14)		(14, 21)		(21, 28)	-	28
2		(7, 14)		(14, 20)	1	(21, 28)		(28, 35)	7	28
3		(14, 21)		(21, 29)		(29, 36)		(36, 43)	8	29
4		(21, 28)	1	(29, 36)		(36, 43)		(43, 50)	7	29

With any of these last four patterns, eight-minute starting intervals would eliminate the waiting on the golf course. But, as above in the comparison of Tables 8.2 and 8.3, it would take longer to move the four groups through the four holes thus reducing the capacity of the golf course. With eight-minute starting intervals, in a sense, each successive group is arriving not "just-in-time," but rather, a minute late. Most groups play most stations in seven minutes, but they are spaced eight minutes apart. While this is a comfortable flow that can be maintained, more "production" takes place with seven-minute tee intervals because each successive group is ready just-in-time (or slightly ahead of time). The "cost" of this approach is the occasional "inventories" of waiting golfers that are allowed to build up. We have now come full circle to the discussion of production theory that opened the chapter. If one "station" on a golf course or one batch of production (group of golfers) takes eight minutes to complete, (all of the time or part of the time) inventory backups will occur (golfers would have to wait) if starting times are seven minutes apart. Production can be smoothed with the ZIP of stretching starting time intervals to eight minutes. This, however, comes at the cost of lower capacity. If efforts could be taken to convert the bottleneck eight-minute station into something that will withstand a seven-minute per group flow rate, then JIT, ZIP, and smoothed production can occur at seven-minute intervals. Furthermore, as the following application illustrates, even if the total production time (what the USGA calls the pace rating or the time-par) is longer, the capacity of the golf course can be increased if the flow rate of production is made faster.

8.6 An Application: Calling Up the Next Group on Par Threes

The final section of this chapter develops a stylized model of the pacing of play on a golf course that has a par three hole that takes eight minutes to play, set into a balanced sequence of stations each taking seven minutes. Four successive stations are illustrated, with the second station being the slow one. As such, it is like the example covered in Tables 8.4 and 8.5. We will track the first 15 groups of golfers but the pattern of what happens will be clear after the first five or six groups, and will continue after the 15th group. Tables 8.10 and 8.11 are the counterparts of Tables 8.4 and 8.5 extended to fifteen groups. Table 8.10 shows the increasing waiting times at the second hole. By the tenth group of the day there will be two groups on the second tee because group 10 arrives after 70 minutes and group 9 does not start the hole until 71 minutes have elapsed. The finishing-time spacing is an even eight minutes but each group takes one minute longer than the group in front of it. It takes a total of 141 minutes to move all 15 groups through this four-station sequence.

Table 8.10 Bottleneck hole # 2 with 7-minute start intervals.

#	w	1	w	2	w	3	w	4	interval	total
1		(0, 7)		(7, 15)		(15, 22)		(22, 29)	-	29
2		(7, 14)	1	(15, 23)		(23, 30)		(30, 37)	8	30
3		(14, 21)	2	(23, 31)		(31, 38)		(38, 45)	8	31
4		(21, 28)	3	(31, 39)		(39, 46)		(46, 53)	8	32
5		(28, 35)	4	(39, 47)		(47, 54)		(54, 61)	8	33
6		(35, 42)	5	(47, 55)		(55, 62)		(62, 69)	8	34
7		(42, 49)	6	(55, 63)		(63, 70)		(70, 77)	8	35
8		(49, 56)	7	(63, 71)		(71, 78)		(78, 85)	8	36
9		(56, 63)	8	(71, 79)		(79, 86)		(86, 93)	8	37
10		(63, 70)	9	(79, 87)		(87, 94)		(94, 101)	8	38
11		(70, 77)	10	(87, 95)		(95, 102)		(102 ,109)	8	39
12		(77, 84)	11	(95, 103)		(103, 110)		(110, 117)	8	40
13		(84, 91)	12	(103, 111)		(111, 118)		(118, 125)	8	41
14		(91, 98)	13	(111, 119)		(119, 126)		(126, 133)	8	42
15		(98, 105)	14	(119, 127)		(127, 134)		(134, *141*)	8	43

Table 8.11 shows what happens for eight-minute tee-time intervals. There is no waiting, groups finish at eight-minute intervals, but it still takes 141 minutes to move 15 groups through these four stations.

Table 8.11 Bottleneck hole # 2 with 8-minute start intervals.

#	w	1	w	2	w	3	w	4	interval	total
1		(0, 7)		(7, 15)		(15, 22)		(22, 29)	-	29
2		(8, 15)		(15, 23)		(23, 30)		(30, 37)	8	29
3		(16, 23)		(23, 31)		(31, 38)		(38, 45)	8	29
4		(24, 31)		(31, 39)		(39, 46)		(46, *53*)	8	29
5		(32, 39)		(39, 47)		(47, 54)		(54, 61)	8	29
6		(40, 47)		(47, 55)		(55, 62)		(62, 69)	8	29
7		(48, 55)		(55, 63)		(63, 70)		(70, 77)	8	29
8		(56, 63)		(63, 71)		(71, 78)		(78, 85)	8	29
9		(64, 71)		(71, 79)		(79, 86)		(86, 93)	8	29
10		(72, 79)		(79, 87)		(87, 94)		(94, 101)	8	29
11		(80, 87)		(87, 95)		(95, 102)		(102, 109)	8	29
12		(88, 95)		(95, 103)		(103, 110)		(110, 117)	8	29
13		(96, 103)		(103, 111)		(111, 118)		(118, 125)	8	29
14		(104, 111)		(111, 119)		(119, 126)		(126, 133)	8	29
15		(112, 119)		(119, 127)		(127, 134)		(134, *141*)	8	29

Now consider what happens if the golf course imposes the policy of calling up the following group on par three holes. Specifically, suppose that the eight minutes it takes to play this hole can be divided as follows: three minutes to hit tee shots toward the green; two minutes to walk to the hole; one minute to hit chip shots to the green; and two minutes to sink putts and clear the green. Traditionally, in between hitting the chip shots and putting, a group can stand aside and wait while the following group plays their tee shots to the green. Then, the first group putts while the following group walks toward the green. If the calling-up convention is not used, there is only one group on the hole at a time, and the green is idle for two minutes out of every eight minutes. By calling people up to the green before putting, there can actually be two groups on the hole for a portion of the time, and the green would be idle for only one out of each seven minutes on average as is verified in the following table. The hole can actually be divided into four stations, labeled 2a, 2b, 2c, and 2d. The pattern of play that develops is illustrated in Table 8.12.

The first group of the day is not affected by the calling-up policy. After they play their tee shots on the second hole (station 2a), walk toward the green (station 2b), and play their chip shots to the green (station 2c) only 13 minutes have elapsed since they started. The second group would not be finished with the first station until time 14 so the first group does not wait to call up the second group, since the second group is not ready. The first group takes two more minutes to putt out (station 2d), the second of which actually delays the second group, and then moves to station 3.

When group 2 comes to station 2, they find that the green is occupied and they have to wait for one minute until time 15. The second group members then play tee shots (time 15 to 18 in station 2a), walk toward the green (time 18 to 20 in station 2b), and play their chip shots to the green (time 20 to 21 in station 2c). At this point they turn back to the tee to see the third group ready to play at time 21. Group 2 then stands aside for three minutes while the third group members aim their tee shots toward the green.

The time is now 24 minutes after the starting time and simultaneously, group 2 is putting on the green (time 24 to 26 in station 2d) while group 3 is walking toward the green (time 24 to 26 in station 2b). It is this simultaneity that allows the gains from this policy. After putting out on the second hole the second group moves through the rest of the course, and finishes 11

Golfonomics

Table 8.12 Bottleneck hole # 2 with 7-minute start intervals, call up next group.

#	w	1	w	2a	w	2b	w	2c	w
1		(0, 7)		(7, 10)		(10, 12)		(12, 13)	
2		(7, 14)	1	(15, 18)		(18, 20)		(20, 21)	3
3		(14, 21)		(21, 24)		(24, 26)		(26, 27)	
4		(21, 28)	1	(29, 32)		(32, 34)		(34, 35)	3
5		(28, 35)		(35, 38)		(38, 40)		(40, 41)	
6		(35, 42)	1	(43, 46)		(46, 48)		(48, 49)	3
7		(42, 49)		(49, 52)		(52, 54)		(54, 55)	
8		(49, 56)	1	(57, 60)		(60, 62)		(62, 63)	3
9		(56, 63)		(63, 66)		(66, 68)		(68, 69)	
10		(63, 70)	1	(71, 74)		(74, 76)		(76, 77)	3
11		(70, 77)		(77, 80)		(80, 82)		(82, 83)	
12		(77, 84)	1	(85, 88)		(88, 90)		(90, 91)	3
13		(84, 91)		(91, 94)		(94, 96)		(96, 97)	
14		(91, 98)	1	(99, 102)		(102, 104)		(104, 105)	3
15		(98, 105)		(105, 108)		(108, 110)		(110, 111)	

minutes after the first group. Group 2 fell behind by four minutes because they waited one minute on the second tee and they waited three minutes on the second green while they called up the group behind them.

Meanwhile, the third group continues to play the second hole. They are ready to hit their chips just as group 2 vacates the green at time 26. This takes one minute. They then see that group 4 is not yet ready to hit their tee shots so there is no one to call up to the green. Group 3 putts out (time 27 to 29) and arrives at the third station only to wait four minutes for group 2 to finish the third station.[10] Meanwhile group 4 arrives at the second tee while group 3 is still putting and has to wait one minute for the green to clear.

After this, the slightly awkward pattern repeats itself with each group waiting a total of four minutes. Some groups have to wait a minute on the second tee and three more minutes on the second green while they call up the group behind them. Other groups are unimpeded on the second hole but have

---

[10]It does not matter whether this group fails to call up the following group. If they do not call up the next group, they end up waiting on the next tee for four minutes as shown in the table. If they do call up the next group, it also slows them by four minutes: one minute of waiting for the next group to arrive on the tee; and three minutes while the next group hits their shots. In this case, they arrive on the third tee just-in-time to tee off.

Table 8.12 (Continued)

2d	w	3	w	4	interval	total
(13, 15)		(15, 22)		(22, 29)	-	29
(24, 26)		(26, 33)		(33, 40)	11	33
(27, 29)	4	(33, 40)		(40, 47)	7	33
(38, 40)		(40, 47)		(47, 54)	7	33
(41, 43)	4	(47, 54)		(54, 61)	7	33
(52, 54)		(54, 61)		(61, 68)	7	33
(55, 57)	4	(61, 68)		(68, 75)	7	33
(66, 68)		(68, 75)		(75, 82)	7	33
(69, 71)	4	(75, 82)		(82, 89)	7	33
(80, 82)		(82, 89)		(89, 96)	7	33
(83, 85)	4	(89, 96)		(96, 103)	7	33
(94, 96)		(96, 103)		(103, 110)	7	33
(97, 99)	4	(103, 110)		(110, 117)	7	33
(108, 110)		(110, 117)		(117, 124)	7	33
(111, 113)	4	(117, 124)		(124, 131)	7	33

to wait four minutes on the third tee. But from the second group on, there is always a group ready to start the third station at regular seven-minute intervals. Therefore, production is smoothed and the seven-minute starting intervals are sustainable.

Standing aside and waiting makes playing the golf course take longer than in the previous case with eight-minute starting intervals. Except for the first group, each group takes 33 minutes to play the course, 29 minutes of playing time and 4 minutes of waiting time. But the 33 minutes can be reached with a starting rate of one group every seven minutes. In Table 8.11, it takes only the actual playing time of 29 minutes to play the course. There is no waiting, but groups can only start at eight-minute intervals. Overall, the calling-up policy increases the capacity of the golf course as it only takes 131 minutes to move 15 groups through these four stations. In Table 8.11 it takes 141 minutes to do the same job.

Undoubtedly, this result will be somewhat counterintuitive to the golfers themselves. Waiting by the green to call up the group behind you seems to be an imposition that slows down your group, and delays the ultimate time when you will finish. How could it actually speed up play overall? Yet it does. It works by smoothing production over the eight-minute bottleneck station essentially by breaking the one eight-minute station into two or more stations that, although they take 12 minutes in total, they can be completed in seven-minute intervals without causing a bottleneck.

In addition to its counterintuitive nature, the calling-up policy can be difficult to implement. Consider group 2 in Table 8.12. They could finish three minutes faster if they did not call up the group behind them. Furthermore, being the first group to call up a following group, it appears as if they are a slow-playing group that cannot keep pace with those in front of them. The group in front of them finishes in 29 minutes while group 2 and all those who follow take 33 minutes. This is a pattern that is similar to the slow group pattern from Table 8.2 or Table 8.3. If there are sanctions for slow play or for not keeping up with the group in front of you, golfers would seem to be justified in being worried about the time it takes to call up the following group.

It is precisely this misunderstanding about the golf course bottleneck as a source of slow play that this chapter is trying to clear up. The managers at some golf courses focus only on gaps between groups. These managers quote silly cliches like, "keeping up with the group in front of you instead of keeping ahead of the group behind you." It is fine to promote fast play tips and ready-golf, but a course may be missing a chance to smooth production through a bottleneck par three hole by, for example, insisting on a calling-up policy that, to the naive, seems only to lengthen the round of golf. Many golf courses have signs at par three holes requiring groups to call up the following group. Unfortunately, it is not often generally understood how or why such a policy works, therefore, the signs go unheeded and the policy goes unenforced.

Other golf courses focus on the time par or pace rating as currently explained in the USGA manual. These courses are not in the position to recognize and smooth bottlenecks that occur on portions of a hole, because the time par is calculated on a hole-by-hole basis and not on a station-by-station basis. Golf courses can choose a lengthened interval between starting times. This reduces waiting and allows a round of golf to be played in a shorter amount of time, but the course may end up with a lower capacity than need be. There is no question that longer starting time intervals will work to reduce waiting on the golf course. The stylized models in this chapter clearly show why. But choosing this path is essentially the equivalent of slowing the production rate of all the machines in the factory to match the speed of the slowest one. By contrast, the insights from economic production theory, especially JIT and ZIP, encourage managers to find the slowest machine and speed it up. On the golf course this means finding the bottleneck and taking efforts to smooth play through it.

Part III

The Back Nine:

The Economics of Professional Golf

Chapter 9

The Business of Professional Golf[1]

Just about every weekend during the year, golf fans can enjoy golf tournaments featuring PGA TOUR, LPGA, or Champions Tour (formerly Senior PGA Tour) professional golfers simply by turning on the television. This convenient source of entertainment requires the work and coordination of several different groups that are involved with the staging of a golf tournament. First of all are the golfers. Without golfers there would be nothing to watch. Second, there are tournament sponsors. Without the sponsors who offer the prize money and who make arrangements at the golf courses where the tournaments take place, the golfers themselves would not show up. And third, performing an important coordinating role as a middleman between the golfers as individuals and the tournament sponsors, is the association of professional golfers that represents the golfers collectively. Without the PGA TOUR, the LPGA, or the Champions Tour acting on behalf of the relevant group of professional golfers, the golfers as individuals (or individually through their agents) would have to negotiate directly with the tournament sponsors.

This chapter presents some of the basic economic problems and decisions faced by the players as individuals, the players as a group, and the tournament sponsors. It describes some of the practical solutions that have arisen to cope with the problems. Ultimately, this chapter develops a coherent understanding of the business side of professional golf by looking at the history of the PGA TOUR and by describing the economic logic of the

---

[1]This chapter draws on conversations with Hans Kramer who graciously explained the workings of the Senior PGA Tour's Transamerica tournament.

decisionmaking of the three above-mentioned groups. PGA TOUR golfers as individuals are treated first, followed by the golfers as a group organized by the PGA TOUR, and, finally, the tournament sponsors.

9.1 The Professional Golfer as an Individual

Professional golfers are the essential input to the game of professional golf. Television sponsors, the PGA TOUR, and tournament promoters are obviously important to today's version of professional golf, but they are not strictly necessary. Even without television, or the PGA TOUR, the accomplished golfers could organize competitions and exhibitions among themselves, paying their own expenses and gambling their own money against all comers. Good golfers, who might be better characterized as hustlers, could earn a living this way, playing golf and gambling. No doubt, there are some who still do. But professional golf has come a long way since its barnstorming days, and now professional golfers have a series of serious business decisions to make.

Perhaps the most basic decision is whether to pursue a career as a tournament player. For superstar players the decision is easy, but for the marginal player, the decision is usually between a comfortable position as a club professional earning a living by giving lessons, selling merchandise, and promoting golf, and the unguaranteed, though potentially lucrative, life of travel to and from tournament venues to compete for prize money. Except for established players and high-profile newcomers who have travel, clothing, and other expenses covered through endorsement contracts and sponsorships, the tournament player has to cover all the costs of travel, lodging, meals, childcare, caddies, equipment, entry fees, etc. Furthermore, entry into tournaments is not guaranteed until one is granted, and maintains, exempt status.[2] Therefore, the newcomer trying to break in has to first win or place highly enough in a qualifying tournament on a Monday in order to gain entry into the tournament proper which starts on a Thursday. Needless to say, for every professional who eventually earns a living through tournament play,

---

[2]The rules for exempt status are explained below in the section on the PGA TOUR.

there are many who make the economic decision to pursue another vocation after trying one or more years to become a successful touring professional.

Supposing one does make it as a touring professional, there is still a large difference between being a superstar and being a marginal player. The *1999 PGA TOUR Media Guide* lists those who won prizes in events in 1998, ranging in order from highest to lowest. David Duval topped the "official"[3] PGA TOUR money list with a then record $2,591,031 earned in 23 events. The record was obliterated the very next year by Tiger Woods who won more than $6,000,000. Tiger Woods has topped the money list every year since 1999. In 2002 he earned $6,912,625 in 18 events. At the low end of the scale, in 248th place, was Bill Glasson who won $4,599 in 13 2002 events. Obviously, the range and scope of possible choices will differ markedly for golfers at these two extremes. For the top 150 or so golfers who have high priority to enter a tournament, the main decision involves which, and how many, tournaments to play. For other golfers with low exempt status, the battle will be to qualify for as many tournaments as possible in order to win as much money as possible. These two extremes will be examined in order.

Since most tournaments admit 144 players, the top 150 golfers on the priority list will generally be able to pick and choose which tournaments to enter. There are official tournaments every weekend from early January to early November, with extra events during the year, particularly in November and December, called the Challenge Season. Some golfers play as many as 35 official tournaments a year but most of the leaders play between 20 and 30 tournaments. The obvious research question, and so far it has been unaddressed by economists, is how these golfers choose which tournaments to enter. The following lists of factors that golfers may. consider when choosing are presented as guidelines to spur future research on this topic.

With respect to how many tournaments to enter, potential variables include: the golfer's age; the golfer's injury status; the timing of a golfer's earnings (a golfer who wins a lot of (little) money early in the year may curtail (expand) his participation in later events); a golfer's "hot hand" status

---

[3]Players can also earn unofficial money in other tournaments or exhibitions. Performance in some of these events counts in determining the worldwide ranking of all professional golfers.

(a golfer who is playing very well (poorly) may desire to continue (or stop) playing while he is "hot" ("cold")[4]); and a golfer's position on different rankings lists (there are extra bonuses for finishing at, or above, certain rankings[5]).

Regarding which tournaments to enter, several factors may be important. The most important is the tournament's status. Several tournaments have achieved a higher stature than others, and traditionally attract the strongest players, not only from the PGA TOUR, but also internationally. These tournaments are known as the "majors," including: the Masters (held every spring at the ultra-exclusive Augusta National Golf Club in Georgia); the U.S. Open (which is hosted at a different golf course each June by the U.S. Golf Association (USGA), the premier organization of golfers and golf courses in the U.S.); the British Open (which has been held every year since 1860 (except for World Wars) rotating among several different courses in the British Isles); and the PGA Championship (hosted at a different course each year by the PGA of America which is the association of golf professionals who do not earn a living predominantly by playing tournaments). In addition to the four majors are two tournaments that have achieved "almost-major" status owing to large prize funds and the strength of the competition, namely, the PLAYERS Championship, and the year-ending TOUR Championship. Virtually all of the highest ranked players will enter these high profile events because of the high prize funds, because they

[4]Recently, Vijay Singh, after winning the 1998 PGA Championship (a "major" tournament), decided to play the very next week and won the 1998 Sprint International. Alternatively, a leading professional, Tom Kite, withdrew from the 1999 British Open (a major event) citing poor recent play as the reason.

[5]The top ten on the Ryder Points list make the Ryder Cup team which represents the United States in an international match against the team from Europe. The top 30 PGA TOUR members are eligible for the year ending Tour Championship in which first place was worth $900,000, and last place $80,000 in 2002. The top 64 on the Official World Golf Ranking are eligible for the $5 million WGC Anderson Consulting Match Play Championship, in which first place was worth $1,000,000. The top 125 on the official earnings list will be fully exempt for the next calendar year. Players "on the bubble" with respect to these thresholds may decide to play in extra tournaments to improve their relative positions.

confer higher exempt status on the top finishers, and because of the potential for extra endorsement money for the winner.

Other factors which may be important to the individual golfer in deciding which tournaments to enter include: the size of the prize fund (for 2002 the so-called "purses" ranged from $3 million to $6 million); the location of the tournament (many players like to play in their home states); defending or past champion status; a player's position in the rankings with respect to certain thresholds (this may be especially important for late season tournaments); the strength of the field (this cuts both ways--it may be easier to win a tournament in which top players are not entered, but winners get more points in the World Rankings based on the strength of the field); the rest of the golfer's schedule (due to fatigue and/or family commitments, golfers will rarely play more than three consecutive tournaments); performance in recent tournaments (the hot-hand phenomenon mentioned above); the characteristics of the golf course (some courses favor long hitters; some favor straight hitters; other courses are windy and favor low ball flight patterns; still others require greater putting skills, etc.); and the scoring conventions used (some players may be better at attempting heroic and risky shots, and the reward for doing so depends on the scoring conventions[6]). Conceptually, each of these factors is quantifiable, and could be included in a statistical analysis of a player's choice to enter a tournament.

Although there may be no fundamental economic or theoretical issues at stake in determining which element or elements in a golfer's vector of skills will be most important at any particular golf course, research along these lines offers four types of potential payoff. First, there are several interesting measurement and econometric issues that can be examined. Second, it may help gamblers or handicappers in setting odds on golf tournaments, thus increasing the value created in wagering markets. Third, it may be important to the golfers themselves to know which of their strengths and weaknesses

---

[6]Some tournaments are conducted at match play instead of stroke play, and some use a modification of the international "Stableford" scoring system. Either of these scoring conventions generally reward low scores on a hole-by-hole basis more than they penalize high scores on a hole-by-hole basis, thus leading to riskier play. Meanwhile, some golfers may have a comparative advantage in playing a risky, go-for-broke style (for example, the legendary Arnold Palmer) while others are known for their prudent course management skills and steady play (epitomized by Jack Nicklaus).

need to be focused on for any particular tournament. Finally, it is the type of information that enthusiastic followers of the sport get great enjoyment from: in conversations with others, in television commentary, and in articles in popular magazines. Suffice it to say that there is much work yet to be done in this area.

The decisions of golfers who have lower status on the exempt lists are actually much simpler. These golfers may not be able to enter the majors or semi-majors. Essentially, these golfers play whenever they can enter a tournament, thus making it into the playing fields at the lesser events with lower purses, weaker fields, and perhaps less desirable placement in the calendar of events (for example, the week after the British Open which will require long travel and resultant jet lag for those elite golfers who do play in it). A potential statistical implication of this is that there will be a lower overall correlation between the decisions of these golfers and the measurable determinants of those decisions suggested above, than for the elite golfers who can pick and choose their tournaments.

The non-elite golfers do have other options. There are professional tournaments and exhibitions held worldwide for which these golfers may be able to qualify. The competition may not be as strong on the South Africa PGA Tour, or the PGA Tour of Japan, so the chance of winning or placing highly is greater; but the courses will not be as nice; the golfers may not be treated with the same celebrity status; the travel expenses will be greater; and the prize funds will be smaller. To justify the travel expense, a golfer will probably have to choose between a lengthy trip to another continent to play in multiple tournaments, and an intermittent schedule of regular PGA TOUR events.

Another option that non-elite golfers have is a type of minor league in the U. S. called the Nationwide Tour (formerly called the BUY.COM Tour, the Nike Tour, and, before that, the Hogan Tour). The prize funds on these minor tours are nowhere near the PGA TOUR. For example, in 2000, the prize funds per event ranged from $400,000 to $500,000 on the BUY.COM Tour, and from $2.2 million to $5 million on the PGA TOUR. Notwithstanding the low prize funds, the top 15 money winners achieve an exempt status that allows them to play in twenty to thirty PGA TOUR events in the following year. In this sense, playing on the Nationwide Tour full time is a kind of investment that pays off in current winnings and in potential future winnings. An interesting line of research would attempt to quantify the value of winning on the Nationwide Tour.

Finally, it is worth remembering that any of the research that might be undertaken with respect to PGA TOUR players, could be repeated for players of the LPGA Tour or the Champions Tour. The women and seniors have their own set of superstars, prestigious "major" tournaments, and a variety of purse sizes and playing conditions. Perhaps the longer series of quality data collected for PGA TOUR players will keep analysis of other tours in the background for the near term.

9.2 The PGA TOUR

The PGA TOUR is an association of touring professional golfers. On the one hand it acts as a middleman between the individual golfers and the tournament promoters, but on the other, it is clearly an agent of the golfers, and looks after the golfers' interests in its negotiations with the tournament sponsors. It was not always this way as revealed in the brief history and chronology of the PGA TOUR that is presented in the *1999 PGA TOUR Media Guide*. Some highlights from that history will help set the stage for this section which examines the economics and business practices of the PGA TOUR.

In the 1920's golfers played their way east from California to Texas to Florida in a series of tournaments during the winter and early spring. Purses were modest; the Los Angeles Open offered total prizes of $10,000 in 1926. In 1930, Bob Harlow became manager of the PGA Tournament Bureau, and raised total prize money from $77,000 to $130,000 in his first year. Little by little, the tour developed its modern characteristics. In 1933, the Hershey Chocolate Company became the first corporate sponsor with the Hershey Open. In 1938, the tour made its first contribution to charity, $10,000 from the Palm Beach Invitational. By the 1950's golf was being televised nationally. In 1961, the Caucasions-only clause was dropped, and by the early 1980's, Calvin Peete became golf's first African-American superstar. Peete represented the United States on two Ryder Cup teams, and won the Ben Hogan Award in 1983 and the Vardon Trophy in 1984.

In 1968, the PGA TOUR split from its parent association of professional golfers, the PGA of America. The split was a natural one because the touring professionals have a set of concerns very different from those of the non-touring pros. The PGA of America itself had been formed in 1916, and had set up the PGA Tournament Bureau in 1930. By 1968, the touring professionals, although outnumbered in the PGA of America by the club professionals, recognized that they held significant financial clout on their own. A separate organization of tournament players, called the Association of Professional Golfers, was formed, briefly, in 1968. With this as leverage, a separate Tournament Players Division of the PGA was established, to be run by, and for, the tournament players. The Tournament Players Division is now known as the PGA TOUR.

In 1983 the "all-exempt tour" established the official priority list for tournament entries leading to the modern form of establishing a tournament field. Finally, starting in 1999, the five most important international mens' tours--the PGA TOUR, the PGA European Tour, the South African PGA Tour, the PGA Tour of Australasia, and the PGA Tour of Japan--formed the International Federation of PGA Tours, and agreed to a format using the Official World Golf Ranking to establish eligibility for the World Golf Championships. In the first year, the World Golf Championships consisted of three events with purses totaling $15 million.

The PGA TOUR plays a valuable role in organizing and judging the competitions; establishing the rules of play; promoting golf; promoting its members; and providing information to its members. But as Rex Cottle[7] has argued, the major role of the PGA TOUR is to organize its members as a cartel in order to extract the largest revenues for its players and the charities they support. Since there are many very talented, professional golfers willing and able to join the *athletic* competition for tournament purses, a problem that golfers have is how to limit the *economic* competition among themselves.[8]

---

[7]Cottle, R. L., "Economics of the Professional Golfers' Association Tour," *Social Science Quarterly*, 62 (December 1981) 721-34.

---

[8]The tension between athletic competition and economic competition has been emphasized by those studying the economics of team sports organized into leagues. See Neale, W. C., "The Peculiar Economics of Professional Sports," *Quarterly Journal of Economics*, (February 1964) 42-56, and Quirk, J. and M. El-Hodiri, "An Economic Model of a

If tournament promoters and golf courses have too much of the bargaining power, then they will attempt to stage tournaments for much lower amounts of prize money, while still attracting respectable talent. Golfers would economically compete with each other by agreeing to play for lower purses. Short of having the players organize with each other, the only thing that would cause the tournament promoters to raise purses would be competition between different tournaments for golfers within the same time period. The industry could be organized with competing tournaments each weekend. But the total value collected by the golfers and the promoters might be higher by staging a monopoly tournament each week, rather than having two tournaments competing with each other. One monopoly tournament at a time could negotiate better television contracts than two tournaments simultaneously trying to sell the event to sponsors. Indeed, it is the usual presumption that one monopolist will earn more profits than will two competing sellers.[9]

Therefore, the best way for the value to be maximized and collected by the golfers is to organize a collective that will bargain with the tournament promoters on behalf of the golfers. This is precisely what the PGA TOUR does in sanctioning one official event for each week of the golfing schedule. The one official event will be able to sell enough tickets and advertising space in the television package to collect the monopoly revenue, much of which, at the insistence of the PGA TOUR, is passed through to the golfers in the form of the prize fund.

Perhaps the success of the PGA TOUR as a cartel of golfers should not be exaggerated. Before the 1998-1999 National Basketball Association (NBA) season, the players' union and the owners came to loggerheads in negotiating a new contract. In the agreement reached, NBA players will earn

---

Professional Sports League," *Journal of Political Economy*, 70 (December 1971) 1302-19. The topic is somewhat richer in the area of professional sports leagues where economic competition can take a variety of forms including bidding more to purchase talent; franchise relocation to cannibalize markets; and rent-seeking through individual sales of television rights. By contrast, in golf the main economic competition is the willingness to compete for lower prize funds.

[9]The PGA TOUR sponsored 75 events in 1973, some of which must have overlapped. Since 1977 the PGA TOUR sponsored between 43 and 49 events each year.

about 50% of the total revenues of the league. It is widely conceded that the players did not get the better of the bargain. Putting the PGA TOUR in perspective, for example, the 1997 U. S. Open, the premier tournament in golf, had a total prize fund under $3 million or less than 5% of the budgeted revenues of about $60 million.[10]

As in any cartel, since the money (probabilistically) flowing to each member is above the member's opportunity costs, the issue of preventing overcompetition and entry into the cartel must be solved. The golfers, through the PGA TOUR, have effectively solved these problems by using predominantly their athletic competition, that is to say, by disallowing economic competition, in determining who gains entry into a tournament. This means that a golfer cannot enter a tournament based upon a promise to return half of his winnings to the sponsor,[11] but can enter a tournament based on being one of the four low scorers in an open qualifying tournament-- usually held on the Monday before the tournament. Actually, being one of the four best in "Monday qualifying" is the 17th category out of 34 possible criteria for tournament admission.

Although the complete list of exemption criteria is too long and too arcane to address here, most golfers gain their exemptions in one of four ways: (1) winning a PGA TOUR approved event (which gives a golfer an exemption for ten, five, three, or two years depending on the stature of the tournament); (2) being one of the previous year's top 125 official money winners; (3) being one of the low 35 scorers (and ties) from the previous year's qualifying tournament, which consists of regional elimination tournaments that set the field for a grueling six-round finals; and (4) being one of the top 15 money winners on the previous year's Nationwide Tour. Of these four categories, placing high enough on the previous year's money

---

[10]Pearlstein, S. "The U.S. Open at Bethesda's Congressional Country Club may look like a golf tournament, but Dennis Spurgeon knows it's really . . . A $60 Million Business," *The Washington Post*, Monday, June 9, 1997; page F19.

[11]Realistically, the "kickback" implied here is probably not the way the competition would work. It is more likely that tournament promoters will offer guaranteed entry into a tournament if the player will commit to enter the tournament even if the prize fund were to be cut in half.

list is the way that established golfers who have not won a tournament maintain their status as exempt members. All of the ways that newcomers can break in to the exempt list are based on golfing merit, either by winning a tournament (perhaps entered through Monday qualifying), or by placing highly in the yearly qualifying tournament or on the Nationwide Tour.

To make room for the new exempt members, existing exempt members will lose their playing privileges if they fall out of the top 125 money winners. To put this in perspective, number 125 on the official money list for 2002 was Jay Williamson who earned $515,455 in 30 events for an average between $17,000 and $18,000 per event. Consistently placing about 40th place would maintain this average. Alternatively, because of the top heavy distribution of prize money, one might be able to stay exempt with only two or three top ten finishes. Clearly, either breaking into the PGA TOUR cartel, or maintaining one's status as an exempt tournament player is based on golfing ability. The PGA TOUR is a true meritocracy.

The arrangements between the PGA TOUR and the tournaments allow for a maximization of the value created by staging golf tournaments. Cartels also have to establish a method of dividing that value among the members. An equal division will surely not do for at least two reasons. First, an equal distribution of the prize fund to the participants does not supply incentives for better play as well as does a prize fund that is weighted toward the winners and top finishers. This will be shown dramatically in Chapter 11. The second reason is that some superstar golfers (Arnold Palmer, Jack Nicklaus, Lee Trevino, Tom Watson, and Greg Norman, in the past; Tiger Woods, Ernie Els, Sergio Garcia, and Phil Mickelson, currently) create more value for the fans because of their exceptional play and personal charisma. Unless these superstars are rewarded for their better play with higher portions of the prize fund, they could weaken the cartel's structure by negotiating for appearance fees separate from the prize money. Tournament sponsors could attract adequate attendance and television ratings with side payments to a few superstars and an underfunded prize fund. The end result of this type of negotiation could lead to something similar to the endless (and pointless) series of made-for-television figure skating "competitions." In fact, in the Challenge Season (mostly in November and December), special events such as the skins game, team events, and mixed events with women and seniors trade on their hand-picked competitors and special formats instead of robust competition for large purses.

With respect to such exhibition golf, the PGA TOUR is treading on thin ice. Recently, the PGA TOUR has allowed head-to-head competitions: Tiger Woods versus David Duval; Tiger Woods versus Sergio Garcia; and, with the LPGA, mixed-team competitions, Tiger Woods and Annika Sorenstam versus David Duval and Karrie Webb; to be played and televised in prime time. The common denominator in each of these events, of course, is the inclusion of Tiger Woods, for whom the appetite of the golf-viewing public seems insatiable. The thin ice is that these special exhibitions enrich Tiger Woods and the other participants at the possible expense of hurting other PGA TOUR members and tournament promoters. It is easy to see how Woods is enriched, and if these special events bring in new consumers and actually increase the demand to see golf on television, then it is a win-win situation. But it is also possible that these events will sate some of the demand to see Tiger play, thus cutting into the ratings of the regular weekend tournaments. Furthermore, it is likely that the greater the number of special events that Woods plays in, the more he will want to, or have to, cut back the number of his appearances in regular events, either to rest or to nurse injuries. If the television ratings for the regular events suffer for either of these reasons, then the level or growth rate of the prize funds will be somewhat depressed, harming the other members of the PGA TOUR.

Therefore, it is not surprising that the PGA TOUR uses the following restrictive practices and enticements to keep its superstar golfers in the fold. First, appearance fees are disallowed in official events. Second, official prize money is distributed using the same proportional breakdown for each event with the first 10 places receiving, in order: 18%, 10.8%, 6.8%, 4.8%, 4%, 3.6%, 3.35%, 3.1%, 2.9%, and 2.7% of the total purse. Prizes are awarded down to 70th place which receives 0.2% of the purse. The top-heavy tournament distribution favors the superstars. Third, the top earners essentially parlay their winnings because they also receive invitations to special, and especially lucrative, year-end and international events. Fourth, the PGA TOUR also requires one to play in a minimum number of rounds, currently 50, to be eligible for certain year-long statistical prizes and for special year-end events regardless of one's money-earned status. And, finally, golfers who meet their minimum requirements in terms of events and official earnings are allowed some freedom to play in foreign exhibitions or to receive appearance fees to play in unofficial events as a way of earning extra money free from the pressure of competing against a field of PGA TOUR players.

All of these institutions are designed to allow the PGA TOUR to assure the promoters of officially sanctioned events that quality golfers will enter in return for negotiating a large prize fund. At the same time these institutions supply some discipline over the cartel members by disallowing chiseling on the cartel, either by golfers competing with each other for the right to play by driving down purses, or by charismatic players attempting to capture larger shares of the value created in staging a tournament independently of the regular PGA TOUR event.

Cottle concluded his analysis of the structure of the PGA TOUR with a warning about the long term stability of the cartel. Echoing the wisdom of many economists, Cottle suggested that the PGA TOUR, like any other cartel, was vulnerable to competition from without, and dissension from within, its membership. As television and transportation make the world smaller, foreign competition can weaken the PGA TOUR monopoly, especially by bidding away the services of the superstars so that PGA TOUR events could not earn as much money from attendance and television, and therefore could not pay as large prizes.[12]

Consider the case of Greg Norman, an Australian-born PGA TOUR superstar of the 1980s and 1990s who won 18 PGA TOUR events and 56 international events, including wins in Australia, Japan, and Europe. On several occasions Norman attempted to bring together the world's best golfers for competitions that would have obvious value to golf fans, but which could lower the value of other events scheduled for the same weekend. Although Norman's individual attempts did not reach fruition, he did get the ball rolling. The PGA TOUR and the other major professional golf tours,

---

[12]Interestingly in this regard, in September 2001, American superstar and fan favorite, John Daly, won the BMW International Open in Munich, Germany capturing all the golf headlines for the weekend along with a first prize of $270,000. The official PGA tournament for the same weekend was the Air Canada Championship in Surrey, British Columbia. Even though the tournament was televised, and even though first-time winner Joel Edwards earned the first prize of $612,000, more than twice as much as Daly, the event received also-ran treatment in the sports pages.

either recognizing the value of the idea, or preempting what would have eventually happened anyway, agreed to sponsor the World Golf Championships starting in 1999. Three events (expanding to four in 2000) with purses totaling $15 million, and open exclusively to the world's best golfers, will allow golf's superstars to significantly increase their earnings, possibly at the relative and/or absolute expense of other golfers and other recipients of golf tournament revenues, for example, charities.

The future success and stability of the golf cartel is worthy of continued observation and study. Superstars with the ability to attract audiences and revenues must be compensated handsomely to avoid the possibility that they break off on their own. But at the same time, the rank and file PGA TOUR members must be compensated. The tournament promoters and the charities they represent must also share in the revenues earned. The following type of research project could be fruitful. A time-series of earnings inequality on the PGA TOUR using a Gini coefficient or a Herfindahl-Hirschmann Index could highlight whether that inequality is waxing, waning, or subject to discrete structural changes due to various PGA TOUR policy changes. Furthermore, whether, and in what direction, that inequality is correlated to the average earnings of all tour players or the earnings of the tournament sponsors and their charities can be determined. The results of the following empirical question could cut either way: Does greater inequality in the earnings of tour professionals that comes from the enhanced income opportunities for superstars increase the fans' enjoyment with positive spillover effects on the rest of the golfers and tournaments, or does any inequality simply represent a siphoning of overall golf tournament revenues to the superstars at the expense of other golfers and tournament sponsors?

Finally, the stellar record of the PGA TOUR in supporting charities must be mentioned, and could be a useful subject of research. Tour events have raised almost $700 million for charity through the end of the 2002 year. In all cases, charities are, if not the total, then at least partial residual claimants of tournament revenues. Evidently, the PGA TOUR has not extracted, solely for its members, all the surplus created by staging golf tournaments. An interesting research project would compare the success of the PGA TOUR in both absolute and relative terms to the charitable donations of other major sporting events. Why has the PGA TOUR been more successful?

9.3 The Tournament Sponsor

The third main participant in staging a professional golf tournament is the group, individual, organization, company, golf course, or combination of the above in charge of running the tournament. This group negotiates with the relevant tour which will supply golfers in return for a guaranteed prize fund. This group negotiates with the golf course and other input suppliers to stage the golf tournament. It negotiates with, and cooperates with, television interests to promote and publicize the event, and to sell the advertising space to sponsors of the tournament. It also coordinates the army of volunteers who help in staging the tournament. Finally, this group takes the risk (if revenues fall short), and acts as residual claimant (if revenues exceed expenses), keeping a profit for the tournament promoters, or passing through all or part of the residual to certain designated charities.

Although any tournament of any size has to confront the same basic issues listed above, there is sometimes an order of magnitude difference that colors how certain arrangements are made. This section draws heavily on a telephone interview with Hans Kramer, former Vice President of International Management Group (IMG) and Executive Director of The Transamerica, a former Senior PGA Tour event held at the Silverado Country Club & Resort in California's Napa Valley, and on an article by Steven Pearlstein in *The Washington Post*,[13] describing the business side of the staging of the 1997 U.S. Open at Congressional Country Club (CCC) near our nation's capital. Therefore, we have as examples a regular event on the former Senior PGA Tour, and arguably the most important major event in golf, the U.S. Open.

As Kramer stressed, there is a vast difference for both the golf course and the surrounding area between hosting a regular Senior PGA Tour event that might draw attendance of 10,000 from the local surrounding area of fans that go home each evening, and the national championship that might draw attendance of over 30,000 from around the country of fans that have to find meals and lodging for the duration of their visits. On the player's side, the

---

[13]Pearlstein, S. "The U.S. Open at Bethesda's Congressional Country Club may look like a golf tournament, but Dennis Spurgeon knows it's really . . . A $60 Million Business," *The Washington Post*, Monday, June 9, 1997; page F19.

usual field for a senior tour event might be 70 golfers for three rounds, compared to the field of 144 for a regular tour event to 156 for the U.S. Open which consists of four days of competition. With respect to corporate hospitality tents, a major revenue item, there may be anywhere from 30 to 50 hospitality tents bringing in over $100,000 apiece for the U.S. Open, while, in 1999 The Transamerica had six hospitality tents going for considerably less.

There are three main cost categories for The Transamerica: the purse; the television contract; and a miscellaneous category that covers everything else. The tournament group must guarantee the prize money for the event. This is what attracts the attention of the Senior Tour and its member players. Since the television broadcast rights for Senior Tour events are not sure money makers, the tournament sponsor was responsible for some of the television related costs as part of the agreement between ESPN, Cadillac, and the Senior Tour to televise 23 events during the 1999 season. The rest of the costs include: set up and operations (such as portable toilets, grandstands, fencing, security); the costs of the pro-am portion of the tournament (mainly parties and gifts and prizes for the amateur contestants), the hospitality tents, parking, transportation, and advertising.

Three categories dominate the revenue earned by The Transamerica. First, the tournament sells packages of benefits to the corporate sponsors of the tournament. Packages may include all or some of the following items: use of a hospitality tent in which corporate displays, merchandise give-aways, and catered food and beverages will be supplied to the guests of the corporation renting the tent; slots in the pro-am tournament for favored employees or customers of the corporation; advertising slots that the tournament committee controls in return for its payments to help produce the television coverage; and tickets for attendance to the tournament itself. Second, the tournament earns revenues from the sale of tickets to the general public. Third, The Transamerica earns from $3,000 to $5,000 per entry from amateur golfers who fill the individual pro-am spots.

The group running the tournament is the residual claimant if the above-mentioned revenues exceed costs. While most tournaments are run as charities, with the charities dividing the residual, some, such as The Transamerica, are actually for-profit ventures. Even the for-profit ventures, however, are proud of their ability to divert significant amounts of cash flow to support local charities in the community where the tournament golf course is located. Economists generally would expect only subtle differences in tournament management to result from this difference in ownership structure. Whoever gets to collect the residual will still want that residual to be maximized and, therefore, will strive to run the tournament in an efficient, businesslike manner.

With the exception of the television package, running a major event like the U. S. Open involves all the same types of costs and revenues, only at a larger magnitude. For example, the 1997 U.S. Open generated about $60 million in revenue and $30 million in profit that was split between the non-profit USGA, CCC, and NBC Sports. For such a large event there is a complex web of risk-sharing and residual claimancy. Everyone knows, for instance, that the television rights are very valuable for such a major event. In this case, NBC, ESPN, and other networks worldwide paid the USGA (an amount estimated to be about $18 million) for the television rights. This places these television networks in the position of residual claimancy with respect to selling the advertising slots. NBC, in fact, sold out all its slots months in advance for a profit estimated at about $8 million. The cause of the difference in the treatment of television rights between this event and The Transamerica is the difference in bargaining power. For a PGA TOUR sponsored event, which has television coverage of every round, the PGA TOUR has the ability to demand payment from the networks for the television rights, and the networks take the risk of selling the advertising. Alternatively, for The Transamerica, the television rights are only marginally valuable and the tournament sponsor or golf course itself will have to take some of the risk by what essentially amounts to prepurchasing some of the advertising slots.

For other revenue items the profit-sharing is based on different formulas. For example, according to the expected division of the 1997 U.S. Open net revenue from the corporate hospitality tents, the USGA got about $4 million while the golf course got about $1.7 million. For the logo'ed merchandise sales, CCC got about $3.5 million while the USGA earned royalties on each sale, that were expected to be about $400,000. The right to sell programs and the advertising space in them were purchased from CCC by *Golf* magazine for an up-front fee of $450,000 and 50% of the residual profits while allowing for a $1 per copy commission to the Boy Scouts who sold the programs at the tournament. Still other arrangements were made for other items. The USGA got all the ticket revenues and paid all the costs of parking, shuttle-busses, scoreboards, fences, grandstands, security, and clean up after the event. And, one-fifth of the gross revenue from food concessions (which was expected to be over $1 million) went to the USGA. Whether, and by what formula, a tournament sponsor will subcontract cost and revenue items is essentially a decision that is negotiated on a case-by-case basis.

Assuming everyone is satisfied with the outcome of a particular tournament, the professional tours usually allow a tournament sponsor and golf course to continue to host tournaments. A tournament's success usually feeds on itself. The local community sees an increase in business. Local charities are funded by the tournament and, in response, are willing to donate thousands of volunteer hours to make it run smoothly. Golfers and golf fans in the community are glad to put up with added congestion and restricted access to the tournament venue and perhaps to nearby golf courses which are used for parking, in order to showcase their city and their golf course, and to get a chance to see a professional event in person. But if the sponsors lose too much money (or expect to lose too much money), or do not get the support of the host golf course and surrounding communities, or if the golfers are too disappointed in the condition of the course, a tournament will be discontinued and replaced by a new tournament.

Given the variety of business arrangements that are used in sponsoring a professional golf tournament, a case-study type of research of a successful (or an unsuccessful) tournament may yield some interesting results. By looking at the administration of one tournament over the years, the special circumstances involved in that particular tournament can be controlled for, and the effects of year-to-year differences in tournament management, weather, strength of field, advertising, and so on, can be highlighted. The results of such analysis would be especially interesting to the respective tours and to the tournament sponsors.

Chapter 10

Practice Makes Perfect[1]

Amateurs and professionals alike are familiar with the perfect golf shot. The shot that seemingly jumps off the center of the clubface and flies straight and true the intended direction, trajectory, and distance. Whenever I hit such a shot I think, "Now why can't I do that every time? If I could, my handicap would surely come down." Then I also realize that since I almost never practice, it is not very likely that I would develop that consistency anytime soon.

Of course, if my livelihood depended on it, I would practice, possibly even to the point where it ceased being a game and became a job. Indeed, with one or two notable exceptions, the PGA TOUR professionals practice more than most avid amateurs play. In my data sample, to be explained below, professional golfers average more than 20 hours per week *practicing* their skills, over and above time spent actually playing rounds of golf either in tournaments or as practice rounds. This practice allows the golfers to develop and finely hone their skills to the high levels displayed every weekend in PGA TOUR events. It also affords the economist with the opportunity to study the relationships among practice, skill development, and income earned in professional tournaments.

There are two areas in economics that can be applied in the study of golfers' practice, skills, and earnings. First, from production theory, there is the basic issue of the relationship between inputs and outputs. Simply stated,

[1]Parts of this chapter were originally published in, Shmanske, Stephen, "Human Capital Formation in Professional Sports: Evidence From the PGA Tour," *Atlantic Economic Journal*, Vol. 20, No. 3, (Sept. 1992) pp. 66-80.

when you use more input, you get more output, at least up to a point. Real world decisions with respect to inputs and outputs necessarily involve quantifying the relationship. How much more output comes from how much more input? But the full economics involves much more. First of all, instead of focusing only on one input and one output, the application of production theory has to consider some cases where multiple inputs go into the production of the output, and other cases where one input could be used to produce a variety of outputs. Second, it is not only, or even primarily, the physical productivity of the inputs that is important, but rather, it is the cost of the inputs used as compared to the value of the outputs created. Golf statistics and the analysis in this chapter will help to illustrate the relationship between inputs and outputs at two levels. At the risk of getting ahead of ourselves, the two levels can be introduced here, briefly. At one level, the single input is the golfer's practice time, and the multiple outputs are the different skills (driving, putting, and so on) that are developed. At another level, the multiple inputs are the skills of the golfer, and the single output is the dollar amount of tournament earnings. Professional golfers use their practice time to "produce" different skills, and they use their skills to "produce" tournament winnings.

The second area in economic theory that informs this research is a branch of labor economics called human capital theory. In labor markets, people earn money by selling (actually renting) their skills to employers. The term, "human capital," comes from the parallel that can be drawn to other markets in which capital owners earn money by lending (in the case of liquid funds) or renting (in the case of land or physical equipment) their capital to firms that will "employ" the capital in their production processes. Capital owners rent their physical capital, and workers rent their human capital. While many, if not most, workers rent their human capital for fixed wages or a fixed salary, some will rent their human capital in contracts that base the pay on the performance of the worker in one way or another; for example, through piece-work, commissions, bonuses, profit-sharing, or in golf, tournament winnings. Tournament-based compensation schemes will be the topic of the next chapter. Here, we focus on another crucial aspect of human capital theory, namely the development and maintenance of that human capital. This might be called the "capital" part of human capital theory. As with any investment that leads to capital formation, costs are incurred first to develop or construct something of value that will last. For most people in labor markets, the investment is in education and training, for professional golfers, it is time spent on the practice range and on the putting green. The next section will introduce the basic jargon and underlying logic of production theory. Additionally, several brief references will be made to previous successful uses of production theory in the economics of professional sports. This section will be followed by a discussion of the golf statistics that are used to quantify the relationships between practice and skills, and between skills and earnings.

Following these preliminaries, the main argument is presented in three parts. The first part is essentially the estimation of a production function. Professional golfers use their different skills: driving; approach shots with irons; putting; etc., to "produce" tournament winnings. One previous study of golf statistics was undertaken by Davidson and Templin.[2] Their results and my results are in general agreement; however, exact comparisons cannot be made because of the ad hoc nature of their statistical approach. I use the skills as regressors for the dependent variable, winnings per tournament, in a regression equation. As such, the coefficient estimates can be interpreted as marginal products (to be illustrated below); or, since the output is measured in dollars, as values of marginal products (VMPs). As we shall see, the truthfulness of the adage, "drive for show; putt for dough," can be examined statistically in a straightforward manner. This part of the chapter treads new ground only to the extent that the regression techniques employed in the analysis of the team sports of baseball, football and basketball, are now applied to the individual sport of golf. The second and third parts of this research, however, offer true advances by examining human capital formation.

The second substantive part of this chapter examines the golfer's production of skills from a fixed input, the stock of received skills, and a variable input, practice time. This part of the chapter addresses issues such as whether the marginal product of practice time is constant or declining, and

---

[2]Davidson, James D. and Thomas J. Templin, "Determinants of Success Among Professional Golfers," *Research Quarterly for Exercise and Sport*, Vol. 57, (No. 1 1986), pp. 60-67.

whether skills depreciate with time. Estimates of the marginal product of practice are developed. There is no existing empirical work in the economics of sports similar to that presented in this section.

The third substantive part of this chapter combines estimates from the two previous sections. Simply, the marginal product of practice in the production of skills is multiplied by the value of the particular skill, in order to obtain an estimate of the VMP of practice. As is explained below, if practice of each skill is equally costly, then efficient use of practice time requires equalized VMPs across the separate skills. The numerical estimates of these VMPs are presented here.

In all three steps of the analysis the regressions are cross section in nature, in that they examine relationships among practice, skills, and earnings for a set of golfers in 1986. Therefore, the maintained assumption is that these relationships are identical for all golfers. To the extent that golfers differ in the production of skills from practice time, the results will yield no systematic tendencies of a statistically significant nature. In general, the regression results yield coefficients that are the anticipated sign, and they are of plausible magnitudes; however, in many cases, the statistical significance levels are low. Nevertheless, there are enough cases of significant coefficients of the theoretically predicted sign to support the contention that systematic relationships between practice and skill, and between skill and earnings, do exist. The low significance levels are the consequence of collinearity and small sample size rather than the lack of any systematic relationships.

10.1 Economic Production Theory

Economic production theory starts from the recognition that there must be a systematic relationship between inputs and outputs. Economists call the relationship, the production function. If we limit ourselves for the moment to only one input and one output, it is possible to illustrate the production function diagrammatically, as is done in Fig. 10.1. Input is measured on the horizontal axis and output is measured on the vertical axis. The production function starts at the origin which signifies, in this case, that if there is no input, there will be no output.[3] The function itself is upward sloping, at least up to a point, indicating that the input is productive in terms of increasing the output. More input leads to more output. Finally, the function does flatten out, indicating that further increases in this input will not increase output.

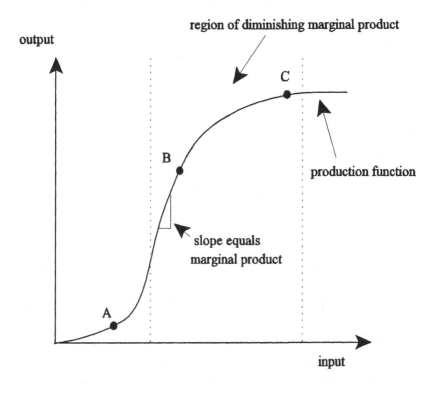

Fig. 10.1 The production function.

The rate of increase of the output due to increases in the input is the crucial target of the economist's attention. This rate is illustrated by the slope of the production function, and is called the marginal product, or the marginal productivity of the input. Simply put, the marginal product tells us how much extra output we will get, starting from any point on the production function, if we increase the input by one more unit. As the diagram indicates, the function need not be linear; the slope need not be a constant; and the marginal product can change depending on how much input we are originally considering. An example might help.

Suppose that the input consists of hours of practice spent on driving the golf ball, and that the output is the driving distance which the golfer achieves. We could consider either a beginner golfer attempting to groove a swing for the first time, or a professional golfer attempting to develop a change in technique that will offer more distance. At first, at a point like A, the production function may be very flat as the practice seems to lead only to frustration for the beginner, and to inconsistency as the accomplished golfer tries to suppress old habits, and learn new ones. As the practice starts to take hold, for example at a point like B, there may be a region where extra practice really starts to lead to the intended results of longer drives. The production function becomes steeper in this region. Finally, at a point like C, when the golfer is approaching the limits of the equipment, or the limits of his own strength and agility, further practice may lead to only negligible, or eventually, even zero increases in distance. The golfer has run into the region of diminishing marginal productivity, in which extra increases in input (practice time), lead to successively smaller increments in output (driving distance).[4] Thus, the production function is traditionally characterized as having an upward sloping and upward curving part, an upward sloping but downward curving part known as the region of diminishing marginal productivity, and possibly, a flat part where output is maximized.

The marginal product is only a technical or engineering relationship between input and output. To economically determine how much input to use requires that we also know the price or cost of the input, as well as the

---

[4]This concept is of such significant importance that economists call it the Law of Diminishing Marginal Productivity; by it, they mean that somewhere before infinity on the horizontal axis, the production function has to start getting flatter.

price or value of the output. To put it in the context of our previous example, consider again, the measurements on the vertical and horizontal axes. The input is measured in hours of practice, and the output is measured in yards of driving distance. Therefore, the slope, or marginal product, is measured in yards per hour of practice. That is to say, the marginal product is the answer to the question, "How many extra yards on the drive will one extra hour of practice lead to?" Without knowing the cost of an hour of practice, or the value of an extra yard on the drive, it is impossible to go any further with respect to analyzing whether a golfer's practice schedule is efficient.

Supposing, however, that we did know the monetary values of the input cost and the output price, we could then determine the best amount of the input. This is done in two steps. The first step is to multiply the value of the output by the marginal product of the input. This, is essence, leads to a dollar value of the additional output created, and is called the "value of the marginal product," (VMP). For instance, if an extra hour of practice led to two extra yards of distance on the drive, and if one extra yard on the drive was worth $100 of extra tournament winnings, then by multiplying the 2 yards per hour by the $100 per yard, we arrive at a VMP of practice of $200 per hour. The second step is to compare the VMP with the cost of the input. If the golfer's time is worth less than $200 per hour, then the golfer can increase his practice time by an hour (which costs less than $200) and gain $200 in benefit. Economic optimization requires the golfer to keep practicing as long as the VMP is greater than the cost of the golfer's time, and to stop practicing when the VMP falls below the cost of the golfer's time. Because of the Law of Diminishing Marginal Productivity, it is assured that the VMP will eventually fall below the cost of the input somewhere before the horizontal axis reaches infinity.[5]

There is another useful result that deductive logic leads to in production theory. If one input is used to produce more than one output, then the VMPs

[5]My own practice regime can be discussed in the same terms. My VMP of practicing driving is very low. Practice would probably lead to longer (and straighter) drives, but the value to me would be relatively low. I might win a few more bets or place higher in a tournament here or there, and I definitely would feel better about my golf game, but the total of these benefits does not amount to very much. Meanwhile, the cost of my time is very high. If I were practicing now, I would not be writing this book!

in the two separate dimensions should be equalized. For example, if the golfer can practice either putting or driving, then the VMP of an extra hour spent driving should equal the VMP of an extra hour spent putting. If the VMPs are not equal, then the golfer should shift his practice time from the lower valued skill to the higher valued skill. For example, suppose that the VMP for practice on driving is $200 per hour and the VMP for practice on putting is $600. The golfer should leave the driving range an hour earlier (thus costing $200), and spend the extra time on the putting green (thus gaining $600). After this reallocation, the golfer is $400 richer without increasing his total hours of practice. Furthermore, the VMP of driving practice goes up, and the VMP of putting practice falls because of the Law of Diminishing Marginal Productivity. While extra practice on putting reduces the marginal product there, the decreased practice on driving increases the marginal product there. Such reallocation of practice time should continue until the VMPs are equalized. Once the VMPs are equalized, no further change in the allocation of a given amount of practice will lead to increased earnings, although the golfer may still choose to add or subtract hours from the total amount of time spent practicing. Even without knowing anything about the cost of the golfer's time, it is possible to comment on the efficiency with which he employs it![6]

Successful examinations of production relationships and labor market institutions have been made using statistics from a number of sports. A common thread in much of the statistical work involving the economics of sports is the attempt to measure the marginal product or VMP of the professional athlete. The skills of the athlete are used as explanatory variables in regressions where the dependent variable measures winning percentage, attendance, team earnings, or salary. A player's salary can then be compared to an estimated value of marginal product to reach conclusions about monopsony power or discrimination. An issue that has not been examined in these settings, however, is that of human capital formation--the

---

[6]There is a hidden assumption here that practice of each skill is equally costly. This may not be true. Practicing driving may be more costly in terms of creating blisters on one's hands; alternatively, practicing putting may be more costly because it puts extra stress on the lower back muscles depending on the particular style or posture that the golfer uses to putt.

development of the athlete's skills in the first place. This chapter uses golf statistics to address this issue, thereby enhancing the received analysis of production relationships in sports, and informing us on human capital formation in sports.

We move next to a description of the data sources.

10.2 The Data

The statistical analysis uses a cross section of golfers for the year 1986. *Golf*[7] magazine and the *Official 1987 PGA TOUR Media Guide*[8] provided the information on golfers' winnings, experience, tournament participation, and statistics on their skills. *Golf* listed complete statistics for the seventy top money winners of 1986. Statistics for ten of these golfers are omitted either because of a lack of enough tournament rounds for the golfer or because the golfer voluntarily withdrew or was disqualified from a tournament.[9] As such, the basic sample uses sixty of the top seventy money winners for 1986.

The golf skills considered are: driving; approach shots; short game; bunker shots; and putting. Summary statistics are presented in Table 10.1.

There are two aspects of driving ability: distance and accuracy. DRIVDIST is the average length of the drive in yards. DRIVACC is the percentage of times the drive ends in the fairway. As Table 10.1 indicates, the average distance for the sixty golfers in the sample is 262.1 yards, and the most accurate golfer, Calvin Peete, hits the fairway 81.7% of the time. Interestingly, the longest driver on tour in 1986 at 285.7 yards, Davis Love III, ranked only 77th on the money leaders list.

[7]*Golf*, George Peper, ed., New York: Times Mirror Magazines, February 1987, p. 54.

[8]*Official 1987 PGA Tour Media Guide*, Ponte Vedra, FL: PGA Tour, Inc., 1986.

[9]Separate prizes are given to the year-end leaders in certain statistical categories. Golfers who withdraw from a tournament after a particularly poor round could affect their individual statistics, and so become ineligible for ranking in the statistical categories.

A second area of skill is reaching the green in regulation, which requires an accurate approach shot that is usually made with an iron.[10] This skill is named GIR, and is measured by the percentage of times the green is reached in regulation, which the PGA TOUR professionals do about two-thirds of the time.

Bunker shot skill, SANDSAVE, is measured by the percentage of times the golfer saves par after hitting into a sandtrap.

Table 10.1 Summary statistics.

Variable	Low in Sample	High in Sample	Average in Sample	Low for all Pros	High for all Pros
DRIVDIST	246.6	277.7	262.1	243.4	285.7
DRIVACC	57.9	81.7	67.8	51.4	81.7
GIR	61.9	72.0	66.5	55.6	72.0
SANDSAVE	36.6	63.8	49.5	29.3	63.8
TOTALPUT	28.39	30.28	29.42	28.39	31.08
PUTTPER	1.736	1.838	1.791	1.736	1.931
SHORTGAM	1.226	1.395	1.342	NA	NA
PRACTIME	5	37.5	20.32	NA	NA
PRACDRIV	.96	5.625	2.744	NA	NA
PRACPUTT	1.2	11.25	5.463	NA	NA
PRACIRON	1	12	5.774	NA	NA
PRACSAND	.25	7.5	2.355	NA	NA
PRACSHRT	.5	7.5	3.231	NA	NA
SKILL	.293	1	.626	0	1
WINNINGS	122,181	653,296	256,407	NA	653,296
WINPER	4,350	34,384	9,634	NA	NA

Notes: DRIVDIST is measured in yards. DRIVACC, GIR, and SANDSAVE are measured in percentage times 100. TOTALPUT, PUTTPER, and SHORTGAM are measured in number of putts. PRACTIME, PRACDRIV, PRACPUTT, PRACIRON, PRACSAND, and PRACSHRT are measured in hours per week. SKILL is measured in percentile from the worst to best skill level in each relevant category. WINNINGS and WINPER are measured in 1986 dollars.

There are two measures of putting ability. TOTALPUT is the total number of putts made per eighteen holes. This measure does not accurately

---

[10]Reaching the green in regulation means hitting the ball on the green in two shots less than par. The golfer is then allowed two putts to obtain par for the hole.

capture putting skill, however, because a player who hits greens in regulation often ends up hitting relatively long putts, while a player who misses the green with the approach shot usually ends up with a short putt. PUTTPER, the average number of putts taken only on greens reached in regulation, corrects this problem. The better measure, PUTTPER, is used in the regressions below. For each putting measure, a lower number indicates a higher skill.

There is no published measure of short game ability. A proxy for this skill can be constructed, however, from the other variables. A player with a good short game is able to hit chip shots close enough to the hole so as to finish the hole with only one putt. More often, a player without this ability will need two putts. Since the short game typically comes into play when the approach shot misses the green, the proxy for the short game skill is the average number of putts on the greens *not* reached in regulation. This variable is called SHORTGAM. Although the PGA TOUR does not keep this statistic, it can be calculated from statistics that the Tour does keep.[11] Again, a lower number indicates a higher skill. It is useful to compare the average PUTTPER in the sample, at 1.791, with the average SHORTGAM at 1.342. As expected, SHORTGAM is lower because the putts left after chips, pitches, or bunker shots will be shorter on average than the birdie putts remaining after a green is reached in regulation.

To obtain data on golfers' practice schedules, the sixty golfers were contacted through their business managers. The business managers agreed to forward a cover letter and a questionnaire on a return postcard to the professionals. The survey asked for the average number of hours per week spent on practice, and for the breakdown of that time among the five skills: driving; putting; irons; sand; and short game. This information led to the formation of the following variables: PRACTIME; PRACDRIV; PRACPUTT; PRACIRON; PRACSAND; and PRACSHRT. Eleven responses were received.[12]

---

[11]Given our notation the formula for SHORTGAM is:
SHORTGAM = ((100/18)TOTALPUT - GIR(PUTTPER))/(100 - GIR).

[12]I am deeply indebted to the following PGA TOUR golfers who graciously responded to my survey: Paul Azinger, John Cook, Rick Fehr, Raymond Floyd, Scott Hoch, Bernhard Langer, Bruce Lietzke, Greg Norman, Nick Price, J. C. Snead, and D. A. Weibring.

The golfers responses to the questionnaire evidenced a great deal of variation. Leading money winner, Greg Norman, took part, indicating that he practiced an average of 35-40 hours per week, which I scaled to 37.5 hours. Norman was the most prolific at practice. At the other end of the scale, the notoriously low practicing, Bruce Lietzke, also took part, indicating that he practiced an average of 5 hours per week. There was also a lot of variation in how these golfers spent their practice time. Five golfers spent more time practicing putting than any other skill, and five golfers spent the most time on their irons. The eleventh respondent, Paul Azinger, reported that he split his practice time evenly among all the skills.

To mitigate the weak results generated by only eleven observations, a pooled sample was created to estimate a generalized skill production function. The pooled sample was created in the following manner. The highest and lowest values for each of the skills over all golf professionals, not just the sixty in the sample, determines the relevant range for each of the skills. For example, for DRIVDIST the range is from 243.4 to 285.7, a distance of 41.3 yards. Each golfer's skill level in each skill category falls somewhere in the middle of the relevant range. Each golfer's raw skill (ie. distance or percentage or number of putts, etc.) was transformed into a percentile ranking over the total distance from the poorest skill level to the highest skill level in each category. For example, a golfer whose driving distance was 253.4 yards (which is ten yards longer than the shortest), would get a percentile ranking of 0.242 which is 10 divided by 41.3. Since all skills are measured on a zero-to-one scale, pooling is made possible. The pooled skill variable is simply called SKILL.

10.3 The Relationship Between Skills and Earnings

A multiple regression determines the relative importance of each of the skills. The first regression uses the total dollar winnings per year, WINNINGS, as the dependent variable. The skills mentioned above are the explanatory variables. In addition to the physical skills, a mental aspect of the game may be important. In part, the mental aspect deals with concentration, and will already be captured in the outcome of the physical skills. There is, however, a mental aspect that has to do with judgment developed through experience.

The first equation to be estimated, therefore, includes EXPERNCE, the number of years the golfer has been a professional.[13] The equation is:

$$\text{WINNINGS} = f(\text{DRIVDIST, DRIVACC, GIR SANDSAVE,}$$
$$\text{PUTTPER, SHORTGAM, EXPERNCE}) \quad (10.1)$$

The functional form is linear, and includes a constant term. All equations are estimated with ordinary least squares. The results appear in Table 10.2. All of the variables have the right sign. Significant regressors are DRIVDIST, IRONS, and PUTTPER.

The interpretation of the results is straightforward. For example, an extra yard on each drive, on average, yields over $6700 extra earnings over the course of the year. An extra percentage point in driving accuracy would yield over $2000 in extra yearly earnings but the result is not significant. Contrary to the expectations of some golf analysts at the time, driving distance is an important skill, even more important than driving accuracy. The mistaken impression that accuracy is more important is created by casual empiricism and Table 10.1, but is not supported by the multiple regression analysis. Table 10.1, for example, shows that the golfer with the overall best driving accuracy, at 81.7%, is among the seventy top money winners, while the longest driver, at 285.7 yards, is not among the seventy top money winners. From this we might be tempted to infer that accuracy is more important. However, when other skills are considered simultaneously, the result is that distance is more important.[14] A new adage,

---

[13]EXPERNCE^2 was also tried. Experience leads to better performance in the golfer's early career or up to a point where advanced age starts to detract from the golfer's earnings. Krohn explores this possibility for baseball players with some good results. See, Krohn, G. A., "Measuring the Experience Productivity Relationship: The Case of Major League Baseball," *Journal of Business Economics and Statistics*, Vol. 1, (Oct. 1983), pp. 273-9. Here, however, EXPERNCE^2 was insignificant.

[14]Multicollinearity is a possible explanation for the insignificance of DRIVACC to the extent that its effect is already captured by DRIVDIST and GIR. Regressions with one of the three variables omitted tend to support this contention. For example, when DRIVACC is omitted, the coefficients and t-values of DRIVDIST and GIR go up. When GIR is omitted, the coefficients and t-values of DRIVDIST and DRIVACC go up, and DRIVACC is now a significant regressor. The other coefficients are largely unaffected by the

"Drive for show, and for dough," may be appropriate. Indeed, John "Grip it and rip it" Daly has had more success than Mike "Radar" Reid.

Table 10.2 O.L.S. estimations of Eqs. (10.1-10.2), (t-statistics).

Equation	10.1	10.2
Dependent Variable	WINNINGS	WINPER
Constant	3,192,571	164,683
	(2.015)	(2.540)
DRIVDIST	6775	341.10
	(2.756)	(3.391)
DRIVACC	2063	170.02
	(.505)	(1.017)
GIR	16,037	495.19
	(2.148)	(1.621)
SANDSAVE	64.99	-4.23
	(.029)	(-.047)
PUTTPER	-2,979,565	-136,040
	(-4.757)	(-5.307)
SHORTGAM	-453,858	-35,549
	(-1.143)	(-2.189)
EXPERNCE	1539	202.52
	(.593)	(1.907)
adjusted R^2	.439	.516
n	60	60

It is also possible to comment on the tradeoff between distance and accuracy. The regression tells us that an extra yard of distance is over three times as valuable as an extra percentage point of accuracy. Consider the following. A PGA TOUR professional may sacrifice 20 yards or more by teeing off with a 3-wood or 1-iron instead of a driver. In order for this to be a reasonable tradeoff, the golfer should desire more than a 60 percentage

exclusion of either DRIVDIST or GIR. To some extent, this should be expected because DRIVACC and GIR measure a skill of accurate shotmaking. However, it is not universally true that accurate drivers are accurate iron players. Furthermore, accuracy off the tee is mostly a matter of direction control, while accuracy on approach shots is a matter of both direction control and distance control.

point increase in accuracy to make up for the lost distance. Since the wildest professional already hits the fairway over 50% of the time, an increase of 60 percentage points would be impossible. These numbers imply that it would be a mistake for professional golfers to hit 1-irons instead of drivers as a general practice. In fact, tour professionals do not make this mistake.

There are situations, however, where the probability of hitting the fairway with a driver is considerably lower than usual. Consider, for example, a tight dogleg where keeping a driver on the fairway would happen only about 20% of the time. Meanwhile, if a 1-iron could be played safely over 80% of the time, then the sacrifice in distance could be made up by the increased accuracy. Such a situation is precisely the time when professionals should, and do, leave the driver in the bag.

Accuracy with irons is also very important; an extra percentage point added to GIR increases yearly earnings by over $16,000.

The putting variable is the most important. One less putt per green reached in regulation yields almost $3 million in extra earnings per year. This, of course, is a terribly large sum for something that is terribly difficult to do. Nevertheless, the magnitude of this coefficient is plausible. Instead of one less putt per green reached in regulation, consider one less putt per tournament. Since tournaments usually consist of 72 holes, with 66.5 percent or about 48 of the holes reached in regulation, the $3 million figure is divided by 48 to yield about $62,500 extra earnings per year. At the sample average of 27.53 tournaments per year this yields about $2270 extra dollars per tournament. This is a reasonable figure. Whereas one putt might mean $40,000 or more for the leaders in 1986, for those in the middle of the pack one less putt means the difference of a thousand dollars or so. At the low end of the winnings, one putt means only ten or twenty dollars.

The least important of the skills is bunker shot ability measured by SANDSAVE. The payoff to an extra percentage point of success in sandsaves is only about $65 per year. Consider a ten percentage point increase in this skill from 50% to 60%. The increased skill will lead to increased earnings of about $650. This seemingly low figure is reasonable considering that a pro who hits into 10 bunkers over the course of a 72-hole tournament will save par six times instead of five for a savings of only one stroke, and will probably not be among the leaders anyway.

As a check on the robustness of these results, several other specifications were tested. In general, the results stand up well. Putting and driving distance are the two most important skills. Accuracy with irons and short game skills are the next most important--always bearing the right sign but sometimes lacking in statistical significance. Driving accuracy is the right sign but not statistically significant. SANDSAVE consistently is insignificant, and, on one occasion, has the wrong sign.

The second equation replaces yearly winnings with winnings per tournament as the dependent variable:

$$\text{WINPER} = f(\text{DRIVDIST, DRIVACC, GIR, SANDSAVE,} \\ \text{PUTTPER, SHORTGAM, EXPERNCE}) \quad (10.2)$$

Except for SANDSAVE, which is not significant, the results agree with Eq. (10.1). DRIVDIST and PUTTPER still have the largest t-statistics. SHORTGAM now is significant while GIR has lost some in terms of significance. Driving accuracy still seems unimportant. However, experience is now a significant regressor. The adjusted R-squared improves from the first equation to .516.

Another variant of this relationship replaced all variables from Eq. (10.2) with their natural logarithms. In such an equation the coefficient estimates may be interpreted as elasticities. All the estimated elasticities were the anticipated sign. Putting and driving distance were still the most important, both in terms of the absolute value of the elasticity and in terms of statistical significance. Even the magnitude of the estimated elasticities corresponds closely to the results of Eq. (10.1). For example, the estimated elasticity of WINPER with respect to PUTTPER was -17.7. This means that a one percent *decrease* in putts taken on greens reached in regulation leads to 17.7 percent higher earnings per tournament. To put this in perspective, a one percent decrease in PUTTPER amounts to a little less than one putt per tournament and yields about $1705 increased earnings per tournament; this result is in line with the $2270 figure calculated above for Eq. (10.1).

This section shows that different skills have different values in terms of producing earnings. However, golfers will not necessarily concentrate efforts on the most valuable skill, since it may also be the hardest to improve. We now turn to the relationship between practice and the achieved skill levels.

10.4 The Relationship Between Practice and Skills

For each of the skills, a separate regression was run using the lagged value of the skill as a proxy for the received stock of skill, which is a fixed input, and the practice hours per week as the variable input. Using S to denote DRIVDIST, DRIVACC, etc., and PRACS to denote PRACDRIV, PRACIRON, etc., the regression equations, one for each skill, are:

$$S = f(S_{t-1}, PRACS) \ . \tag{10.3}$$

The results, in Table 10.3, for practicing driving distance and putting are significant, and in the expected direction. An hour of practice per week increases the average drive by 1.79 yards; an hour of practice per week on putting decreases putts taken per green reached in regulation by .006. The remaining results are disappointing. Most of the estimated coefficients are insignificant and, curiously, a significant negative coefficient is calculated for practicing driving accuracy.[15]

The coefficient of the lagged level of skill allows for a discussion of the depreciation of the human capital that has been previously developed. If skills did not depreciate with time, then last year's skill level should give a perfect prediction of this year's skill level, and the estimated coefficient should be equal to one. Practice would serve to increase the skill level but would not be needed to maintain whatever skill was already there. To the extent that the estimated coefficient is less than one, however, it means that a portion of the skills disappear through time. For example, if the coefficient

---

[15]This result might be understandable. Ordinarily, a golfer would not practice a skill if the outcome of practice was to decrease the golfer's ability in the skill. For driving, however, the golfer may simultaneously practice for distance and accuracy. Since distance increases with practice, the gains in increased distance may offset the loss from poorer accuracy. Indeed, Eqs. (10.1) and (10.2) indicated that distance was important and accuracy was not. In another light, increased distance may make accuracy harder to achieve as well as less important. For example, a long drive that just rolls slightly off the fairway may still be a better shot than a shorter drive in the same direction that stays in the fairway.

is 0.75, it means that 25% of last year's ability will disappear if not maintained and replaced through current practice.

Table 10.3 O. L. S. estimations of Eqs. (10.3), (t-statistics).

Dependent Variable	Constant	S_{t-1}[a]	PRACS[b]	adjusted R^2
DRIVDIST	64.15	.732	1.789	.670
	(1.054)	(3.152)	(2.400)	
DRIVACC	11.19	.903	-1.102	.814
	(.788)	(4.354)	(-3.159)	
GIR	42.16	.375	-.095	.152
	(2.010)	(1.229)	(-.491)	
SANDSAVE	59.08	-0.180	1.446	0
	(1.775)	(-.271)	(1.405)	
PUTTPER	1.950	-.074	-.006	.616
	(3.085)	(-.213)	(-4.233)	
SHORTGAM	1.706	-.301	-.004	0
	(3.007)	(-.670)	(-.645)	

Notes: S_{t-1} is the lagged value of the dependent variable. PRACS stands for PRACDRIV, PRACIRON, PRACSAND, PRACPUTT or PRACSHRT whichever is relevant.

The results for the lagged skill level are encouraging. The variable is significant for driving distance and driving accuracy, less so for accuracy with irons, and unimportant for sand shots, short game, and putting. These results are plausible. The skill of hitting drives and iron shots should not deteriorate that rapidly. However, putting, short game, and bunker shots, all of which require a lot of touch, will be less related to their past levels because these skills deteriorate more rapidly.

Several other specifications of the skill production function were estimated to improve the poor results, and to check the robustness of the good results. The insignificant lagged skill level from Eq. (10.3) was dropped: the practice time was entered as a quadratic to check for diminishing marginal productivity: and the practice time was entered as a square root to force a diminishing marginal product. The results for relationships between practice and driving distance, and between practice and putting, are robust. These estimations yielded significant coefficients with the correct sign in each of the functional forms. However, while some specifications lead to good results for the remaining skills, most of the time the coefficients are insignificant.

There are too many permutations to report all the results. Table 10.4 lists a sample of the results, choosing one equation for each of the skills. Except for the driving distance equation, the results reported are those equations with the highest adjusted R^2. Keep in mind, however, that robust inferences are warranted only for the cases of driving distance and putting ability. Table 10.4 shows that the best form of the skill production equation is quadratic for driving accuracy. The best form for SANDSAVE and PUTTPER is a constant MP with no received stock of skills. The best form for SHORTGAM and for GIR has no received stock of skills and a declining marginal product because PRACSHRT and PRACIRON are entered as square roots.

Table 10.4 Various estimates of skill production functions, (t-statistics).

Dependent Variable	Constant	S_{t-1}	PRACS	PRACS^2	PRACS$^{1/2}$	adj.R^2
DRIVDIST	47.24 (.768)	.781 (3.315)			5.635 (2.201)	.646
DRIVACC	17.13 (1.405)	.868 (4.986)	-4.037 (-2.846)	.439 (2.114)		.870
GIR	-3.012 (-2.45)				1.29 (2.414)	.305
SANDSAVE	49.25 (15.987)		1.395 (1.456)			.101
PUTTPER	1.815 (207.9)		-.006 (-4.490)			.657
SHORTGAM	1.341 (50.35)				-.020 (-1.284)	.056

Note: The result in Table 10.3 is actually a better fit for DRIVDIST. This result is presented for comparison.

Undoubtedly, a problem with discovering robust relationships lies in the small sample size rather than in the lack of systematic relationships between practice and skill level to begin with. To explore this possibility, a pooled data set was created to estimate a general skill production function. The dependent variable, SKILL, ranging from zero to one, is the percentile ranking of the individual golfer's skill over the range of that skill, from worst to best, for all golfers.[16] The simplest formulation is:

$$SKILL = f(SKILL_{t-1}, PRACTICE) \quad . \qquad (10.4)$$

Table 10.5 lists the results. One minus the coefficient of the lagged dependent variable is the depreciation rate of the golfer's skill averaged over all skills. The coefficient is .285 which means that the depreciation rate is 71.5%. Remember, however, that complete depreciation drops one's skill level to zero, which as far as this data is concerned, is not too bad, because zero, here, means the lowest of all professional golfers which is still very good on an absolute scale.

The coefficient of the practice variable represents the average MP of practice. One hour per week more of practice leads to a 2.7 percentage point increase in the percentile ranking of the golfer's skill. Some numerical examples will put this in perspective. In driving distance, the shortest yardage for 1986 was 243.4 yards, and the longest yardage was 285.7. The difference in these distances is 42.3 yards, so that each percentage point of improvement translates into .423 yards. An additional hour per week of practice on driving would increase driving distance by 1.14 yards (.423 times 2.7).

For putting the numbers are as follows. The worst putter took an average of 1.932 putts per green reached in regulation. The best putter took an average of 1.736 putts per green reached in regulation. The difference between these figures is .195 so that a one percentage point improvement translates into .00195 fewer putts per green reached in regulation. Therefore, an additional hour per week of putting practice would lead to .005256 fewer putts per green reached in regulation. Since on average about

---

[16]Both putting and short game ability are now measured with higher numbers indicating higher skill. Therefore, a positive coefficient with respect to practice time is expected.

48 greens are reached in regulation in a 72-hole tournament, the latter figure translates into about .25 fewer putts each tournament.

Table 10.5 O. L. S. estimations of Eqs. (10.4) and (10.6), (t-statistics).

Equation	10.4	10.6
Dependent Variable	SKILL	SKILL
Constant	.336	.403
	(3.458)	(2.967)
SKILL$_{t-1}$	.285	.033
	(1.793)	(.139)
PRACTICE	.027	
	(3.946)	
PRACDRIVDIST		.025
		(1.031)
PRACDRIVACC		.109
		(1.713)
PRACIRONS		.030
		(1.783)
PRACSAND		.041
		(1.659)
PRACPUTT		.044
		(3.812)
PRACSHORT		.0007
		(.038)
adjusted R^2	.184	.254

Other functional forms for this production function were also examined. In a result not reported here, there was no evidence in favor of a declining marginal product of practice from the inclusion of PRACTICE^2 to Eq. (10.4).

Perhaps the MP of practice should not be the same for golfers situated differently with respect to the received level of skill. Indeed, maybe the fixed input, received skill, as well as the variable input, practice hours, are mutually detracting. In a certain sense this has to be true since the golfer who starts out near the top of the percentile ranking for a particular skill cannot improve appreciably, no matter how much time he spends practicing the skill. The way to explore this possibility is to add to Eq. (10.4) a term composed of the product of the practice time and the lagged skill level, as in:

$$\text{SKILL} = f(\text{SKILL}_{t-1}, \text{PRACTICE}, \text{SKILL}^{t-1} \text{xPRACTICE}) \quad . \quad (10.5)$$

The expected sign for the interactive variable is negative. The data do not support this possibility. The coefficient of the interactive variable is insignificant and the significance of the practice variable itself disappears.

The result of one more regression is reported in Table 10.5. It is possible to calculate separate marginal products of practice for each of the skills. Let D be a set of vector dummy variables, where each vector separates out the effect of one of the skills. When D is interactive with PRACTICE we get different marginal products for each of the skills. Formally:

$$\text{SKILL} = f(\text{SKILL}_{t-1}, \text{DxPRACTICE}) \quad . \quad (10.6)$$

This formulation offers a slight improvement over Eq. (10.4). In Eq. (10.6) the marginal product of practice is still constant with respect to practice but can be different for each skill. The magnitude of these estimates runs from 10.9 percentage points for driving accuracy to practically zero (seven-hundredths of a percentage point) for the short game. As has been consistently the case, the putting variable is the most significant.

10.5 The Value of the Marginal Product of Practice

By combining the estimates from the previous two sections it is possible to calculate the VMP of practice time for each skill. Value maximization requires these VMPs to equal the marginal cost of practice time for each skill. If the VMPs are not equal across skills when the marginal costs of practice are, then the golfer's practice time can be spent more profitably.

Given that the most robust inferences from above concern putting ability and driving distance, the most interest surrounds the calculation of VMPs for these two skills. Estimates of the VMPs for the other skills will be presented but generally have large standard errors owing to the imprecision of the relevant estimates from above. There were two calculations of the value of each skill, one from Eq. (10.1) with the dependent variable equal to yearly winnings, and one from Eq. (10.2) for winnings per tournament. Furthermore, there were several different calculations of the marginal product of practice for each skill. Thus, there are many permutations that can be used in the calculation of the VMPs. Table 10.6 lists the results, indicating which combination of the above regressions was used.

To understand Table 10.6, consider the calculations behind just one of the entries, the $302 figure listed for the VMP of practice on putting calculated from Eqs. (10.1) and (10.4). Equation (10.4) tells us that an extra hour per week of practice will increase a skill by .027 or by 2.7 percentage points. Putting skill has a total range of .195 putts per green in regulation which comes from the best and worst values for putting skill of 1.736 and 1.931. Therefore, each percentage point is worth .00195 putts per green, which, multiplied by 2.7 percentage points, yields an improvement in putting of .05265 putts per green. Multiplying this *decrease* by -2,979,565, which is the coefficient of the putting variable in Eq. (10.1) yields a yearly increase of $15,687. Since this comes from an increased practice of an hour *per week*, we must divide by 52 to obtain the value of $302 per hour which appears in the table. The other figures are calculated accordingly.

In Table 10.6 the column headed DRIVDIST lists the estimates of the VMP of one hour per year of practice on driving distance measured in dollars of extra earnings per year. The estimates range from $138 per hour to $323 per hour. Meanwhile, the range for practicing driving accuracy is from negative to $298 per hour. The rest of the columns are interpreted in the same manner. Each entry is the estimated VMP of one hour of practice on the indicated skill. Practice on putting has the biggest payoff, ranging from a low of $302 per hour to a high of $618 per hour. The pros not only "putt for dough," they practice putting for dough.

Since practice on driving distance and driving accuracy are undertaken simultaneously, perhaps these two columns should be added to get the total return to practice on driving. Reading across the table shows that the VMP of practice on putting is still greater than that for practicing driving. That is, the sum of the numbers in columns headed DRIVDIST and DRIVACC is less than the VMP reported for practice on putting in the column headed PUTTPER. These numbers indicate that extra practice time would be better spent on putting than on driving.

These numbers also uncover the following conundrum. Economic theory indicates that VMPs should be equalized when the same input can be used to produce different outputs. But the statistics developed here indicate that

Table 10.6 Estimates of the VMP of practice of various skills.

Equations	DRIVDIST	DRIVACC	GIR	SANDSAVE	PUTTPER	SHORTGAM
10.1 and 10.3	233 (134)	(-)	(-)	2 (76)	344 (110)	35 (78)
10.1 and Table 10.4	221 (134)	(-)	83 (54)	2 (73)	344 (107)	48 (66)
10.1 and 10.4	149 (67)	32 (66)	128 (70)	1 (36)	302 (101)	44 (41)
10.1 and 10.6	138 (151)	131 (310)	142 (110)	2 (81)	492 (168)	1 (35)
10.2 and 10.3	323 (170)	(-)	(-)	(-)	432 (132)	75 (132)
10.2 and Table 10.4	307 (171)	(-)	70 (55)	(-)	432 (127)	105 (102)
10.2 and 10.4	206 (82)	74 (71)	109 (75)	(-)	379 (121)	95 (51)
10.2 and 10.6	191 (185)	298 (357)	121 (109)	(-)	618 (202)	2 (58)

Notes: Estimates are in dollars per year per hour of practice. The first column lists the equations used to calculate the dollar estimates of VMP. Each VMP estimate is essentially the product of two random variables (the coefficient estimates) drawn from separate distributions. The resulting distribution is not normal but means and variances can be calculated, see Frischman[17]. The standard errors are in parentheses.

[17]Frischman, Fred, "On the Arithmetic Means and Variances of Products and Ratios of Random Variables," in G. P. Patil et. al. (eds.), *Statistical Distributions in Scientific Work*, Vol. 1, D. Reidel Publishing Company, (Dordrecht-Holland, 1975), pp. 401-406.

practice on putting has a higher payoff than practice on driving. This is a paradox suggesting that the professional golfers do not know what they are doing. Perhaps the resolution of the paradox is simple. The differences in the VMPs are not always significant with a high statistical level of confidence. In this sense, the hypothesis that the golfer equalizes VMPs across skills, cannot be rejected.

But the point estimates do differ systematically. Practice on putting is always worth more. If we wish to reject neither the theory nor the numbers, there must be some reconciliation to the paradox. I can think of two possibilities. First, remember that VMPs should be equalized only if the marginal cost of practice is equal across skills. There is a significant amount of anecdotal evidence that practicing putting is especially hard on the muscles of the lower back. If practicing putting is more strenuous than the other skills, then the maximizing golfer will stop practicing putting even though it has a higher VMP than some other practice activity.

The second possible explanation goes back to human capital theory. Practicing golf skills is a costly (in the sense that it takes time) investment that pays off in the future. The payoff can occur in the near term only, or over an extended future, depending on how quickly the skills deteriorate. We have seen that putting skills depreciate almost fully each year but that roughly 75% of the skill measured by DRIVDIST does not depreciate. This means that the practice time spent on driving will pay off this year, and will pay off again to a 75% extent next year, and will pay off again to 75% of a 75% extent the year after, and so on. At this 25% depreciation or discount rate, the present value of the long term series of gains is roughly four times the current gain. Even after considering additional discount factors to take care of the market rate of interest, and the risk of shortened time horizons due to possible injury or impending retirement, the VMP of practice on driving, as reported in the table, could still be enhanced by a factor of two or three which would bring it into line with the VMP of practice on putting. Either of these two explanations means that the statistics developed here are consistent with economically rational behavior on the part of professional golfers.

Regarding the other skills, the standard errors are high with respect to the estimates themselves, so not too much attention is worthwhile.[18] Practice on approach shot accuracy as measured by GIR is the next most important after putting and driving. It is worth about one hundred dollars per hour, although the range for this VMP goes from negative to $142. Short game skills are the next most valuable to practice. The VMP for practice on the short game ranges from $1 to $105 per hour. Practice on bunker shots is consistently the least important.

These results indicate that golfers could more profitably use their practice time by spending less on bunker shots, where they spend very little anyway; by spending less on the short game and irons, where they spend a great deal; and by spending more on putting and driving in that order.

All of the results enumerated here, of course, are averages. For some professionals, or for some skills, the figures may be more or less. However, this is at least a first attempt to develop some objective figures on the value of one of the things that professional golfers do so much. Television coverage of tournaments has made the payoffs and glamour of winning on the PGA TOUR very visible. Behind the scenes, however, there are hours and hours of practice to build up and maintain the skills necessary to win in the first place. Instead of "drive for show; putt for dough," the statistics calculated here tell a story that brings to mind a different adage, "Practice makes perfect."

---

[18]The reporting of standard errors of the value of marginal product of practice is also an improvement over much of the literature in other sports which reports only point estimates.

## Chapter 11

Tournament Compensation in the Boardroom

A controversial issue in today's economy is the astronomical level of compensation earned by the C.E.O.'s of many large corporations. Including current salaries, bonuses, and lucrative deferred compensation in the form of stock options and pensions, as well as expense accounts and fringe benefits, many C.E.O.'s earn multiple millions of dollars per year. Could they really be worth that much? Except for some who are simply envious of those earning more, it is easy to answer in the affirmative if the company in question is growing rapidly and increasing its earnings and its stock price. If the C.E.O. earns millions but the company's stockholders collectively earn multiple billions, then the stockholders in question would not be unhappy. The idea that pay for performance is efficacious has a well-established pedigree. If the company has performed handsomely, and salaries are connected to performance, why begrudge the lavish payments made to those in charge?

But what if the market is falling? Can the firm that is downsizing, losing profits, and seeing a decline in its stock value still justify the large salaries? If the idea is "pay for performance," and if the firm is losing money, then maybe the C.E.O.'s salary should be low or even negative. Yet there are many cases where those who preside over money-losing companies still earn multiple millions. Some people draw the conclusion that the management teams in these companies are able to pull the wool over the eyes of the stockholders. But most find that this argument is not a convincing one because, in most cases of large corporations paying multimillion-dollar salaries, the stockholder groups are dominated by savvy institutional investors who both know better, and have the power to instigate change. The question remains, why or how are the multimillion-dollar salaries of upper-echelon executives justified?

This chapter draws on an important insight from modern labor economics to shed light on the question of why corporate executives earn so much, and, particularly, why they earn so much more than their immediate subordinates. In an important paper by economists Edward P. Lazear and Sherwin Rosen[1], an analogy is drawn between the pay scales at the upper levels of corporate management and the distribution of prize funds in a typical sports tournament. The link to golf comes from ingenious tests of the theory that economists Ronald Ehrenberg and Michael Bognanno carry out using golf statistics.[2] In this chapter we have an example in which something immediate and important about the world outside of golf can be tested by examination of sports statistics.

The remainder of the chapter is divided into three sections. First, the essence of tournament compensation is described as it applies, literally, to golf tournaments and, figuratively, in managerial compensation packages. Second, some of the underlying economic problems that arise in trying to develop salary and promotion packages are highlighted, as are the ways that tournament-reminiscent salary schemes address those problems. Finally, in the third section, evidence from golf tournaments is brought to bear on the implications of the theory.

11.1 The Essence of Tournament Compensation

There are two things about tournament compensation that are important for our purposes. The first is that relative performance matters while absolute performance does not. The second is that the reward to superior relative performance, in terms of the prize that the competitor wins, is not linearly

---

[1]See, Lazear, E. P. and S. Rosen, "Rank-Order Tournaments as Optimum Labor Contracts," *Journal of Political Economy*, 89 (October 1981), pp. 841-64.

[2]See, Ehrenberg, R. G. and M. L. Bognanno, "Do Tournaments Have Incentive Effects?," *Journal of Political Economy*, 98 (December 1990a), pp. 1307-24, and Ehrenberg, R. G. and M. L. Bognanno, "The Incentive Effects of Tournaments Revisited: Evidence from the European PGA Tour," *Industrial and Labor Relations Review*, 43 (Supp. February 1990b) pp. 742-88s.

related to one's finishing rank in the tournament. These will be explained in turn.

The issue of relative performance versus absolute performance is a common theme in the economics of competition. To win a sports competition, for example, one does not have to meet any preset standard, one only has to beat all of the other contestants. Furthermore, whether one wins by a lot or a little has no bearing on the division of the prizes. A horse race could be won in a photo finish or by several lengths; a golf tournament could be won in a playoff or by ten or more strokes. Spectators may be especially awed by large margins of victory, or by record-setting performances, but, in most cases, a win is a win is a win, and the payoff is the same.[3]

Relative performance is also important in economic competition. There are many cases in which a consumer has to decide between or among competing manufacturers of a product. When buying a printer for a computer, for example, the manufacturer can never be assured of a sale simply by meeting some absolute, preset standard; say, in terms of pages per minute. Even if consumers only care about the speed of the printer, sales are guaranteed only to the fastest printer (a standard that changes relative to the offerings of competitors). Obviously, consumers care about dimensions other than speed. They also care about price, durability, reputation, and so on, though the principle remains the same. The consumer looks at all the factors he or she deems relevant, then chooses the best printer. Each consumer chooses one printer, the one he or she deems to be better than all the others. This is a relative standard. In an absolute standard, the consumer would buy every printer, or perhaps the first printer sampled, that met all of the multidimensional preset criteria; for example, every printer under $200 that could print both in black and white and in color, at least 8 pages per minute, carrying a 3-year warranty, etc. This is not the way consumers make decisions.

[3]There are exceptions. A record-breaking or tying performance is judged against a pre-existing absolute standard, and may carry with it a special prize. But the existence of special prizes for special absolute feats (for example a special prize for setting a course record or hitting a hole-in-one) is not the part of the compensation that is germane to our argument.

For economic decisions, whether a relative standard or an absolute standard is used depends on the importance of the decision and the cost of using each standard. The more important the decision, the more likely that a relative, rather than an absolute, standard will be used. Furthermore, many decisions may actually require a combination of absolute and relative standards. Consider an unimportant decision like picking an avocado at the supermarket. I desire a suitably ripe avocado, and start squeezing them in the produce section. If I am in a hurry I will probably take the first one that feels suitably soft but not overly soft. This is a pure absolute standard. I would not use a relative standard in this case because it is too costly in terms of time to sample each fruit and then choose the best one.

If I am in less of a rush, I might squeeze other avocados even after finding a suitable one, and then choose the one that is best, relative to the others, among all those I have sampled. But, assuming I encounter an avocado display of at least moderate size, I would probably not squeeze every avocado in the store. This is a combination of a relative standard and an absolute standard.

If the decision were important, suppose, fantastically, that there was a large monetary prize for choosing the best avocado in the store, then I would sample every one, and choose the best. This would be a pure relative standard.

The issue of relative standards versus absolute standards pops up in a variety of settings. Some colleges admit as freshman any student who meets a predefined standard in terms of high school grade point average and standardized test scores. This is an absolute standard. Other colleges can limit the number of applicants who get serious consideration by using absolute standards in a first cut; but the ultimate decision as to entry depends on each application's relative standing among those who make the first cut. The latter type of college is usually the more academically exclusive. Getting into medical school involves a relative competition against all other applicants for entry. However, becoming a licensed doctor (or a licensed driver, for that matter), requires a specific level of absolute performance on a certification examination, regardless of how well all the other test takers perform. Admission to the bar to practice law has, in some cases, been controversial because of the differences between relative and absolute standards. The secretive and somewhat subjective nature of the grading of bar exams, and the self-interest that members of bar associations have in limiting entry, cause some to suspect that a relative standard of passing only the top x%, however good or bad they are, is being used instead of an absolute standard of passing everyone who demonstrates the required minimum level of competence.

To get a glimpse of why the difference between a relative performance standard and an absolute performance standard is important, reconsider the college admission example. In particular, consider the effort that prospective applicants have to put forth if they want to enter either of the two types of schools. With an absolute standard, the student can stop working as soon as the standard is met, and still be guaranteed an offer of admission. With a relative standard, the student can never be sure of admission because it depends on the achievements of all the other applicants. The student who really wants to go to the exclusive campus with the relative standards has to keep working even after the minimum absolute standards are met. The fact that trying to meet a relative standard causes one to put forth more effort is a crucial feature that the relative performance standard brings to the table.

The second issue in this section has to do with the pattern of tournament winnings as they relate to one's placement in the order of finishers. Economists believe that the highly nonlinear relationship between one's finish in a tournament and the prize he receives is an important factor. The relationship can be illustrated diagrammatically or in a tabular fashion. Figure 11.1 illustrates the percentage breakdown of the prize fund for the first 20 places in a PGA TOUR sanctioned golf tournament. The nonlinear relationship can clearly be seen. Table 11.1 lists the actual percentage breakdown and dollar amounts for all money winners in a PGA TOUR event with a total prize fund of $4,000,000. As is typical in tournaments, an outright winner must be declared for first place, and this might necessitate a playoff. However, ties for all other places will be left as they stand with the money prizes for the effected places simply added together and divided equally among all those in the tie. In a three-way tie for second place for example, the sum of the second, third, and fourth prizes is divided by three to determine the prize each will receive. The next best finisher gets the fifth place prize money, etc.

In sports competitions, in particular for golf tournaments, we have seen how prizes are related to relative performance in a highly nonlinear fashion.

The pattern of salaries in upper level management positions is somewhat reminiscent of the pattern of money prizes in a typical golf tournament. In particular, as one works one's way up the pyramidical structure of management to higher and higher positions of authority, the increases in salary get larger and larger. That is to say, a substantial raise may accompany being promoted from assistant vice president (of which the company might have hundreds) to vice president (of which the company

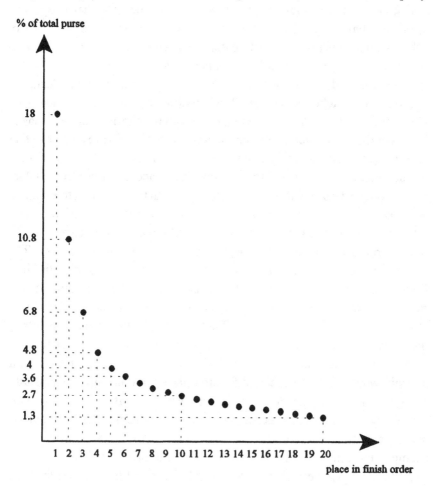

Fig. 11.1 PGA TOUR prize distribution percentages.

Table 11.1 Prize distribution table.

Place	% of Purse	$ amount	Place	% of Purse	$ amount
1	18.0	720,000	36	.515	20,600
2	10.8	432,000	37	.49	19,600
3	6.8	272,000	38	.47	18,800
4	4.8	192,000	39	.45	18,000
5	4.0	160,000	40	.43	17,200
6	3.6	144,000	41	.41	16,400
7	3.35	134,000	42	.39	15,600
8	3.1	124,000	43	.37	14,800
9	2.9	116,000	44	.35	14,000
10	2.7	108,000	45	.33	13,200
11	2.5	100,000	46	.31	12,400
12	2.3	92,000	47	.29	11,600
13	2.1	84,000	48	.274	10,960
14	1.9	76,000	49	.26	10,400
15	1.8	72,000	50	.252	10,080
16	1.7	68,000	51	.246	9,840
17	1.6	64,000	52	.24	9,600
18	1.5	60,000	53	.236	9,440
19	1.4	56,000	54	.232	9,280
20	1.3	52,000	55	.23	9,200
21	1.2	48,000	56	.228	9,120
22	1.12	44,800	57	.226	9,040
23	1.04	41,600	58	.224	8,960
24	.96	38,400	59	.222	8,880
25	.88	35,200	60	.22	8,800
26	.8	32,000	61	.218	8,720
27	.77	30,800	62	.216	8,640
28	.74	29,600	63	.214	8,560
29	.71	28,400	64	.212	8,480
30	.68	27,200	65	.21	8,400
31	.65	26,000	66	.208	8,320
32	.62	24,800	67	.206	8,240
33	.59	23,600	68	.204	8,160
34	.565	22,600	69	.202	8,080
35	.54	21,600	70	.2	8,000

Notes: The % breakdown is the same regardless of the total purse. The dollar amounts are calculated for a $4,000,000 tournament.

might have dozens). An even larger raise would accompany a promotion from one of the dozens of vice president positions to one of a handful of positions at the senior or executive vice president level. And a still larger raise accompanies being promoted to C.E.O. status.

In addition to the larger and larger salary increments as one moves up the corporate ladder, there is another similarity between tournament compensation and boardroom compensation. The similarity is in the prime importance placed on relative competition. That is, openings in senior management are often filled from within the firm by choosing the best or most competent employee from the immediate subordinate level. This is a relative standard. An absolute standard would hardly work. How could it be that everyone in the firm who passes some preset absolute threshold would be promoted? A firm would be fortunate if many of its vice presidents actually had the ability to move up to senior vice president status, but only one can be chosen to do so when an opening develops. Firms tend to choose the best one, (a relative standard) rather than simply choosing randomly from among all those eligible for promotion. Moving up the corporate ladder is like moving up in the finishing order in a tournament. What is important is that you beat everyone else who is also trying to move up, and the prize for the winner is very lucrative.

11.2 Information, Scarcity, and Management Compensation

One of the basic tenets in labor economics is that employees are paid according to the value that they add to the firm. The basic idea is very simple. If an employee, before being paid, can add $100,000 of profit to a firm, then his or her salary would be $100,000. Certainly, the firm will not want to pay more than $100,000. Meanwhile, if the employee can produce and get paid $100,000 of value elsewhere, he or she will not want to work for less.

Unfortunately, the world itself is not as simple as this basic idea. Production in firms typically involves teamwork, and in team production it is generally impossible to determine exactly how much profit is attributable to each individual team member.[4] If the measurement of the values of the marginal products (VMPs) were easy, then salary could be directly tied to the VMPs. Those who produce more, earn more, in direct proportion to the extra production. Alas, economic scarcity makes the needed information unavailable at a reasonable cost (or perhaps at any cost), and another method is required to align pay with productivity.

The usual answer to measuring an individual's productivity in order to compensate the individual appropriately involves managers who monitor the performance of the members of the team. In the absence of an objectively measurable signal of the individual's value, the subjective ranking or rating of employees by a manager becomes necessary. Furthermore, because of the measurement difficulty and the subjective component, mistakes will be made. Some workers will be paid more than they are worth while others will be paid less than they are worth. The extent of overpayment or underpayment becomes clearer only after the fact, but even then, it may never be completely clear how valuable an individual employee is.

In this environment of incomplete, costly, and scarce information, the firm still has to make decisions about salaries and promotions. From an *ex-ante* point of view, the firm attempts to pay all workers appropriately. Given competitive and market pressures, the firm cannot afford to pay workers more or less than they are worth on average. This means that at any level in the firm, the salary will be set near the average of the VMPs at that level. This implies that the less competent employees at this level are actually overpaid relative to their productivity and that the more competent are underpaid. Through time it can be determined with increased confidence who the best workers are and who the worst workers are, relative to each other. The worst workers will tend to stagnate in their career growth, while the best workers are promoted when upper level positions become available. In a sense, the overpayment to the worst workers is a cost of obtaining information about which employees are the best.

Here is where it gets interesting. Firms are always on the lookout for competent, dynamic employees, and are willing to hire a competitor's up-and-coming stars if only they could determine who they are. While firms cannot

---

[4]See Alchian, A. A. and H. Demsetz, "Production, Information Costs, and Economic Organization," *American Economic Review*, Vol. 62, No. 5, (Dec. 1972), pp. 777-95.

observe the day-to-day diligence of the employees of other firms, they can observe the acts of promotion. That is, firms could discover their competitor's best employees by observing who gets promoted, thereby gaining information without going through the costly process that entails possible overpayments to less competent employees. This information will allow a firm to make employment offers to its competitor's best employees, perhaps enticing them to switch companies, unless the promoting firm also includes a significant increase in salary along with the promotion. At least in part, the promoting firm can justify the sizable jump in salary that accompanies the promotion, as a makeup for the past relative underpayment during the period in which the employee was at the previous level. Thus, relative competition among employees at each level to determine who gets promoted, along with substantial raises at the point of promotion, in essence, a tournament-like salary structure, solves economic problems that arise in salary setting and employee retention.

There is more. The link between higher performance and higher pay is a two-way street. The previous paragraphs have focused on rewarding the more productive with promotions and higher salaries. This is the link that runs from higher productivity to higher pay. But there is also a link that runs from higher pay, or at least the prospect of higher pay, to higher productivity. That is, the employment and promotion process is not simply a matter of the discovery of which employees are the most productive, and their subsequent reward in the form of a raise. The employment and promotion process also involves the spur or incentive to be more productive that is brought out in the first place by the prospect of the substantial raise.

If the raise that accompanies a promotion is not substantial, then the extra effort that employees might expend to relatively outshine their peers will not be that substantial either. An employee might decide that a featherbedded position at the current salary level, involving low effort (or, from a different point of view, high shirking of responsibility), might be preferable to putting forth high effort, if the reward to high effort is only a meager raise. Again we see the implications of viewing salaries and promotions as a tournament. The relative (as opposed to absolute) competition among all the peers at one level, to be the one or few that are promoted, brings forth greater effort and productivity, as long as the salary increase between steps is sufficient.

This is the prevailing wisdom's explanation of the overwhelmingly large compensation packages of senior corporate officials. In this view, the incredibly large salaries of senior executives are not statements about an executive's VMP in his or her current position, as much as they are rewards for past superlative performance in lower positions, and as much as they provide incentives that spur employees at lower levels of the pyramid to try to outdo each other by supplying the extra effort. The large increment in salary that comes with promotion gives incentive to all members at any given rank to work hard to attain promotion; such hard work translates into efficient operations and, ultimately, into higher profits.

The above argument rests on the proposition that the greater the potential reward, the greater the effort expended. Economists, no doubt, are comfortable with this proposition. As long as effort is not a constant, as long as effort can be increased, at a cost, or decreased, for some saving in cost, then it is true that if the return to effort goes up, the amount of effort supplied will also go up. Many people, however, would be skeptical about the proposition. Non-economists may start from the proposition that effort is fixed, that people will always work hard. Undergraduate students in my Economics of Sports classes often claim that athletes, especially high level professional athletes, always give 100%. Certainly the whole Soviet system was based on the premise that workers would give their best regardless of their own personal reward. Invariably, socialists and communists are unhappily surprised to find that equal sharing of output destroys the incentive to work hard and produce in the first place. Into this milieu step economists Ronald Ehrenberg and Michael Bognanno, who use golf statistics to illustrate the links between rewards, effort, and performance, in a setting where many would be surprised to find that any correlation existed.

11.3 Rewards, Effort, and Performance: The Evidence from Golf

Viewing corporate compensation schemes as akin to prize distributions in tournaments, and arguing that they are an effective means to bring forth effort and reward performance, relies on the proposition that greater effort will be forthcoming when the potential rewards are higher. In order to test this proposition in golf tournaments, we must carefully consider all of the following: what it means to supply effort; how to measure performance; and how to measure the rewards.

First of all, the supply of effort must be a variable that is under the control of the golfer in question. If it is not, then the reward-effort linkage will be nonexistent. Ehrenberg and Bognanno consider this question, here is what they say:

> Of course, one may argue that treating the effort/concentration levels of professional golfers as choice variables does not make sense because professionals *always* play as hard as they can. What this criticism ignores, however, is how difficult it is even for professionals to maintain their concentration levels over tournaments that typically last four days per week and that involve four to five hours of physical effort per day. Furthermore, playing on the PGA European Tour involves weekly international travel and living out of hotel rooms. At the very least, one might expect fatigue to set in during the latter days of each tournament and players' ability to maintain their concentration to diminish at these times.[5]

Indeed, single-minded concentration on one's golf game cannot always be at a maximum. If it could, it would imply that concentration is not subject to scarcity, that one could maintain maximum concentration on golf, without sacrificing or trading off any other thought patterns that are also competing for attention. But there are always distractions. Successful professionals might be able to concentrate more fully than would casual amateurs, but even they will have times of being more focused or less focused, times of being "in the zone" and times of suffering mental lapses that lead to poor judgment on the golf course. Regardless whether one is persuaded by these *a priori*, introspective arguments about the variability of effort, the proof is in the statistical tests. If effort/concentration/performance cannot be influenced by the reward structure in the prize fund, then the statistical tests reported here will not show any significant correlations.

[5]Ehrenberg, Ronald G. and Michael L. Bognanno, "The Incentive Effects of Tournaments Revisited: Evidence from the European PGA Tour," *Industrial and Labor Relations Review*, Vol. 43, Special Issue (February 1990b) p. 75-S.

We next turn to the issue of measuring performance. As it turns out, golf tournaments are ideal for our purposes. Scores are available by player, by tournament, and by round for almost all professional golf tournaments. Ehrenberg and Bognanno use 39 official PGA TOUR events in 1984 and 23 tournaments on the 1987 European Men's PGA Tour in two similar research papers. The results in the two studies are consistent with each other, and I report here on the results from the United States.

Professional golfers' scores in tournaments will be affected by many things. Certainly the par, the length, and the difficulty rating of the tournament venue are important. Since all golf tournaments consist of relative competition, the strength of the field of competitors will also be important. Furthermore, in assessing any one golfer's score, that particular golfer's level of skill should be an important explanatory variable. Even the weather on the days of the tournament can be controlled for as an influence on a golfer's performance as measured by his scores.

For the purposes of their research, Ehrenberg and Bognanno, placed specific attention on the financial (and other) rewards to performing well in a tournament. Therefore, prize money is included in the regression equation. The higher the prize money, so the argument goes, the more concentration and effort, and therefore, the lower the scores. In addition to prize money, there are other rewards to good performance in terms of publicity and potential endorsements, and in terms of passing certain thresholds that might confer on a particular golfer a special exempt status, or an invitation to a special competition such as a spot on the Ryder Cup team. It is generally difficult to capture these other rewards in a statistical model. However, it is possible to single out the four tournaments known as the majors to see if they might bring forth an extra level of preparation, concentration, and effort, potentially leading to lower scores than otherwise would be achieved.

Given these multiple factors, Ehrenberg and Bognanno perform a multiple regression analysis on the following equation:

$$
\begin{aligned}
\text{FINALSCORE} = \; & b_0 + b_1\text{TPRIZE} + b_2\text{PAR} + b_3\text{DIST} + \\
& b_4\text{RATING} + b_5\text{WAVE} + b_6\text{MAJ} + \qquad (11.1) \\
& b_7\text{SCOREAVE} + b_8\text{FCUT} + b_9\text{FRACT} + \\
& b_{10}\text{MPERAVE} \; ,
\end{aligned}
$$

where the variables will be described below along with the results. The
results are listed in Table 11.2.

Table 11.2 Coefficient estimates for Eq. (11.1), (t-statistics).

Dependent Variable: FINALSCORE	
variable	coefficient
constant	-324.099
	(-13.1)
TPRIZE	-0.011
	(-6.9)
PAR	1.495
	(8.5)
DIST	0.006
	(7.4)
RATING	0.211
	(20.5)
WAVE	2.394
	(13.3)
MAJ	-0.698
	(-1.3)
SCOREAVE	4.059
	(14.0)
FCUT	4.346
	(3.0)
FRACT	4.277
	(2.1)
MPERAVE	0.042
	(10.6)
adjusted R^2	0.421
n	2,432

Note: From Table 1, p. 1314, Ehrenberg and Bognanno (1990a).

The dependent variable in the regressions is the total score for all four
rounds. The sample includes pooled data across 39 tournaments and the top
160 players for the year. In total there were 2,432 observations. Overall the

results are very good, with the adjusted R-squared of .421 loosely meaning that about 42% of the variation in final scores is explained in the model.

The main variable of interest is TPRIZE, which is the total purse for the tournament in question measured in thousands of 1984 dollars. The coefficient estimate of -0.011 means that for each $100,000 increase to the prize fund, each golfer's score goes down by 1.1 strokes on average. The t-statistic of -6.9 means that the result is statistically significant. It appears that golfers play better when more is at stake. The best explanation of the result that I can think of is that the golfers are trying harder because of the extra potential winnings. Thus, there is strong support for the existence of incentive effects from tournament compensation schemes.

It is clearly not the case that the result is spurious, as it would be, for example, if the high money tournaments were played on easier golf courses, thus accounting for the correlation. We know that this is not the case because the difficulty of the golf course is controlled for in three separate ways, each of which is the right sign and statistically significant. The variable, PAR, is the par for the golf course on which the tournament is played. The coefficient is 1.495, meaning that courses with higher par lead to higher scores. The variable, DIST, is the length of the golf course in yards. Here, too, the coefficient is positive and significant, as expected, with a value of 0.006, which means scores increase by six-tenths of a stroke for every additional 100 yards of distance. Finally, the variable, RATING, is the course difficulty rating (measured in strokes), and is also a significant positive factor in explaining final scores.

The weather is also significant as captured by WAVE, which is "the average of three raters' perceptions of the number of days during the tournament in which the weather significantly influenced player performance."[6] According to the statistically significant estimate, 2.394, each day of bad weather adds between two and two-and-a-half strokes to the final scores.

MAJ is a dummy variable equal to one if the tournament in question is one of the majors. This variable is included because there are benefits over and above the prize fund that the winner of a major will receive. As such,

---

[6]Ehrenberg, R. G. and M. L. Bognanno, "Do Tournaments Have Incentive Effects?," *Journal of Political Economy*, 98 (December 1990a), p. 1312.

the majors should bring forth extra effort which will reduce scores. One might think that the majors are played on especially tough golf courses which will lead to higher scores, but remember, the difficulty of the course is already captured with the PAR, DIST, and RATING variables. Here, as expected, the coefficient is negative; scores in majors are almost seven-tenths of a stroke lower than otherwise. Caution should be exercised, however, because the estimate is not statistically different from zero.

SCOREAVE and FCUT are both measures of the individual golfer's skill. SCOREAVE is the player's average score per round on all rounds played in 1984. A higher value of SCOREAVE means the player is not as good, and should be positively related to his score in a tournament, which it is. Even the magnitude of the coefficient, 4.059, is right on the button. This coefficient means that every additional stroke per round for the golfer over the course of the year, translates into four more strokes in the final score over a four round tournament. An unexpected result is achieved, however, for FCUT. FCUT is the fraction of tournaments in which the golfer made the cut in 1984. Since better golfers make the cut more often, and since better golfers shoot lower scores, the expected result here is a negative coefficient. Instead, however, the coefficient is significantly positive. Evidently, this variable is capturing something other than the golfer's skill, but it is not clear what. Ehrenberg and Bognanno make no mention of the curious result, or even why they chose to include the variable, other than to say that it captures a player's ability. Since SCOREAVE seems to be the direct way of capturing a player's ability, and since it clearly works to do so in the expected direction, it is curious that FCUT is also included.

Finally, MPERAVE and FRACT are separate ways of measuring the skill of all the golfers who made the cut in a particular tournament. MPERAVE is the year-long performance average of the players who made the cut. It is measured in such a way that a higher value indicates a higher skill. FRACT is the fraction of the players who made the cut in a particular tournament who were among the top 160 money winners for the year. Each of these measures is expected to have a negative effect on final scores because, when playing in a relative competition against better opponents, one has to shoot lower scores than otherwise to win any given prize amount. If the relative competition part of the tournament compensation scheme brings forth better performance, then the coefficients of these two variables should be less than zero. Unfortunately, these variables yield significant positive coefficients. Neither the original authors nor I have a good explanation of this result. Evidently, this curious anomaly will have to await further exploration.

These results already support the view that higher potential rewards bring forth greater effort and better performance. The most intriguing results, however, are yet to come. Ehrenberg and Bognanno perform a highly innovative microanalysis of the fourth round scores, exploiting information about where the golfer stands in the tournament after three rounds to get a finer view of the actual money incentives that are operative for the final round. Because of the top-heavy distribution of the tournament prize structure, golfers near the top of the leader board after three rounds have much more at stake than golfers in the middle or at the bottom of the pack.

Consider a tournament with a purse of $400,000 which was fairly typical in 1984. The figures in Table 11.1, divided by 10, can be used to indicate the prizes as a function of the order of finish. In such a tournament, moving up from second place after the third round to a first place finish will increase the winnings from $43,200 to $72,000, for a gain of $28,800. Meanwhile, moving up from 32nd place to 31st place will increase the golfer's paycheck by only $120. Near the back of the pack, moving up from 62nd place to 61st place is worth only $8. It is obvious who has the most at stake, who will be concentrating fully, and who will having fun, going through the motions, experimenting with untested routines, and/or thinking of the plane trip home or on to the next tournament site. Ehrenberg and Bognanno calculate the actual amount of extra winnings for moving up one place (measured in thousands of dollars) for each golfer in each tournament, and form a variable called UPRIZE3. Then, they use this variable on the right hand side with a set of control variables similar to those in Eq. (11.1) in a regression with the fourth round score as the dependent variable. The result for this coefficient only is reported in Table 11.3.[7] As the table shows, for each $1,000 of extra prize money at stake for a particular golfer who

---

[7]The authors indicate that the other variables behave as expected.

improves his position, his score falls by almost one quarter of a stroke. And the result is statistically significant.

Table 11.3 Coefficient estimates (t-statistics) for various measures of monetary rewards to performance in the fourth round.

Dependent Variable: Score in Fourth (final) Round	
variable	coefficient
UPRIZE3	-0.236
	(-3.5)
DPRIZE3	-0.042
	(-2.7)
MIDPRIZ3	-0.212
	(-3.3)
LES3PRIZ	-0.049
	(-2.0)
LES2PRIZ	-0.088
	(-2.6)
LES1PRIZ	-0.181
	(-2.7)

Note: From Table 3, p. 1321, Ehrenberg and Bognanno (1990a).

Due to a quirk in the measurement of UPRIZE3, Ehrenberg and Bognanno consider a couple of variations on the theme. The quirk is that the leader after three rounds has nowhere to go but down. The leader, therefore, would have a zero value of UPRIZE3 because he cannot improve his position. Clearly, however, the leader has incentive to perform well in the last round lest he fall back in the standings and lose a sizeable amount of prize money. So Ehrenberg and Bognanno also calculate DPRIZE3, which is the amount of money, measured in thousands of dollars, that a golfer will lose if he falls back one place in the standings. While UPRIZE3 is a reward for moving up, DPRIZE3 is a penalty for falling back. The authors also use the average of UPRIZE3 and DPRIZE3, which they call, MIDPRIZ3. The estimates of these coefficients are also included in Table 11.3. As the table shows, each of these variables has the expected negative sign (that is, more money at stake leads to lower scores), and is statistically significant. A comparison of the estimates indicates that golfers might be motivated more by a positive incentive to do well than by a monetary penalty for backsliding, a result that would be consistent with the prevailing wisdom in behavioral psychology. Due to the measurement quirk in UPRIZE3, however, perhaps the most reliable formulation of this variable is MIDPRIZ3. To me, these results already offer very clear evidence of the incentive effect in action. Nevertheless, as if to put an exclamation point on it, the authors take it even one step further.

UPRIZE3 captures the monetary gain of moving up one place, but it does not capture how easy or difficult it would be to move up one place. For example, if a golfer was one stroke behind the leader (or one stroke behind the golfer just ahead of him in the standings), it would be very possible to overcome the deficit and move up in the standings. Concentration and effort in this instance could clearly pay off. Alternatively, if the golfer in question was four or five strokes behind the player in front of him, although it would be possible, it would not be all that likely that the golfer could overcome the gap. Instead of calculating the gain from moving up by one place, Ehrenberg and Bognanno calculate the gain from moving up by one stroke relative to the other golfers in the tournament. A one-stroke gain is very possible, and it could mean a substantial money gain if the golfer was tied after three rounds with many other golfers, or was one stroke behind a logjam of golfers tied ahead of him. Alternatively, a one-stroke gain might not affect one's position or money winnings at all. The authors construct the variable, LES1PRIZ, which is the gain, measured in thousands of dollars, from moving up by one stroke relative to the rest of the field. Movements of two or three strokes relative to the rest of the field are also well within the realm of possibility and the authors also construct LES2PRIZ and LES3PRIZ which are defined as the marginal gain measured in thousands of dollars for gaining two or three strokes, respectively, on the rest of the field.

Once constructed, these variables are used in regressions in the same way that UPRIZE3 was used above. The results are also listed in Table 11.3. Again, the results are in the expected direction and are statistically significant. The coefficients seem small but a quick example will put them in perspective. Consider the coefficient of LES3PRIZ equal to -.049. For each $1000 potential gain, the golfer concentrates more and saves slightly less than 1/20 of a stroke. This may not seem like a lot. But consider a golfer who is in tenth place after three rounds but only 3 shots out of first place. In a $400,000 tournament, this player's earnings would increase from $10,800 to $72,000, for a gain of $61,200, which means LES3PRIZ equals 61.2. Controlling for everything else, this golfer would be expected to shoot 3 strokes (61.2 times .049 equals 2.9988) better than otherwise. This does not mean that the golfer will make up the three-shot deficit because those golfers in first through ninth places (including ties) also have a great deal of incentive to play well. But it does show that when more extra money is at stake, effort and concentration increase, and scores improve. As such, the results of this research cause us to reject with great confidence the type of reasoning which asserts that golfers always do their best, or always try their hardest, or always give 100%. I do not believe that there is any reason to think that employees competing with each other to move up the corporate ladder will act any differently in response to the potential rewards for increased effort and performance.

Chapter 12

Gender Discrimination?[1]

Another controversial issue in today's economy is the difference between the income levels of men and women. Many women's groups are fond of proclaiming that for every $1 earned by a man, a woman earns only 72 cents.[2] Such proclamations are meant to attract attention to gender discrimination, and to raise consciousness. Unfortunately, the statistics, as cited, are not logically sufficient to prove anything about discrimination. Male/female earnings differentials can be caused by differences in schooling, education, or skills; differences in job tenure or experience; differences in hours worked; and/or underlying discrimination. Simply quantifying the existence of earnings differentials in no way proves that they come from discrimination. Keep in mind, however, that the existence of other reasons for differentials in earnings in no way proves that the earnings differentials do not come from discrimination.

It is obvious that we require statistics on earnings that control for all causes of any differentials that may exist. A stronger case that

---

[1]Parts of this chapter were originally published as, Shmanske, Stephen, "Gender, Skill, and Earnings in Professional Golf," *Journal of Sports Economics*, Vol. 1, No. 4, (Nov. 2000), pp. 400-415. They are reprinted with permission of Western Economic Association International.

[2]The website of the National Committee on Pay Equity lists the women's wage as only 72 cents for every dollar that men earn as of 1999. The Feminist Women's Health Center website lists the women's wage at 74 cents to the dollar for March 1998. See also, Moberg, David, "Bridging the Gap: Why Women still don't get Equal Pay," *In These Times.Com*, Jan. 8, 2001, who uses 72 cents to the dollar as the relevant figure.

discrimination exists, and a better measure of the extent of discrimination, comes from the examination of earnings differentials that remain after controlling for skills, experience, and the rest. Unfortunately, even the controlled statistics can never be absolutely conclusive. Any wage differential that remains after controlling for everything that it is possible to control for, might be due to discrimination, or might be due to other factors that are still omitted from the analysis. Some of these factors may even be impossible to control for.

One of the payoffs of sports economics is the abundant availability of statistics that make it possible to control for almost all of the obvious factors in a much clearer fashion than for a typical white or blue collar employee. As such, the sports economics literature has expended considerable effort examining the discrimination issue.[3] The existing literature, however, is almost exclusively concerned with men only, looking at black versus white, Hispanic versus white, or, in ice hockey, French-speaking versus English-speaking. This chapter uses golf statistics to undertake the first large-scale statistical analysis of gender discrimination in sports.

This chapter proceeds by developing a simple numerical example of earnings differences. The example shows wherein the basic statistical problems lie. Following this, the chapter reports on an analysis of the earnings differentials between the men on the PGA TOUR and the women on the Ladies Professional Golf Association Tour (LPGA).

12.1 A Simple Model of Earnings and Discrimination

Consider a simple model in which there is one skill or attribute that employers find desirable, x, and two types of people, A and B. Each type of person, i = A or B, sells his or her amount of skill, x_i, for a per unit price of P_{xi}, thus earning income of Y_i, which is equal to x_i times P_{xi}, or:

---

[3]See, Kahn, Lawrence M., "Discrimination in Professional Sports: A Survey of the Literature," *Industrial and Labor Relations Review*, Vol. 44, No. 3, (April 1991) pp. 395-418, for a useful survey of the literature. In a nutshell, the results of many of these studies confirm the existence of measurable discrimination, especially in the earlier periods considered. The trend seems to be that discrimination has dramatically decreased through time, and in many cases, has disappeared altogether.

$$Y_i = (x_i)(P_{xi}) \quad \text{For } i = A, B \quad . \tag{12.1}$$

For example, if A had 10 units of x and sold them each for a price of 10, A's income would be 100. If B also had 10 units of x to sell for 10 apiece, then B's income would also be 100, and we would not be talking about earnings differentials or possible discrimination.

Suppose, however, that B's income is only 90. B earns only 90% of what A earns. This could happen in a variety of ways, but consider the following two scenarios. In scenario one, B has only 9 units of x to sell and sells them for 10 apiece. In scenario two, B has 10 units to sell but can only receive a price of 9 for each. Most people would say that there is no discrimination in the first case, but that there is discrimination against B in the second case, quantifiable as a 10% discounting of the price paid for each unit of x. It is clear from these simplest examples that simply looking at overall earnings, 100 for A and 90 for B, cannot distinguish between these two scenarios and, therefore, cannot prove or disprove the existence of discrimination. Nevertheless, statistics about average differences in earnings or income are often quoted in the context of discrimination. In that context, one has to wonder why anyone would quote the overall statistics as conclusive; why journalists would uncritically report about someone quoting the overall statistics; or why anyone would be willing to draw conclusions about discrimination from the overall statistics. The earnings differences only make sense as a measure of discrimination if we add the untenable assumption that the skills or attributes that the A's and the B's have to sell are equal.

Obviously, the two scenarios considered above do not cover all the possibilities; in fact, they do not even bracket the possibilities. Discrimination could even be more than the 10% difference in earnings. Suppose that B actually had 15 units of x to sell but could only sell them for a price of 6. B's income would be 90, but the extent of discrimination would be measured by a 40% discount in the price that B could receive. Furthermore, discrimination could even go against A even though A earns more in total. For example, A could have 12.5 units of x to sell, but because of discrimination against A, perhaps he/she could only sell them for a price of 8, thus earning 100 in total. Even though A earns more in total, there is discrimination in the form of a price discount of 1/9 (if B earns 9 for each unit of x) or approximately 11% *against* A in this example.

In this simple example, earnings are the product of the number of units of some skill or attribute, and the price per unit. There are three values in the equation: skill; price; and income. If analysts can observe only the product, income, then the breakdown between skill differences and price differences remains elusive. If, however, analysts can observe the total earnings and the amount of skill or attribute supplied, then the price per unit can be determined, and statements about discrimination can be supported. Therefore, the intermediate goal in the assessment of discrimination and earnings differentials is the refinement in the measurement of the skills that different employees bring to the market. This is exactly where the economics of sports fits in. There are better measurements and more agreement about which things to measure in sports examples than there are in most industrial settings. In golf, for example, earnings are available from the lists of money leaders. Golf skills are measured by the array of performance statistics that are available. Then, using earnings as the dependent variable, and skills as the explanatory variables, the prices or values of each skill are estimated by the coefficients of the skill variables in a regression equation.

Before turning to these statistics for the case of golf, there are a couple of extensions of the simple example in this section that need to be addressed. The first extension is to capture arithmetically the extent of discrimination from the statistics. To do this, subtract Eq. (12.1) evaluated for i = B, from Eq. (12.1) evaluated for i = A, and derive an expression for the differential in earnings between A and B:

$$Y_A - Y_B = (x_A)(P_{XA}) - (x_B)(P_{XB}) \quad . \tag{12.2}$$

Then, by adding and subtracting the amount $(x_A)(P_{XB})$ from the right hand side of Eq. (12.2) and rearranging we obtain:

$$Y_A - Y_B = (x_A)(P_{XA} - P_{XB}) + (P_{XB})(x_A - x_B) \quad . \tag{12.3}$$

Equation (12.3) divides the total differential in earnings into two parts. The first term on the right hand side is a measure of discrimination; it is composed of the difference in prices weighted by the amount of skill of A.

The second term on the right is the portion of the differential due to the difference in skills between A and B. This part is not due to discrimination. Finally, by dividing each term in Eq. (12.3) by $Y_A - Y_B$, the left hand side becomes one, and the right hand side consists of two terms which sum to one, and which represent, respectively, the proportions of the earnings differential due to discrimination and to differences in skills.

A few examples will illustrate the basic calculations. For each case below, assume A earns 100 from the sale of 10 units of x for 10 apiece. Now suppose B earns only 90 from the sale of 10 units of x because of a 10% discriminatory price discount. Equation (12.3) would become:

$$100 - 90 = 10(10 - 9) + 9(10 - 10) \qquad (12.3a)$$
$$10 \; = \; 10 \; + \; 0 \; ,$$

and dividing by 10:

$$1 \; = \; 1 \; + \; 0 \; .$$

This signifies that 1 or 100% of the difference in earnings is due to discrimination, and 0% to skill differences, as assumed in this case.

Now suppose that the reason for the earnings gap is the skill difference. Equation (12.3) becomes:

$$100 - 90 = 10(10 - 10) + 10(10 - 9) \qquad (12.3b)$$
$$10 \; = \; 0 \; + \; 10 \; .$$

Dividing by 10 this time reveals that 0% of the gap is due to discrimination as captured in the first term and $10/10 = 1$ or 100% of the gap is due to the difference in skills.

These are the easy cases. Now suppose that B's earnings of 90 are less than A's earnings of 100 due to both discrimination and a lower level of skills. With a slight rounding error, suppose that B sells 9.5 units of x for 9.47 per unit.[4] Now, Eq. (12.3) becomes:

[4] 9.5 times 9.47 equals 89.965. It is apparent by the construction of this simple example that the breakdown between discrimination and skills is roughly 50-50, with just slightly more of the difference coming through prices, that is, from discrimination.

$$100 - 90 \cong 10(10 - 9.47) + 9.47(10 - 9.5) \qquad (12.3c)$$
$$10 \cong \quad 5.3 \quad + \quad 4.735 \ .$$

Dividing through by 10 this time indicates that .53 or 53% of the differential is due to discrimination, as captured in the first term, and roughly 47% is due to the difference in skill levels.

Before moving on to the second extension, it is necessary to point out a minor quibble with the decomposition of the earnings differential that is developed in Eq. (12.3). There is nothing wrong with the derivation of Eq. (12.3), except that it is not the only way to do it. Starting again from Eq. (12.2), this time add and subtract the amount $(x_B)(P_{XA})$ from the right hand side and rearrange. The result is:

$$Y_A - Y_B = (x_B)(P_{XA} - P_{XB}) + (P_{XA})(x_A - x_B) \ . \qquad (12.4)$$

The difference is that this time the price difference is weighted by the amount of skill of B, and the skill difference is weighted by the price that A receives. Before, these weights were reversed. For the most part the differences are minor. There will be no difference to the conclusions drawn in Eqs. (12.3a) or (12.3b) above. In the case comparable to that calculated in Eq. (12.3c), the decomposition of the earnings differential becomes:

$$100 - 90 \cong 9.5(10 - 9.47) + 10(10 - 9.5) \qquad (12.4c)$$
$$10 \cong \quad 5.035 \quad + \quad 5 \ .$$

This time, dividing through by 10 reveals that the percentage of the gap that is due to discrimination is roughly 50%, and the percentage of the gap due to skill differences is also 50%. These numbers are within three percentage points of those calculated above.

The second extension is to note that the real world is never as simple or clear cut as these illustrative examples. The skills that employees have that are valuable to employers are never one-dimensional. A multidimensional skill vector will have to be measured for each worker, and a price imputed to each dimension of skill. It may turn out that women and men have vastly different types of skills, and that the returns, or prices, for these different types of skills could vary widely. It is even possible that women are paid more than men for some types of skills but that men earn more than women overall because the most valuable skills are those of which men have relatively more. Conclusions about discrimination in such a setting will be even more difficult to draw out. Luckily, the basic logic of the simple, one-dimensional examples developed above does extend to multiple dimensions. We will be able to attribute the total difference in earnings between men and women professional golfers to differences in prices and differences in skill levels over a number of different skills. These calculations come at the end of the chapter. First, however, it is useful to get an overall feel for the comparison of men and women professional golfers, and to develop a diagrammatic exposition of the relationship between skill and earnings. The next section starts by so doing.

12.2 Discrimination Between Men and Women Professional Golfers

Useful comparisons between men and women can be made by examining the relationship between skills and earnings on the PGA TOUR and the LPGA. Men on the PGA TOUR play for bigger purses than do the women in the LPGA tournaments. But men also play more rounds of golf over longer golf courses in front of more spectators, and exhibit greater levels of skill than women. Our goal is to determine how much of the larger earnings on the PGA TOUR is due to the differential in skills, and how much could be attributed to discrimination.

In the 1998 season, the purses for the 45 official PGA TOUR tournaments ranged from $1.5 to $4 million, with an average of $2,144,444. In the same year, women competed in 36 official LPGA events for purses ranging from $0.5 to $1.5 million and averaging $788,500. The leading money winner on the PGA TOUR was David Duval who set a then record (since obliterated in 1999 by Tiger Woods who earned over $6 million) yearly amount of $2,591,031. Annika Sorenstam topped the LPGA earnings list with $1,092,748.[5] Some would say that this illustrates a gender bias in

---

[5]Purses have continued to grow rapidly. For the 2000 season, Woods led the PGA TOUR with $9,188,321. Fourteen other PGA TOUR golfers won over $2,000,000. Karrie Webb led the 2000 LPGA money list by winning $1,876,853. In each of the 1999 and 2000 seasons, three LPGA golfers went over the $1,000,000 mark. In 2002, five LPGA golfers

earnings, although given the arguments offered in the beginning of this chapter, it is clearly not conclusive. No one accuses any tournament promoter of being sexist, but perhaps golf fans themselves are gender-biased. Actual attendance and television ratings are lower for LPGA events, and this translates into lower prize funds. But the question remains whether fan support is lower because of gender discrimination or because men are better players. Neither lower attendance nor lower prize funds are proof of discrimination because the men play more rounds of golf over longer golf courses (see Table 12.1), and because higher earnings (and higher attendance) are justified to the extent that men exhibit higher levels of skill (see Table 12.2, below).[6] Multiple regression techniques are used herein to determine the extent to which the earnings differential is explained by differences in skills and the extent to which it is discrimination.

Most casual observers of golf conclude that the larger physical stature of men allows them to drive the golf ball greater distances than women. On average, male professional golfers hit the ball about 33 yards farther than their female counterparts. This is so, notwithstanding that driving distance is more a function of technique than brute strength, and that several smaller men are among the long drive leaders. It is also true that fans of golf are awed by the great distances that the professionals can hit the ball, and enjoy watching this aspect of the sport. The fan's awe and enjoyment explain the first part of the adage "drive for show, putt for dough." But if the second part of the adage is also true, it is the putting skills that are more important to winning tournament prizes. And there would seem to be no apparent gender-based reason why women could not be able to putt as well as men.

---

earned more than $1,000,000 and Sorenstam earned $2,863,904 surpassing Duval's PGA TOUR record of 1998.

[6]The LPGA statistics are listed two ways in Table 12.2. There were 130 PGA TOUR golfers who played enough rounds of golf to have their statistics counted as "official." For the LPGA the number was 178. For a simple comparison of means, the women's means would be biased downwards by the presence of golfers ranked 131st to 178th, therefore, the part of the table using only the top 130 women should be used for this purpose. The regressions, however, use all 178 data points for the women because the goal is not a comparison of skill levels, but rather the comparison of the relationship between skills and earnings. The information in the lower tail of the women's distribution should not be discarded for this purpose.

In fact, given that LPGA courses are shorter than PGA TOUR courses, putting may be even more important for the women. Statistical analysis can shed light on the relative importance of driving and putting skills on the PGA TOUR and the LPGA.

Table 12.1 Comparison of PGA TOUR with LPGA, 1998.

TOUR	PGA	LPGA
EVENTS	45 (plus 7 unofficial)	36 (plus 6 unofficial)
WITH 2 ROUNDS	0	1 (rain shortened)
WITH 3 ROUNDS	2 (both rain shortened)	12 (1 rain shortened)
WITH 4 ROUNDS	41	23
WITH 5 ROUNDS	2	0
AVERAGE YARDAGE	6998	6282
LONGEST YARDAGE	7559	6460
SHORTEST YARDAGE	6478	6024
AVERAGE PURSE	$2,144,444	$788,500
LARGEST PURSE	$4,000,000	$1,500,000
SMALLEST PURSE	$1,500,000	$500,000

Note: The sources for all data are the *1999 PGA TOUR Media Guide* and the *1999 LPGA Media Guide*.

The underlying intuition for the analysis can be illustrated in Fig. 12.1. In each panel, the earnings per tournament entered are measured on the vertical axis and some skill is measured on the horizontal axis. Suppose that point M measures the averages of these amounts for the men on the PGA TOUR and point W measures these amounts for the LPGA. As shown, the men earn more, and exhibit a higher level of skill. Panel A shows two regression lines, one for the PGA TOUR and one for the LPGA. The lines, by definition, go through the sample averages. If the actual regressions match the pattern in Panel A, one could conclude that men and women are earning the same marginal payoff to talent (that is, the same prices for that particular skill), but that an earnings bias equal to the vertical distance between the lines exists. However, if the two lines are essentially the same line as shown in Panel B, then no bias exists. Unfortunately, life is not this simple. The actual linear regressions exhibit the pattern shown in Panel C, implying that women and men earn more as a function of their skills playing on their own

separate tours.[7] If Panel B was called "separate but equal," then Panel A
would be "separate and unequal," and Panel C might be playfully described

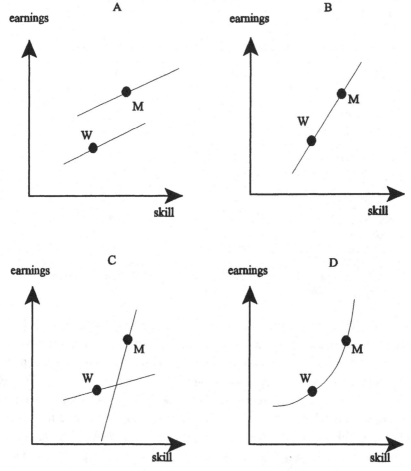

Fig. 12.1 Possible patterns of earnings and discrimination.

[7]This conclusion follows because point W lies above the regression line calculated for the
men. This means that if women golfers were paid like their male counterparts, they would
earn less than they currently do. Similarly, point M lies above the regression line
calculated for women.

as the oxymoron, "separate and more than equal." The actual pattern exhibited in Panel C and the theoretical issues considered when compensation is determined nonlinearly by tournaments, as discussed in Chapter 11, indicate that a nonlinear functional form to the regression might be appropriate. Indeed, the pattern in Panel D, with no gender bias actually describes the data the best.

The statistical regressions reported in this chapter are very similar to those used in the first part of Chapter 10. Various measures of earnings are used as dependent variables, and the skills are used as explanatory variables. The estimated coefficient of each of the skills is the monetary value or price or value of the marginal product of that skill. Once the earnings and the amounts of skills and the prices or values of each skill are calculated, implications about the male/female earnings differential can be drawn.

The skills that golfers use to win shares of tournament purses fall into five categories, driving distance, driving accuracy, reaching greens in regulation, bunker shots, and putting. These will be discussed in order.

Driving skill is measured in two dimensions. DRIVDIST is the distance in yards that the golfer averages on his or her drive. DRIVACC is the percentage of the time that the drive ends up in the fairway. Summary statistics for these and all variables used are listed in Table 12.2. As the table shows, men outdrive women by an average of about 33 or 35 yards, and the difference is statistically significant. Nevertheless, the distributions of driving distance do overlap a little. The longest driver in the LPGA, Caroline Blaylock, at 267 yards, is 18 yards longer than the shortest hitter on the PGA TOUR, Corey Pavin, who averages 249 yards. Accuracy, on the other hand, seems to be a dead heat between the men and the women, each hitting the fairway about 69-70% of the time.

Both tours attempt to squeeze the two driving measures into one dimension, TOTDRIV, by adding the rankings of each golfer in the separate skills. As will be shown below, this *ad hoc* combination does not perform as well as the two separate measures in the regression analysis. Furthermore, since women are ranked only against other women, and men only against other men, TOTDRIV overstates the driving performance of women relative to men. For example, if the longest driver was also the most accurate driver on each tour, then each would be ranked first in each of those skills, and would get a measure of 2 in the constructed variable, TOTDRIV.

Table 12.2 Summary statistics.

130 PGA TOUR Golfers

Variable	Mean	Std. Dev.	Minimum	Maximum
FEMALE	0	0	0	0
TOTPUTT	29.148	.41585	28.22	30.54
EVENTS	254.46	157.40	19	659
EVENTS98	26.154	4.3571	15	35
Y98	623,400	500,330	10,870	2,591,031
SCOREAVE	70.902	.72062	69.13	73.86
DRIVDIST	271.25	7.7995	249	299.4
DRIVACC	69.774	4.9314	52.4	80.4
TOTDRIV	180.78	55.319	62	348
GIR	65.624	2.6794	55.5	71.3
PUTTPER	1.7783	.022289	1.724	1.865
PUTTPRED	1.7783	.019590	1.734	1.845
SANDSAVE	52.455	5.7492	36.2	69.8
WINPER	25,123	22,065	374.7	112,700

top 130 LPGA Golfers

Variable	Mean	Std. Dev.	Minimum	Maximum
FEMALE	1	0	1	1
TOTPUTT	30.192	.50587	28.74	31.90
EVENTS	231.18	160.95	14	649
EVENTS98	23.338	3.9894	13	32
Y98	186,010	195,630	27,720	1,092,748
SCOREAVE	72.438	.77765	69.99	74.14
DRIVDIST	238.00	8.8340	215.1	260.4
DRIVACC	70.001	5.6971	56.30	83.20
TOTDRIV	176.01	51.146	47	312
GIR	65.788	3.8620	55.60	78.10
PUTTPER	na	na	na	na
PUTTPRED	1.8150	.025835	1.734	1.870
SANDSAVE	39.753	7.2003	21.90	62.20
WINPER	7,750.90	8032.8	1,517	52,040

Table 12.2   Summary statistics (continued).

178 LPGA Golfers

Variable	Mean	Std. Dev.	Minimum	Maximum
FEMALE	1	0	1	1
TOTPUTT	30.300	.59097	28.74	32.35
EVENTS	232.61	161.66	13	649
EVENTS98	21.640	5.0011	10	32
Y98	139,440	183,890	587	1,092,748
SCOREAVE	72.918	1.1604	69.99	78.38
DRIVDIST	236.63	9.7834	208.2	267.0
DRIVACC	69.065	6.1864	50.90	83.20
TOTDRIV	191.22	58.652	47	380
GIR	64.035	4.9294	46.10	78.10
PUTTPER	na	na	na	na
PUTTPRED	1.8267	.033392	1.734	1.926
SANDSAVE	39.208	7.2220	19.50	62.20
WINPER	5,872.80	7,529.6	34.53	52,040

Note: The sources for all data are the *1999 PGA TOUR Media Guide* and the *1999 LPGA Media Guide*.

Although measured the same, 2, the man would clearly be the better driver, outdistancing the woman by 32, yards and giving up less than 3 percentage points in accuracy. Since TOTDRIV would overestimate the woman's skill, using it in the statistics would place more of the earnings differential in the discrimination category as opposed to the skill differential category. Consequently, if TOTDRIV is used to (mis)measure the driving skills, it will look as if women are discriminated against. This is a significantly important point and a warning. The statistics used to capture skills must be carefully measured and theoretically supported. If not, claims of discrimination or its absence will be spuriously supported.[8]

[8] I mention the need for theoretical support as a criticism of some of the statistical record keeping that the PGA TOUR and the LPGA do. As mentioned, each tour measures total driving by adding the ranks in driving distance and driving accuracy. Additionally, the PGA TOUR also prominently displays what they call "all-around" by adding the ranks of all the other skill categories. Certainly it is easy to calculate such a statistic but it is next to meaningless. First of all, it weights each category equally, whereas the careful statistical work done by myself and others shows that putting is the most important, and that relative

The skill of approach shot accuracy is called GIR, which measures the percentage of the time that the golfer reaches the green in regulation. Like driving accuracy, this skill also seems to be a dead heat. The difference between the levels of GIR is not statistically significant. Interestingly, GIR seems to be measuring a skill of accuracy with irons from similar distances. Table 12.1 pointed out that the average PGA TOUR course was about 716 yards longer than the average LPGA tournament venue. Divided by 18, this corresponds to about 34.2 extra yards per hole. Since the men drive the ball, on average, between 33 and 35 yards farther than the women, a crude approximation indicates that the approach shots are taken from about the same distances.[9]

If either the drive or the approach shot is misplayed, the ball may end up in an area of sand known as a bunker. The golfer may be able to recover from the bunker and still make par. The percentage of times that this happens is measured in SANDSAVE. Therefore, SANDSAVE is a measure of skillful play from the sand bunkers. Men are significantly better than women in this area.

There are two measures of putting skill. TOTPUTT is the total number of putts taken on the greens during a round. This measure is a little misleading, however, because if a player often misses the green and has a low GIR, then the player is often hitting very short range shots that end up close to the hole from where the player can finish the hole with only one putt. A player, who is just as good a putter but has a higher GIR, will more often be taking two putts on a green, because the approach shot, although on the green, will not be as close as the third shot of the player with a low GIR. The way to control for this is to count only the average number of putts taken on greens that were hit in regulation, called PUTTPER. PUTTPER

differences in some skills hardly matter. Perhaps even more important, adding ranks distorts the measurement of the actual differences in the skills. In the middle of the pack two golfers might be separated by one-tenth of a yard in driving distance, and their difference in ranks would be one unit. Meanwhile, at the top or bottom of the distribution, two golfers adjacent in rank might be separated by two yards or more. One would think that a two-yard differential is more important than a one-tenth yard differential, but in this case, they would have the same effect on the measurement of "all-around."

[9]The approximation is crude because par fives often involve two maximum distance shots akin to driving, and most par threes do not require a drive at all.

is the superior measure, but unfortunately, only the PGA TOUR keeps track of it. We will revisit this problem below.

Thus, the five main skills used to explain earnings are driving distance, driving accuracy, accuracy with approach shots, sand bunker shots, and putting.

Although measured in the same way, there is still some concern that these statistics might not measure the same thing. For example, in comparing the PGA TOUR to the LPGA, the fairways may be wider or narrower; the greens may be larger or smaller; and the sand bunkers may be deeper or shallower. At least one systematic difference that makes reaching the green in regulation harder for men is the extra length of the average golf course on the PGA TOUR. There are a few occasions when men and women professionals play the same course, but perhaps still from separate tees. A micro analysis of performance on such a course is a potentially fruitful future research topic.

The rest of the measures can be explained briefly. EVENTS is the total number of tournaments that the golfer has played during his or her career. It is a measure of experience, and because many tournaments repeat the same golf courses year after year, it may have power especially in deriving a prediction equation for PUTTPER. EVENTS98 is the number of tournaments entered in the 1998 season. Y98 is the official tournament earnings of the golfer during the 1998 season. WINPER, the earnings per tournament, is derived by dividing Y98 by EVENTS98. SCOREAVE is the average score per 18-hole round for the golfer. Finally, FEMALE is a dummy variable equal to 1 for women golfers.

All the data come from the *1999 PGA TOUR Media Guide* and the *1999 LPGA Media Guide*. Each tour keeps track of statistics on player performance, and considers those statistics to be official if the golfer plays at least a certain number of rounds (different for each tour). In 1998 there were 130 men with official statistics on the PGA TOUR and 178 women with official statistics on the LPGA. These are the statistics used in the regression analysis.

A simple comparison of means is facilitated by looking only at the top 130 women for comparison to the top 130 men. A recap of these comparisons indicates that the men are clearly better in driving distance, putting, and sand saves. Women are slightly better at driving accuracy and greens in regulation, although, statistically, these two categories are dead heats. Men earn more than three times as much per tournament on average, but overall play better golf, averaging over 1.5 fewer strokes per round which would translate to six strokes over a four-round tournament. Comparing the top 130 men to the top 178 women, men earn closer to four times as much per tournament, and average about 2 fewer strokes per round.

There is one additional variable listed in Table 12.2 called, PUTTPRED. I have argued above, that putts per green in regulation is a way of measuring putting skill that is superior to simply counting the total number of putts taken. However, because the LPGA does not keep track of this statistic, we shall have to construct it in an indirect way. It is possible to get a prediction equation for PUTTPER by finding out the relationship between PUTTPER and all the other statistics that are kept for the PGA TOUR. Using PUTTPER as the dependent variable, and all the other data series as explanatory variables, the following prediction equation is estimated (t-statistics in parentheses):

$$\text{PUTTPER} = .4985 + .05529 \text{ TOTPUTT} - .000009540 \text{ EVENTS}$$
$$(1.65) \quad (13.18) \qquad\qquad (-1.40)$$

$$+ .00009976 \text{ EVENTS98} - .000000003189 \text{ Y98}$$
$$(0.38) \qquad\qquad\qquad (-0.90)$$

$$- .003371 \text{ SCOREAVE} + .0003272 \text{ DRIVDIST} \qquad\qquad (12.5)$$
$$(-0.87) \qquad\qquad\qquad (0.97)$$

$$+ .001099 \text{ DRIVACC} + .00008382 \text{ TOTDRIV}$$
$$(2.01) \qquad\qquad\qquad (1.72)$$

$$- .004484 \text{ GIR} + .0004332 \text{ SANDSAVE} ,$$
$$(-5.52) \qquad\quad (2.26)$$

$$\text{adjusted } R^2 = .753 \qquad \text{observations} = 130 .$$

The coefficients in this equation are then used to form a prediction series for PUTTPER called PUTTPRED for all the observations. PUTTPRED is used in the rest of the regressions. Experiments using TOTPUTT instead of PUTTPRED do not yield any different inferences *vis a vis* discrimination, but the t-statistic on TOTPUTT is lower and the adjusted R-squared is lower in the experiments. These experiments support the argument that PUTTPER or its stand-in, PUTTPRED, is a better measure of putting skill than TOTPUTT.

A look at the prediction equation and a comparison of PUTTPER and PUTTPRED for the men indicate that a nice correspondence has been achieved. Over 75% of the variation in PUTTPER is explained by Eq. (12.5). As Table 12.2 shows, the means of PUTTPER and PUTTPRED are identical, and there is slightly less variation in the predicted levels of PUTTPRED than there is in PUTTPER. Furthermore, the minimums and maximums for PUTTPER and PUTTPRED are almost identical. From Eq. (12.5) itself, it is interesting to note that TOTPUTT is very important, that most of the other skills variables are statistically important, but that scoring, events, earnings, and the constant term are not statistically significant. It is difficult, however, to attach any intuitive meaning to the levels of the coefficient estimates in such a prediction equation. No attempt to do so will be made here.

The first set of main results is listed in Table 12.3. WINPER is the dependent variable, and the regressors include the skill variables and the FEMALE dummy variable when appropriate. Equations (12.6) and (12.7) separate the sample by gender with 130 in the PGA TOUR sample and 178 in the LPGA sample. Equation (12.8) is the combined sample with the dummy variable. Upon comparison of Eqs. (12.6) and (12.7) one concludes that there is no support for the proposition that men and women professional golfer's incomes depend on skills in the same way. All the variables have the right sign, and about half are statistically significant, but the men earn much more per skill for every skill except the insignificant SANDSAVE. In terms of statistical significance, putting and driving distance dominate for the men, and putting and greens in regulation dominate for the women.

For the men, the coefficient of DRIVDIST reveals that earnings per tournament will increase by $980 for each extra yard of distance. This amount is approximately three times as much as was calculated and reported in Chapter 10 using the 1986 data. The coefficient on PUTTPRED is also three times the size of the corresponding coefficient for 1986. Between 1986 and 1998, the purses have grown dramatically, but relative value of the two most important skills, putting and driving distance is remarkably similar.

Table 12.3 Regressions of earnings per tournament on skills, (t-statistics).

Equation	12.6	12.7	12.8	12.9
sample	men only	women only	combined	combined
dep. variable	WINPER	WINPER	WINPER	WINPER
Constant	334,476	117,193	102,461	273,336
	(1.809)	(4.000)	(1.516)	(4.330)
FEMALE			9136.14	-9076.99
			(1.777)	(-3.628)
DRIVDIST	980.499	47.1722	527.503	
	(3.560)	(0.724)	(4.004)	
DRIVACC	832.748	42.8813	501.202	
	(1.729)	(0.489)	(2.611)	
TOTDRIV				-63.8489
				(-3.417)
GIR	1381.27	656.092	232.120	381.899
	(1.673)	(5.069)	(0.812)	(1.400)
SANDSAVE	31.1046	35.3340	139.199	121.454
	(0.106)	(0.663)	(1.179)	(1.025)
PUTTPRED	-408,078	-92,432.2	-156,287	-150,763
	(-4.704)	(-7.100)	(-5.246)	(-5.046)
R-squared	.360	.560	.454	.446
adj. R-squared	.334	.547	.443	.437
observations	130	178	308	308

As in the earlier chapter, the coefficient of the putting variable is overwhelmingly large. A $408,078 gain per tournament for a one putt decrease on each green reached in regulation is a fantastically large amount for an impossible feat. To put the coefficient on PUTTPRED into perspective, consider one less putt per tournament. Since about two-thirds, or 48 of the 72 holes during a tournament are reached in regulation, one less putt would lower PUTTPRED by about 1/48. Therefore, one less putt would raise earnings by approximately $8,500, a reasonable figure. While one shot for the leaders might be worth more than $200,000, a one-stroke difference for those in the middle of the pack might be worth $500 or less.

Equation (12.8) forces the slope coefficients to be equal for men and women. The coefficients are the right sign and mostly significant, and of reasonable magnitudes. However, given the results in Eqs. (12.6) and (12.7), the PGA TOUR and the LPGA should probably not be combined. Nevertheless, combining them and examining the coefficient of the FEMALE dummy variable, provides one type of test for discrimination or gender bias. As it turns out, the coefficient is not even negative, and is borderline significantly positive. Controlling for their skill levels, women earn over $9,000 *more* per tournament than do men.

Suppose, however, that the driving skill was mismeasured by the *ad hoc* variable TOTDRIV. Equation (12.9) lists the results for the combined sample with a dummy variable, and with DRIVDIST and DRIVACC replaced by TOTDRIV. The coefficient of TOTDRIV is negative because TOTDRIV assigns lower numbers to those with better rankings. As the R-squared and adjusted R-squared show, the use of TOTDRIV costs a little in terms of the precision of the equation. Noteworthy for our purposes is the now significant negative coefficient of the FEMALE dummy. Controlling for skills, it appears that women earn about $9,000 less than men. What is really going on is much different. In fact, women are not actually being paid in accordance with the overstated measurement of their driving skill, but the equation assumes that they are. This means that the estimated return to driving, as measured by the coefficient of TOTDRIV, multiplied by the women's overstated rankings, gives a number that is too high for the women. The overage is offset for the women by the significant negative coefficient of the FEMALE dummy variable. Ordinarily, one might interpret the coefficient of -9,079.99 as a $9,000 underpayment of women due to discrimination. But in this case, it is actually an adjustment for the overly-high predicted earnings for women that stems from the overmeasurement of their driving skill, when TOTDRIV is used.

Equation (12.8) shows that there is no support for the pattern of regression results in Panel A of Fig. 12.1. Meanwhile, Eqs. (12.6) and (12.7) show that there is no support for the pattern of regression results in Panel B of Fig. 12.1. In fact, the regressions in Eqs. (12.6) and (12.7) show a pattern found in Panel C as the following simulations will confirm.

A simulation technique that can be used to ferret out discrimination is to estimate an equation for one group, and substitute the means from the other group (or values from a specific observation) to compare the predicted earnings from the equation with the actual earnings based on the means (or on a specific observation). For example, the men's mean value of WINPER is $25,123. When the men's average skills are placed into the women's function in Eq. (12.7), the predicted value for WINPER would be only $13,517. For the men, playing in PGA TOUR tournaments is more lucrative. Correspondingly, the women's mean value of WINPER is $5,873. When the women's means are placed into the men's function in Eq. (12.6), the predicted value for WINPER would be -$31,762. Clearly, the women earn more in LPGA tournaments than they would in PGA TOUR tournaments, and the men earn more on the PGA TOUR. This is the pattern indicated in Panel C of Fig. 12.1.

It is also interesting to consider specific cases. Annika Sorenstam was the leading money winner on the LPGA averaging $52,036 in earnings per tournament. When Sorenstam's statistics are evaluated in the men's function, the predicted earnings are $27,127. Sorenstam earns more with her skills playing on the LPGA circuit than she could by playing for bigger prizes against better competition on the PGA TOUR. But it is dangerous to place too much emphasis on one simulation like this. Sorenstam was also an outlier on the LPGA. Her predicted WINPER from the women's function in Eq. (12.7) was only $20,179.

These simulations, the pattern of results in Eqs. (12.6) and (12.7) as shown in Panel C of Fig. 12.1, and the theoretical implication of nonlinearities in the earnings function suggest the use of the logarithm of earnings per tournament as the dependent variable. The results of these regressions are listed in Table 12.4. Equations (12.10) and (12.11) separate the men from the women, and Eq. (12.12) uses the combined sample.

Overall, the results of the logarithmic models are superior to the linear models. The R-squared goes up dramatically, and there are more significant coefficients. In fact, of the 15 skills coefficients in the table (five coefficients in each of three equations), all are the right sign, and all but two are significant at the 99% level. The magnitudes are also reasonable. From Eqs. (12.10) and (12.11), the coefficient of DRIVDIST indicates that an extra yard increases average earnings for the men by about 3.6% and for the women by about 1.6%. Driving distance is once again more important for the men than it is for the women. Putting is still by far the most important

Table 12.4 Regressions of earnings per tournament on skills, (t-statistics).

Equation	12.10	12.11	12.12
sample	men only	women only	combined
dependent variable	LNWINPER	LNWINPER	LNWINPER
Constant	23.8913	31.0894	28.6281
	(4.024)	(9.637)	(10.09)
FEMALE			.285914
			(1.324)
DRIVDIST	.036237	.015740	.023267
	(4.099)	(2.195)	(4.205)
DRIVACC	.051119	.016830	.027148
	(3.307)	(1.743)	(3.367)
GIR	.075187	.122250	.110121
	(2.836)	(8.578)	(9.172)
SANDSAVE	.003976	.015854	.012031
	(0.422)	(2.700)	(2.427)
PUTTPRED	-18.3444	-19.9488	-19.6158
	(-6.588)	(-13.916)	(-15.68)
R-squared	.535	.819	.847
adj. R-squared	.516	.814	.844
observations	130	178	308

skill, yielding roughly the same percentage payoff for the men as it does for the women.

For the combined sample in Eq. (12.12), the skills ranked in order of importance are putting, greens in regulation, driving accuracy, driving distance and sand saves. Over 84% of the variation is explained, and there is no evidence of a bias against women. In fact, the coefficient of FEMALE is once again positive but statistically insignificant.

Neither do the simulations show any evidence of gender bias against women. The women's average LNWINPER (the natural logarithm of WINPER) is 7.9862, which translates to about $2,940. When the LPGA means are placed in the PGA TOUR function, the predicted LNWINPER is only 7.4573, which translates to about $1,732. Also consider the special example of Annika Sorenstam, who earned $52,036 per tournament in 1998. Her predicted earnings using the men's logarithmic regression in Eq. (12.10) would have only been $29,821, while the prediction from Eq. (12.11) is $60,872. That is, Sorenstam definitely earns more playing in the LPGA. If anything, the simulations show a slight bias against men whose average LNWINPER was 9.8078, which translates to $18,175 per tournament but whose predicted LNWINPER on the LPGA is 9.9124, which translates to $20,179.

A third set of regressions is reported in Table 12.5. These regressions use the logarithmic transformation of the dependent and the independent variables, and the coefficient estimates are interpretable as elasticities. The format is the same as the previous tables, with the first two columns, Eqs. (12.13) and (12.14), separating the PGA TOUR from the LPGA, and the third column, Eq. (12.15), combining the samples. Again 13 of the 15 coefficients are significant, the right sign, and of reasonable magnitudes. Putting, driving distance, and greens in regulation are the most elastic, in that order, for the men. For the women it is putting and greens in regulation, followed by driving distance that are the most elastic. In the combined sample, adding the dummy variable changes the elasticities only slightly, and the dummy itself is again positive and again insignificant. No apparent gender bias is uncovered. Also, the magnitude of the putting elasticity is consistent across all formulations. An increase in putts taken of one percent, which represents a decrease in skill, will reduce earnings by about 32 to 36%.

Table 12.5 Regressions of earnings per tournament on skills, (t-statistics).

Equation	12.13	12.14	12.15
sample	men only	women only	combined
dep. variable	LNWINPER	LNWINPER	LNWINPER
Constant	-63.2962 (-4.447)	-27.4525 (-2.939)	-39.7325 (-5.029)
FEMALE			.268135 (1.250)
LNDRIVDIST	9.99581 (4.162)	3.50643 (2.023)	5.63003 (4.008)
LNDRIVACC	3.57149 (3.407)	1.10408 (1.526)	1.81214 (3.258)
LNGIR	4.71910 (2.741)	7.65401 (8.361)	6.87640 (8.792)
LNSANDSAVE	.206765 (0.427)	.615072 (2.789)	.527967 (2.626)
LNPUTTPRED	-32.3304 (-6.515)	-36.6501 (-13.83)	-35.6859 (-15.60)
R-squared	.539	.815	.845
adj. R-squared	.520	.810	.842
observations	130	178	308

Finally, it is possible to formally extend the simulation experiments calculated above along the lines of the example in the first section of this chapter. This will allow us to decompose the difference between men's and women's mean earnings into parts where each part is attributable either to a skill difference or a difference in the payoff structure. The derivation follows Oaxaca.[10] Consider that:

$$Y_m - Y_w = (B_m - B_w)X_w + B_m(X_m - X_w) \quad , \qquad (12.16)$$

where the subscripts distinguish the men's values from the women's, where Y is the mean of the dependent variable, where X is a vector of the mean values of the explanatory variables and where the first element of X is equal to one for the constant term, and where B is a vector of estimated coefficients whose first element is the constant term. According to this decomposition, the difference in average earnings between men and women is composed of two terms. The first term is equal to the part due to the difference in coefficients (including the constant term), weighted by the averages of the men's values. This is the discrimination part. The second term is the part due to the difference in skills, weighted by the women's coefficients. This is the part of the earnings gap that is not attributable to discrimination. In assessing gender discrimination, only the first part could be considered directly due to discrimination. Furthermore, each of the two main terms in the equation above is actually composed of several terms, one for each dimension of the vector of explanatory variables. This allows an inspection of the gender differential on a skill by skill basis. Before moving to the results, three important ambiguities should be recalled.

The first problem with this method is that the weights on the coefficient differences and the skill differences could be reversed. That is, the equation above could be written:

$$Y_m - Y_w = (B_m - B_w)X_m + B_w(X_m - X_w) \quad , \qquad (12.16a)$$

for a different breakdown of the total difference between skill differences and discrimination. Oaxaca noted in his original paper that this is essentially an index number problem. I report the detailed results using the first decomposition, and mention the overall breakdown for the second decomposition in the footnote.

---

[10]Oaxaca, Ronald, "Male-Female Wage Differentials in Urban Labor Markets," *International Economic Review*, 14 (October 1973) 693-709.

The second ambiguity, pointed out by Oaxaca and Ransom,[11] is that the breakdown of the discrimination part between the individual skills and the constant term depends on the measurement of the skills in a way that the underlying regression results do not. For example, PUTTPRED is measured as the number of putts taken on greens reached in regulation and, as such, is negatively correlated to the skill of putting, since fewer putts are better than more putts. Consequently, the coefficient of PUTTPRED is negative. Without changing the statistical properties of the regression (except for the constant term), one could form a new putting variable, PUTTPRED* = 1.926 - PUTTPRED, by subtracting PUTTPRED from the highest (worst) measured level of that skill in either the men's or women's sample. Thus, PUTTPRED* measures the level of putting skill positively as the improvement in skill over the worst in either sample. This completely arbitrary change in measurement protocol does not change the decomposition of earnings between the skills part and the discrimination part. It does, however, change the breakdown within the discrimination part between that due specifically to the difference in payoff to the putting skill, and that due to general discrimination and captured in the constant term.

The third problem is that the numbers reported in any such decomposition are essentially combinations of other statistics with a variety of statistical properties. To my knowledge, no one successfully attempts to derive confidence intervals or standard errors associated with the resulting numbers. As such, the results are useful for illustrative purposes but not for classical hypothesis testing.

Table 12.6 reports the results of one such decomposition. The dependent variable is the natural logarithm of earnings per tournament as in Table 12.4. In light of the second ambiguity above, the explanatory variables have all been rescaled to be measured as the improvement in that skill category over the worst in either sample. Thus all skills are positively correlated to their measured level, and zero indicates the lowest recorded level for each skill. This rescaling does not change the coefficient estimates or t-statistics (except by a negative sign for PUTTPRED, and, of course, except for the constant term) or the R-squared. The difference between LNWINPER for the PGA TOUR and the LPGA is 1.8216 log points. The separate terms in the

[11]Oaxaca, Ronald and Michael R. Ransom, "Identification in Detailed Wage Decompositions," *The Review of Economics and Statistics*, 81 (February 1999) 154-7.

decomposition equation are all divided by 1.8216 so that the numbers in Table 12.6 are the percentages of the earnings differential due to each factor.

Once again, Table 12.6 shows evidence that women are not discriminated against, overall. While 32% and 34% of the earnings gap could be attributed to discrimination in the payoff to driving distance and driving accuracy respectively, these figures are more than offset by negative discrimination (that is women earn more) in the payoff to reaching greens in regulation and in the constant term. On the skills side, the men's greater performance on driving distance and putting alone can explain over 100% of the differential in earnings. As noted in the footnote to Table 12.6, neither is there overall discrimination when the alternate weighting scheme is used.

Table 12.6 Decomposition of PGA TOUR - LPGA earnings differential.

| Variable | (unadjusted differential = 1.8216) | |
	% of gap due to differences in estimated coefficients	% of gap due to differences in average skill levels
Constant	-.272	0
DRIVDIST*	.320	.689
DRIVACC*	.342	.020
GIR*	-.463	.066
SANDSAVE*	-.129	.029
PUTTPRED*	-.088	.487
total	-.290	1.291

Notes: The above table weights the % of the gap due to differences in estimated coefficients by the women's mean skills and the % of the gap due to differences in average skill levels by the men's estimated regression coefficients. When the alternative weighting scheme is used the totals are -.057 for discrimination and 1.055 for skill differences.

The calculations presented here do not support the contention that women golfers are discriminated against. Women earn less than men, but when their differing skill levels are taken into account there does not seem to be a gender bias against women.

The effects of skills on earnings confirm earlier work. Putting is the most important skill for men or women, followed by driving distance for men, and greens in regulation for women.

The separate linear equations predict that men earn more on the PGA TOUR than they would earn on the LPGA, and women earn more on the LPGA than they would on the PGA TOUR. The combined sample in the linear formulation yields evidence, if anything, that women are overcompensated relative to their skill levels.

The nonlinear formulations confirm the results of the linear models. If anything, a bias against men exists. The most variation (over 84%) is explained in the combined model with both men and women and an insignificant dummy variable. To highlight perhaps the best result, the elasticity of earnings per tournament with respect to putting skill is on the order of 32 to 36, and is consistently measured in the combined and gender-separated equations.

Given that the percentage increases in earnings due to putting skills are about the same for men and women, but given that women earn less than men because of their lower achievement in other skills, the absolute dollar payoff to improvement in one's putting skills is higher for men. Is this still discrimination? Probably not, but the differing dollar payoff does provide an answer or explanation to a different question, namely, why are the men on the PGA TOUR better putters than the women in the LPGA? There is no apparent gender-based or physical reason why women should not be just as good. Given the greater number of dollars at stake on the PGA TOUR, and the longer playing schedule, perhaps the men practice more.

In conclusion, maybe none of these results should have been surprising. After all it is the LPGA that discriminates by not allowing men rather than the PGA TOUR which has a non-discrimination clause in its by-laws forbidding discrimination based on race, religion, sex, or national origin. Presumably, if a woman attempted to qualify for a PGA TOUR event and succeeded, she would be allowed to play. Given the relative strength of the competition, the woman would probably be taking a pay cut to do so. Nevertheless, I predict that it is only a matter of time before a top woman golfer decides to forego the extra earnings, and grab the notoriety, and all the approbation and condemnation that will go with it, and attempt to compete in a PGA TOUR event. It may take a while for any such attempt to meet with significant success, but I have no doubt that in the long run, it will be good for women's golf. Furthermore, it will be good for women in general and good for golf in general.[12]

---

[12]These sentiments were originally written in early 2000. In 2003, women played in two PGA TOUR events. Annika Sorenstam received a sponsor's exemption to play in one tournament. Suzie Whaley won a local qualifying tournament (albeit from the women's tees). Neither woman made the cut in her respective tournament. However, several upcoming teenage women seem to have the training and conditioning to drive the ball prodigious distances and may end up competing directly against the men.

Part IV

The Nineteenth Hole

Chapter 13

The Nineteenth Hole

This chapter is to the book as the nineteenth hole is to a round of golf. After playing eighteen holes, it is traditional to relax in the clubhouse, restaurant, or bar, while having a snack, or a drink or two with your playing partners. Golfers will replay the round of golf in their minds, making mental notes of triumphs and mistakes, trying to figure out what went right and what went wrong. To the extent that this review is successful, the golfer draws conclusions, and resolves to practice this or that, to employ the insights in the next round of golf, or to somehow avoid the mistakes that tarnished the just-finished round. Sometimes the introspection about the completed round leads to no conclusions in particular. The golfer simply decides to play again soon or to take a lesson. Similarly, this chapter will review some of the things we have learned in the book, and point out lessons still to be learned. Recapping the inferences that are drawn from *Golfonomics* is analogous to a golfer's mental replay of the just-finished round. Applying these inferences in our golf games, our golf course management, or our future economic research, is tantamount to the resolve that a golfer forms about fixing mistakes in his or her next practice session or round of golf. Finally, several new questions brought up by *Golfonomics* require further research, either in the form of obtaining more data, or developing a new model. In the extended simile, obtaining more data is analogous to playing another round of golf, while developing a new model is the counterpart of taking a lesson.

Golfers do not always systematically review their rounds in hole-by-hole chronological order. A career shot leading to a birdie or eagle on the fifth hole, or a spectacular flub somewhere on the back nine may stand out foremost in the golfer's memory. So, too, one particular result (or one glaring error) in the preceding pages may be all that the reader can recall in an instant. Unlike golf, however, where everyone in the foursome will remember the same career shot made by anyone in the foursome, the specific memories taken from this book may be different for each reader. Therefore, in the interest of being thorough, I have organized this chapter in the same order that topics appear in the book.

Let us start with Chapter 2, where the primary purpose is to warm up the reader to the types of statistical jargon that economists often use in testing or illustrating their theories. The chapter introduces regression analysis, slope coefficients, t-statistics, and r-squareds, setting up the background for the analysis in the rest of the book. In the specific example that is examined, we learned that there is a positive, statistically significant, but negligible relationship between a golfer's weight and his driving distance. Something like 90% of the variation among the PGA TOUR golfers is due to factors other than height and weight. Obviously, there is still a lot to learn. The topic, however, is not predominantly an economic one. Those in the field of kinesiology, or those doing research on movement and exercise, may be able to fruitfully employ measures of upper body strength, measures of muscle mass and body fat percentages, or measures of quick-twitch and slow-twitch muscle fibers, as improvements over the simple weight measures that I use. There may also be a chance to exploit male and female anatomical differences to learn more about the weight/driving distance connection, although these efforts are hindered by the LPGA's tactful avoidance of the weight issue in their player biographies. Finally, a time-series analysis of the weight/driving distance relationship offers a chance to study the influence of technology and equipment changes that have occurred, contemporaneously, with changes in nutrition and exercise regimens.

Chapter 3, To Ride or Not to Ride, develops the basic theory of the demand curve, and applies it to the example of the demand to rent golf carts. Along the way we explored some interesting nuances in the measurement of prices (having to do with whether carts were mandatory). We also learned that a subjective measurement of golf course hilliness could more appropriately capture the effect of hilliness on demand than an objective measurement could. As for the results themselves, price, hilliness, and the percentage of the time that carts were required, all significantly affect, in the expected direction, the demand to rent carts. The regression also tells us which variables do not significantly affect demand in this sample, namely; golf course yardage, restrictions to cartpaths only, and the income level of the golfers. The coefficient of price indicates that each $1 increase in price would lead to a 3.6 percentage point decrease in cart rentals. When transformed into an elasticity, the result is that the demand to rent golf carts is inelastic at the average price.

There are still lessons to be learned about golf cart economics, some of which are highlighted by the results achieved, or not achieved, in this chapter. A better measure of the income effect is clearly called for. The results here indicate that golfer income does not influence cart rental rates, but this result may be caused by the imprecise measurement of income rather than the lack of a relationship. In my view, however, the most intriguing riddle uncovered in Chapter 3 concerns the finding that demand is inelastic at the average price. Economists immediately recognize this as a puzzle because raising price would guarantee more profit, both by lowering cost, and by increasing revenue. Why would golf courses leave money on the table? Worse yet, some golf courses implicitly set the price for carts at zero, or require that carts be paid for, and used, even when so doing imposes costs on both the golfer and the golf course. The explanations that have been offered for these practices do not generally hold water, so a puzzle remains. A possible answer that, if pursued and documented, would make a nice research project, involves the possibility of price discrimination against golfers who prefer to walk.

Chapter 4 explores the issue of whether a golfer who had just finished a poor round of golf would give biased answers to interviewer questions about subjective course characteristics. Although no evidence of a "bad-mood" bias was uncovered, there is evidence of a slight gender bias (males rate course beauty more harshly than females), and some evidence of a home course bias in which golfers rate the beauty of their home course more highly than visitors do. An interesting question remains whether this home course bias is caused by pride, or by the ability to develop, over time, a familiarity with, and appreciation for, the aesthetics of one's home course. Either way, an interesting marketing angle presents itself. If visitors are not able to fully appreciate the beauty of a golf course after having played it once, then, perhaps, targeted price reductions can be used to encourage what economists and marketing professionals call "repeat purchases." As always, the difficulty in any such targeted price-reduction scheme is keeping regular, full-price customers from taking advantage of it. One method that a multiple golf facility owner might be able to exploit is suggested in the chapter.

The targeted price reduction mentioned above is just one example of a pricing practice that economists call price discrimination. Describing the theory of price discrimination, and illustrating the implications of price discrimination for statistical work are the topics of Chapter 5. A variety of nice results is the reward. First, from the theory and the numerical example, we see how to differentiate among several forms of price discrimination, each of which has its own pattern of effects on quantity, average revenue, total revenue, profits, consumer surplus, and social welfare.

Second, comparing the results of a seller employing price discrimination to a simple uniform price monopolist, clearly illustrates that the monopoly "problem" as commonly understood, and as depicted in most economics textbooks, is misstated. The problem of underproduction by the uniform price monopolist can be substantially mitigated when the seller uses multiple price strategies, as all sellers do. The inapplicability and inadequacy of the standard monopoly model, with its single price assumption, is not nearly well-appreciated enough in textbooks, in statistical work, or even in many advanced theoretical papers.

Third, the chapter shows how to implement the effect of multiple price strategies in a statistical model. A generic measure of price dispersion, such as the standard deviation of prices, can be a significant explanatory variable in a multiple regression setting. Furthermore, an industry specific measure capturing third-degree price discrimination, namely, the difference between the regular weekday price and the weekend price, is shown to work even better than the generic measures.

When it comes to the regression coefficients, we can learn several things about the demand to golf at specific golf courses. For example, requiring carts to remain on cartpaths decreases demand by almost 10,000 rounds of golf per year. The regression also shows a significant negative coefficient for the subjective Hilliness variable, and a significant positive coefficient for the Beauty variable, thus confirming the usefulness of measuring subjective quality variables with survey data. The results also imply that demand is very inelastic. I believe that this result is best understood as evidence that the municipal golf courses in the study are not maximizing profits. Indeed, confirmation of this tendency appears when another variable shows that municipal courses use two-part pricing differently (and not to maximize profit!) from the way that for-profit golf facilities do.

There is still work to be done, especially in taking stock of the effect that a golf course capacity constraint has on the pricing decisions of the golf courses. Such a model would pay off handsomely in the economics of sport literature where the demand to attend team sports events has to be estimated in the presence of a sometimes-binding capacity constraint.

Overall, the chapter presents important lessons for golf course managers about the effect that additional complexity in the pricing structure will have on quantity, revenue, and profit. There are important lessons for golfers who are attempting to seek out good deals to stretch their golfing budgets. There is also a warning to non-golfing residents of a city that they are subsidizing their golfing neighbors if their city has a municipal golf course that grants resident discounts. Finally, there is the demonstration to economists that complex pricing is important and that efforts should be made to capture it when undertaking statistical demand studies.

Chapter 6 further exploits the data set on golf course characteristics, golf course policies, golf course costs, and golf course revenues, by calculating the marginal cost and marginal revenue of golf course condition and golf course beauty. To get the ball rolling, the chapter explains and illustrates the simple economics of quality decisions. As always, the relevant marginal cost should be set equal to the relevant marginal revenue. But once we move beyond this abstraction to an actual statistical implementation of the theory, subtle differences arise between the quality dimensions of condition and beauty; differences that should show up in the regression results.

In particular, golf course condition was shown to be positively related to both current costs and current revenues by the same magnitude, as it should be if the marginal cost of condition is equal to the marginal revenue of condition. This part of the theory was confirmed. Furthermore, on the margin, condition should not be related to profit because the profit function should flatten out at the optimal level of condition. In this part of the statistical test, our theory is the null hypothesis, and the statistics fail to reject it. Thus, the hypothesis that golf courses optimally set the level of condition through their yearly maintenance expenditure is confirmed in one test and not rejected by another test.

By contrast, golf course beauty, although measured by the same survey technique as condition, and although positively correlated to condition, reacts differently in the regression equations. Beauty affects revenues, as indeed it should. But beauty should not be positively correlated to ongoing, yearly maintenance expenditures, because beauty is more a function of the original cost of the golf course's location and construction, than it is a function of current maintenance expenditure. This is precisely what happens in the results. Taken together with the results for condition, we have additional strong confirmation that the survey correctly captures these subjective quality variables.

With respect to the coefficient estimates of the control variables, several interesting results turn up. The marginal cost of a round of golf in terms of extra maintenance expenditures measures about $3, measured in 1994 dollars. We also learn that the golf course property costs about $2,000 per acre to maintain but yields revenue of about $3,000 per acre. The $1,000 per acre difference gives a capitalized value of the land of about $20,000 per acre. This amount does not seem out of touch with reality.

We also learn important lessons from variables which do not show up significantly in the regressions. Important information for golf course managers can be gleaned from the fact that none of the following affect maintenance expenditures for a given level of course quality: lakes; bunkers; hilliness; and interestingly, whether carts have to stay on cartpaths. This last item is especially eyebrow-raising. It is usually presumed that carts are restricted to paved cartpaths in an attempt to save wear and tear on the golf course turf. But perhaps this is not true. It is interesting in this regard that at least one golf course manager claimed that paved cartpaths themselves cause maintenance problems with respect to water drainage and runoff during rainy seasons. It is also interesting in this regard that at least one seminar participant claimed that the experience in his neighborhood association with paved paths proved that they were not one-time capital expenditures as one might assume, but rather, that they posed a continuing maintenance expense for their upkeep. Given my aversion to carts and the related paved pathways, I wonder if any golf course managers will reconsider the expenses associated with them. My continuing casual empiricism indicates that golf course managers will not. Paved paths are spreading and multiplying on the golf courses that I play. Perhaps, however, there is another angle to the cartpaths-only rule. Instead of avoiding wear and tear on the turf, the policy is avoiding wear and tear on the carts themselves. It seems likely that a smooth ride on paved paths will extend the useful life of the typical golf cart. Clearly, more work on the economics of carts and the economics of cartpaths is called for.

Finally, with respect to Chapter 6, we can also learn lessons from statistical techniques that do not work. I attempted to use nonlinear forms in the regressions to test for increasing marginal cost and decreasing marginal revenue. These attempts brought only insignificant coefficients. I also tried, unsuccessfully, several multiple equation specifications. There are many possible dimensions to the cost and revenue equations, but only 46 data points. Future research with a larger data set would seem to be fruitful.

The economics of location, also called spatial competition, provides the setting for Chapter 7. Golf courses must compete among themselves for customers who are spread out in geographical space. A golf course located in a densely populated area will, all else equal, be able to draw more customers than one located in a sparsely populated area. An accurate measure of the size of the population that any golf course can count as its "captive" market is essential to any study or forecast of the demand to golf at that particular course. This chapter develops four different ways to count population, and illustrates them in two stylized numerical examples. The point of these exercises is to show the importance of this often overlooked measurement issue, that is, to highlight that different ways of measuring population can have major effects on relative rankings of golf courses by relevant market size. After illustrating the stylized cases, the real-world application is also calculated. Without exception, the more sophisticated the measurement protocol, the better the statistical results.

Several interesting theoretical and statistical results present themselves. In particular, when population is measured as the population living within a certain radius of the golf course, the relative rankings of the courses, and even the overall variation between courses, is not invariant to the radius chosen. A large radius tends to lump all nearby courses into the same market, and attribute to each the same population measure. A small radius tends only to capture the local population density, and may also fail to distinguish between courses. Furthermore, choosing to use a market radius that highlights differences between courses may not correspond to the market radius that one would choose based on an intuitive feel for the market. The proper size to use for a market radius is an important issue that deserves more research.

The statistical regressions show that the best way to capture the relevant population in this study is to divide up the market based on which course each person lived closest to. The r-squared increased by ten percentage points as population measurement became more refined. If this technique were shown to work in other markets and in other settings, then it would establish an important protocol for the measurement of the relevant population in a demand study. Currently, population is included in most studies in an ad hoc manner. So, this is a potentially important result for economists working on spatial demand studies. It is also an important result for golf course managers and potential golf course investors. The better the relevant market can be defined and measured, the better the forecasts of future demand, and the better the understanding of how that demand might be affected by a new, nearby entrant to the market. Notwithstanding these improvements, further improvements should be attempted. My population figures use measurements of distance that are calculated "as the crow flies." Golfers may chase after "birdies," but they do not fly; they drive along indirect routes with varying degrees of traffic congestion. Perhaps in the future some clever economist will develop a workable technique to assign golfers to courses based on travel time instead of simple linear distance.

Finally, with respect to Chapter 7, two ancillary results pop out of the summary statistics and the regression results. The first is that there were, on average, approximately 124,000 people per public access golf course facility in the San Francisco area. This compares unfavorably, if you are a golfer, to the national average of roughly 63,000 people per golf course in 1989. The San Francisco area would seem to be underserved.[1] The second notable result concerns the coefficient of the dummy variable separating municipal

---

[1]Since 1993, one of the courses in the study has closed, but not because of a lack of demand. The land was required as a depository for mud dredged from the bay. The dredging plan called for the building of a new golf course on the land when the project was completed, and the new course is now open. Also, several other new courses have opened. Population has also increased. I make no attempt to calculate the current ratio of people per course, but it is clear that the number of courses would have to approximately double to bring San Francisco up to the national average, and it has not.

courses from profit-seeking courses. The estimate is on the order of negative $400,000. That is, municipal golf courses earn revenues that are $400,000 lower than comparable for-profit courses, controlling for population, beauty, condition, hilliness, etc. This result is consistent with earlier results.

Chapter 8 introduces more economic theory and more economic language, this time from management science and production theory, in order to get a better understanding of slow play on golf courses. The chapter draws a parallel between players on a golf course and partially-completed inventory in a factory. Having done so, the chapter is able to employ concepts from inventory management including: zero inventory policies, production smoothing, and just-in-time production. The payoff comes along the lines of both themes of the book, that is, using golf to help understand economics, and using economics to help understand golf.

In using economics to help golf, there is the important illustration of the crucial difference between the volume capacity of a golf course and the rate capacity of a golf course. This difference stems from the unappreciated difference between the time it takes to play a hole (measured in minutes per hole), and the rate at which golfers can finish a hole (measured in groups per hour). In tackling the slow play problem, the USGA is only cognizant of the importance of the first of these, and, as such, has an incomplete understanding of all of the causes and remedies for slow play. Once the difference between these measures is appreciated, clearer focus is brought to bear on three separate causes of long rounds of golf, namely: slow average play by individual groups; group-by-group and/or hole-by-hole variance in the time it takes to play; and the golf course bottleneck. The improved focus extends to the analysis of the effectiveness of policies that golf courses adopt to speed the pace of play. Lengthening the interval between reservations may help in some cases, and hurt in others. Sometimes a bottleneck can be addressed by the redesign of a hole. Furthermore, the stylized model that is developed shows striking calculations of what happens on a golf course when play is not "smoothed." Finally, a dramatic illustration is made of the somewhat counterintuitive way that "calling up the following group on par threes" speeds play, and increases capacity even though each group takes slightly longer than absolutely necessary to play the whole golf course.

The theme of using golf and golf institutions to help economics is captured in two ways. First, the chapter spurs new empirical research by presenting a clear testable implication. The model in the chapter predicts that increasing the tee time interval will not decrease golf course capacity if the problem causing slow play is a bottleneck. Alternatively, if the problem is a slow group, then increasing the tee time interval will decrease the capacity of the golf course. On a more general level, different causes of long rounds of golf lead to slightly different variations in the pattern and spacing of finishing times compared to starting time intervals. Further research on rate or flow timing and overall length of rounds can now be carried out with a unifying theoretical structure.

Second, the chapter discovers a new theoretical issue that arises in a discrete or batch production process, namely, the possibility that a unit of partially completed output may be in two steps simultaneously. This problem is related to the possibility of dividing existing steps in a production line into multiple parts so that, in essence, two units of partially completed output can be sharing, simultaneously, the same step. The golf course example may supply a valuable laboratory for study of what seems to be intermediate to a discrete process and a continuous process, and what might be called a "fractal-discrete" production process. Further study of this possibility could prove to be fascinating.

In Part III of the book the setting shifts to professional golf. Chapter 9, The Business of Professional Golf, is primarily a descriptive account of the way professional golf tournaments work. There are three major agents that must cooperate to stage a tournament, namely, the golfers, the professional golf association, and the tournament promoters. The chapter describes the three-way interaction.

The analysis of the golfers highlights the factors that influence their choices concerning how many, and which tournaments to enter. There are many hypothetical factors to consider, from golf course characteristics to each golfer's place on the money leader's list, as well as idiosyncratic factors like a golfer's home state, a golfer's "hot hand," and a golfer's status as a defending champion. Each of these factors is a potential explanatory variable in a statistical study of the golfer's choice. Future work in this area will offer a variety of benefits. There are payoffs to economists in terms of interesting econometric issues to tackle. There are payoffs to professional golfers in terms of understanding the connections between their own strengths and weaknesses and the unique challenges posed by any particular golf course. Golf fans will also benefit. They are major consumers of the interesting tidbits of information about the sport that such analysis will reveal.

The section on the PGA TOUR reveals the history of the association, and describes and explains many of the unusual rules and institutions that have developed. Underlying the explanations is the recognition that the professional golfers, as a group, want to allow their sporting competition to flourish while eliminating economic competition between the golfers as individuals. Economic cartel theory goes a long way toward coherent explanations of many special PGA TOUR rules and regulations, including: required minimums for number of rounds played; the top-heavy distribution of prize funds; the prohibition of appearance fees; the establishment of lucrative world-wide competitions for superstars; and the establishment of a priority list for tournament entry. One of the potentially more exciting propositions that could be tested with readily available data concerns the relationship between the average earnings of professional golfers and the variance (or some other measure of inequality) of those earnings.

The section describing the costs and revenues of staging a golf tournament reveals several interesting differences based on the size of the tournament. Risk-sharing and revenue-sharing formulas seem to be determined on a case-by-case method depending on the bargaining power of the interests involved. There is much more that can be learned from an in-depth, case-study analysis of any particular tournament over the years.

Chapter 10 reports on my very first paper on golf and economics. The chapter uses production theory and human capital theory to explain and quantify the relationships between practice and skill development, and between skill levels and tournament winnings. The underlying theory and its statistical implementation yield a number of new and interesting results.

First of all, the description of different professional golfer's practice regimens is fascinating in its own right. Greg Norman could be classified as a "range rat," practicing between thirty-five and forty hours per week. The average practice time for the golfers in the survey was twenty hours per week. Family man and notoriously low practicing, Bruce Lietzke, only averages five hours of practice per week

Second, the chapter introduces the logic of the production function that captures the relationship between inputs and outputs. An important, deductive, theoretical result is explained, namely, that when an input can be used to produce more than one output, the VMPs between the two dimensions should be equalized. As it turns out, an economic puzzle arises regarding this result. In particular, the VMP of practice on putting is estimated to be in the range of $300 to $600 per hour, measured in 1986 dollars, while that for practicing driving is roughly half as large. The chapter offers two explanations to the riddle: one based on the fact that practicing putting may be more costly (in terms of back strain) than practicing driving distance; and the other based on the fact that these statistics only measure the current year payoff to practice, and, as such, relatively underestimate the payoff to practicing driving, because driving skills do not deteriorate as rapidly as putting skills do.

Along the way to these results many other numerical estimates are calculated. Saving one stroke per tournament on the greens is calculated to be worth about $2000 per tournament in 1986. Increasing driving distance by one yard yields over $6,000 per year in extra winnings. Meanwhile, an extra one hour per week practicing driving pays off in roughly one or two yards of extra distance. An hour spent practicing putting saves about .005 to .006 putts per green reached in regulation, which translates, on average, to about one-quarter of a stroke per tournament. Other results indicate that the skill of putting deteriorates rapidly, with a depreciation rate of 100% per year. Meanwhile the depreciation rate for driving distance is only about 25%. There are many other coefficients estimated, and many different functional specifications tried. The bottom line is that there are consistent relationships between practice and skills and between skills and earnings for putting and driving distance. These results nicely confirm and quantify what we expected to be the case.

Chapter 11 presents and tests the "tournaments" model of salary determination. In so doing, the chapter explains: how tournaments work; the difference between relative performance and absolute performance, in particular, the ability of a relative performance standard to encourage extra effort; and how information and measurement problems in a firm can be overcome through promotion tournaments. The essence of the model is that large salary differentials accompanying promotions are efficacious because they bring forth extra effort.

After explaining the theory the chapter moves on to present the ingenious tests that were performed by Ronald Ehrenberg and Michael Bognanno. Using total scores in professional golf tournaments as the dependent variable, Ehrenberg and Bognanno show a significant relationship between the size of the purse and the finishing scores. The main result is that for each $100,000 increase in the prize fund, scores drop, that is, improve, by about 1.1 strokes. Other interesting results come from some of the control variables. For example, scores increase in bad weather, or on longer, more difficult courses, with higher levels of par. These results are all to be expected. A curious result that remains unexplained is that scores increase when the field of golfers is composed of golfers who have better year-long records. Ordinarily, one would expect the scores to improve when playing against better competition. The resolution of this paradox will have to await further study.

Ehrenberg and Bognanno also perform tests with the fourth round score as the dependent variable. They cleverly develop several different measures of how much a professional golfer really has at stake in the final round. How much is really at stake depends not only on the prize fund, but also on the golfer's ranking going into the final round, and on how many golfers are bunched together with similar scores. These tests offer strong evidence of the incentive effects of tournaments in action, thereby confirming a crucial assumption in the tournaments model of executive compensation. Once again, the two themes of the book are exhibited. Economics caused us to focus on golf in a specific way, allowing us to gain novel insights about final round scores in golf tournaments. And, by using certain statistics from golf, an important economic proposition about salary formation is tested and confirmed.

The final substantive chapter reports on a comparison of the PGA TOUR and the LPGA that was designed to ferret out whether gender discrimination exists in professional golf. The chapter begins by explaining the logical problem with often quoted figures of the type that women earn only so many cents for each dollar that men earn. Such figures are meaningless, and the chapter shows why. The chapter also uses a simple arithmetic example to show exactly what has to be measured and compared, in order to uncover the existence of gender discrimination. The chapter shows how diagrams and algebraic manipulations can be used to decompose the earnings gap between men and women into a part attributable to skills differences and a part due to discrimination.

Moving from economic theory to golf, the summary statistics on PGA TOUR and LPGA golfers indicate several differences between the two groups. Basic comparisons of means show that the men play more rounds of golf on longer golf courses for larger purses. The comparisons also show that men drive the ball about 33 yards farther than women (although the distributions overlap), are better at bunker play, and putt better than women. Driving accuracy and reaching greens in regulation percentages are dead heats. The result for driving distance may not be surprising, but there is no physical reason why men should be better putters. A possible explanation of this result is that men practice more because there is more at stake, but a conclusive explanation will have to await future research.

Many other results come out of the regression equations. For example, for PGA TOUR golfers, the coefficients of the driving distance and putting variables are almost precisely three times as large in the 1998 data as they are in the 1986 data examined in Chapter 10. This implies that the relative returns to putting and driving have not changed over the years. The fact that these estimates are consistent across time and across minor variations in the specification of the equations is comforting. It is also comforting that an equation using an ad hoc mismeasurement of driving skills leads to a distortion in the results that, given the nature of the mismeasurement, is in the expected direction. In the logarithmic equations, 13 out of 15 coefficients are statistically significant in the expected direction. Also, putting skill is the most important, as expected, with the highest elasticity. A one percent improvement in the putting skill is associated with somewhere between a 32% and 36% increase in earnings per tournament, and the estimate is consistently estimated across different specifications of the model. All of these results establish confidence that the underlying data measurements, and the model specifications are sound.

When one is examining a sensitive issue like gender discrimination, confidence in the statistics is absolutely necessary, if one is to persuade readers about a provocative result such as the finding here. Overall, no discrimination is found. In professional golf, women earn less than men, but once the differing levels of skills are taken into account, it might even be the case that women are relatively overpaid. This conclusion is robust. It stands up in linear and non-linear specifications. It stands up in *ad hoc* comparisons of one golfer's (Annika Sorenstam) skills and earnings. It stands up to a comparison of the average skills and the average earnings. And, it stands up to the formal wage-gap decomposition technique.

This research, however, will not, and should not, be taken as the last word on the subject. Purses are growing rapidly on both the PGA TOUR and the LPGA. Golfers, both male and female, are starting younger. The potential rewards to stardom in women's golf are certainly large enough to bring forth the kind of effort, dedication, and practice that will allow women to improve their skills, and close the skill gap between the PGA TOUR and the LPGA. As the skill gap closes, so should the wage gap. At the very least, future work should attempt to confirm or overturn these results as new data become available.

There is always a little sadness upon leaving the nineteenth hole. Each enjoyable day spent on a golf course must eventually come to an end. So, too, with *Golfonomics*. When driving from the parking lot, one can appreciate the beauty of the golf course for another brief moment, and then start to look forward to the rest of the day, and to the next scheduled round of golf. While writing the words that close this research, I am already looking forward to my next research project on the economics of golf.

References

1995 USGA Pace Rating System, United States Golf Association, Far Hills, New Jersey, 1995.

1999 LPGA Media Guide, Ladies Professional Golf Association, Daytona Beach, FL. 1999.

2003 PGA TOUR Media Guide, PGA TOUR, Ponte Vedra Beach, FL. (2003)

Adams, C., Cramer, J., Patterson, L., Senko, D. and Wiles, J. (1999). *1999 PGA TOUR Media Guide*, Ponte Vedra Beach, FL.

Alchian, A. A. (1950). Uncertainty, Evolution, and Economic Theory, *Journal of Political Economy*, 58, pp. 211-221.

Alchian, A. A. and Demsetz, H. Production, Information Costs, and Economic Organization, *American Economic Review*, 62, pp. 777-795.

Blauvelt, H. (2001). Survival of the Fittest, *Golf Magazine*, 43, pp. 120-125.

Cottle, R. L. (1981). Economics of the Professional Golfers' Association Tour, *Social Science Quarterly*, 62, 721-734.

Davidson, J. D. and Templin, T. J. (1986). Determinants of Success Among Professional Golfers, *Research Quarterly for Exercise and Sport*, 57, pp. 60-67.

Do, A Q. and Grudnitski, G. (1995). Golf Courses and Residential House Prices: An Empirical Examination, *The Journal of Real Estate Finance and Economics*, 10, pp. 261-270.

The Economic Impact of Golf Course Operations on Local, Regional, & National Economies, The National Golf Foundation, Jupiter, Florida, November 1992, p. 3.

Ehrenberg, R. G. and Bognanno, M. L. (1990a). Do Tournaments Have Incentive Effects?, *Journal of Political Economy*, 98, pp. 307-324.

Ehrenberg, R. G. and Bognanno, M. L. (1990b). The Incentive Effects of Tournaments Revisited: Evidence from the European PGA Tour, *Industrial and Labor Relations Review*, 43, pp. 74S-88S.

Frischman, F. (1975). On the Arithmetic Means and Variances of Products and Ratios of Random Variables, in G. P. Patil et. al. (eds.), *Statistical Distributions in Scientific Work*, Vol. 1, D. Reidel Publishing Company, (Dordrecht-Holland, 1975), pp. 401-406.

Goldman, M. B., Leland, H. E. and Sibley, D. S. (1984). Optimal Nonuniform Prices, *Review of Economic Studies*, 51, pp. 305-319.

Golf Consumer Profile 1989 Edition, National Golf Foundation, Jupiter Florida, August, 1989, pp. 39-40.

Hazlitt, H. *(1996)*. *Economics in One Lesson*, Laissez Faire Books, San Francisco, CA.

Hotelling, H. (1929). Stability in Competition, *Economic Journal*, 39, pp. 41-57.

Jensen, K. C., Kamath, S. and Bennett, R. (1987). Money in the Production Function: An Alternative Test Procedure, *Eastern Economic Journal*, 13, pp. 259-269.

Kahn, L. M. (1991). Discrimination in Professional Sports: A Survey of the Literature, *Industrial and Labor Relations Review*, 44, pp. 395-418.

Krohn, G. A. (1983). Measuring the Experience Productivity Relationship: The Case of Major League Baseball, *Journal of Business Economics and Statistics*, 1, pp. 273-279.

Lazear, E. P. and Rosen, S. (1981). Rank-Order Tournaments as Optimum Labor Contracts, *Journal of Political Economy*, 89, pp. 841-864.

Maskin, E. and Riley, J. (1984). Monopoly with Incomplete Information, *Rand Journal of Economics*, 15, pp. 171-196.

McCloskey, D. N. and Ziliak, S. T. (1996). The Standard Error of Regressions, *Journal of Economic Literature*, 34, pp. 97-114.

Moberg, D. (2001). Bridging the Gap: Why Women still don't get Equal Pay, *In These Times.Com*, Jan. 8, 2001.

Neale, W. C. (1964). The Peculiar Economics of Professional Sports, *Quarterly Journal of Economics*, 78, pp. 42-56.

Oaxaca, R. (1973). Male-Female Wage Differentials in Urban Labor Markets, *International Economic Review*, 14, pp. 693-709.

Oaxaca, R. and Ransom, M. R. Identification in Detailed Wage Decompositions, *The Review of Economics and Statistics*, 81, pp. 154-157.

Official 1987 PGA Tour Media Guide, Ponte Vedra, FL: PGA Tour, Inc., 1986.

Pearlstein, S. (1997). The U.S. Open at Bethesda's Congressional Country Club may look like a golf tournament, but Dennis Spurgeon knows it's really . . . A $60 Million Business, *The Washington Post*, Monday, June 9, p. F19.

Peper, G. ed. *Golf*, New York: Times Mirror Magazines, February 1987, p. 54.

Quirk, J. and El-Hodiri, M. (1971). An Economic Model of a Professional Sports League, *Journal of Political Economy*, 70, pp 1302-1319.

Shmanske, S. (1996). Contestability, Queues, and Governmental Entry Deterrence, *Public Choice*, 86, pp. 1-15.

Shmanske, S. (1999). The Economics of Golf Course Condition and Beauty, *Atlantic Economic Journal*, 27, pp. 301-313.

Shmanske, S. (2000). Gender, Skill, and Earnings in Professional Golf, *Journal of Sports Economics*, 1, pp. 400-415.

Shmanske, S. (1992). Human Capital Formation in Professional Sports: Evidence from the PGA Tour, *Atlantic Economic Journal*, 20, pp. 66-80.

Shmanske, S. (1998a). Price Discrimination at the Links, *Contemporary Economic Policy*, 16, pp. 368-378.

Shmanske, S. (1998b). Subjective Measurement and 'Bad-Mood' Bias, *Briefing Notes in Economics*, 35, pp. 1-4.

Wilson, C., Higgs, S., Neal, L., Reid, N., Rovnak, P., von Louda, D., Widick, K. and Shelly, L. (2003). *2003 LPGA Media Guide*, Ladies Professional Golf Association, Daytona Beach, FL.

Index

Printed in the United States
By Bookmasters